Marcion, Mu

Marcion, Muhammad and the Mahatma

Exegetical Perspectives on the Encounter of Cultures and Faiths

Heikki Räisänen

The Edward Cadbury Lectures at the University of Birmingham 1995/96

SCM PRESS LTD

0 334 02693 8

First published 1997 by
SCM Press Ltd
9–17 St Albans Place London N1 0NX

Typeset by Regent Typesetting, London
and printed in Finland by
Werner Söderström Oy

Contents

Preface

In March 1996 I was honoured with the task of delivering the Edward Cadbury lectures at the University of Birmingham. I wish to express my gratitude to my hosts, especially to Michael and Clare Goulder, for their wonderful hospitality, and to all my hearers for their keen interest in the lectures. I learned much from the discussions, and they have led to many revisions in the text which follows.

The lectures comprised what are now Chapters 1, 3, 5, 6, 8, 10, 11 and 12 of the present book. In Chapters 2 and 4 some assertions about Romans and Luke-Acts, made rather quickly in Chapter 1, are given a firmer foundation. Chapters 7 and 9 consist of material which I would also have liked to discuss, but could not find room for in the lectures.

The design of the book is explained at the end of Chapter 1. In a nutshell, the general idea is to illustrate some ways in which a biblical scholar may contribute to the encounter of faiths and world-views. One way is to analyse critically ancient encounters of this kind; I shall do this in Chapters 2–4. A less common approach is to study the reception of the Bible, or of Jewish-Christian tradition, by outsiders (or by insiders considered heretical by the mainstream tradition); case studies of this fascinating phenomenon are undertaken in Chapters 5–6 and 9–11. In Chapters 6 and 7 (on the Qur'an), insights gained in critical study of the Bible are applied to the exegesis of another scripture.

Throughout the book I am asking what mainstream Christians might learn from a confrontation with others who read their scripture with more critical eyes. However, it also becomes necessary to ask in reverse: could not people of other faiths, in this case Muslims, also learn something from the enterprise of biblical criticism while wrestling with the interpretation of their sacred tradition (Chapter 8)?

Different chapters can be read independently from each other, but an effort is made in the concluding chapter to tie them together. In a rather coherent way they seem to point in a direction which may be called 'the pluralist imperative'.

The area covered is vast, and it would have been possible, perhaps desirable, to spend a much longer time working through the secondary literature in the various areas. I chose rather to make my soundings available right away – in the hope that they might stimulate further discussion about the tasks and possibilities of biblical scholarship in the 'global village'.

Most chapters draw on previous work of mine, though none is fully identical with anything published earlier.

Chapter 1 uses parts of my Manson Memorial Lecture 'Liberating Exegesis?' (*Bulletin of the John Rylands Library* 78, 1996, 193–204).

Chapter 2 brings together parts of a German article and of three English ones on Romans 9–11: (*a*) 'Römer 9–11: Analyse eines geistigen Ringens', *Aufstieg und Niedergang der Römischen Welt* II.25.4, 1987, 2891–939; (*b*) 'Paul, God and Israel: Romans 9–11 in Recent Research', in *The Social World of Formative Christianity and Judaism, Festschrift H.C. Kee*, ed. Jacob Neusner et al., Philadelphia 1988, 178–206; (*c*) 'Romans 9–11 and the "History of Early Christian Religion"', in *Texts and Contexts. Essays in Honor of L. Hartman*, ed. T. Fornberg and D. Hellholm, Oslo, etc. 1995, 743–65; (*d*) 'Faith, Works and Election in Romans 9', in *Paul and the Mosaic Law*, ed. J.D.G. Dunn, Tübingen 1996, 239–46.

The substance of Chapter 3 appeared with the same title in *Temenos* 31, 1995, 163–80.

Chapter 4 is a slightly revised version of an article with the same title in P. Luomanen (ed.), *Luke-Acts: Scandinavian Perspectives*, Helsinki and Göttingen 1991, 94–114.

Chapter 6 updates 'The Portrait of Jesus in the Qur'an: Reflections of a Biblical Scholar', *Muslim World* 70, 1980, 122–33, an article based in its turn on *Das koranische Jesusbild*, Helsinki 1971.

Chapter 7 updates and abbreviates a chapter in *The Idea of Divine Hardening*, Helsinki 1976.

Chapter 8 expands on 'Islamsk koranutläggning och kristlig bibelexeges', *Svensk Exegetisk Årsbok* 51–52, 1986–87, 203–13.

Chapter 10 partly overlaps with 'Joseph Smith und die Bibel', *Theologische Literaturzeitung* 109, 1984, 81–92.

Chapter 11 is based on 'Mahatma Gandhi and the Sermon on the Mount', *Temenos* 27, 1991, 83–108; this has been abbreviated, but new material has also been added.

Chapter 12 combines fresh material with passages from 'Liberating Exegesis?' (see on Chapter 1) and from 'The New Testament in Theology', in *The Companion Encyclopedia of Theology*, ed. J.L. Houlden and P. Byrne, London 1995, 122–41.

Helsinki, November 1996

I

A Biblical Critic in the Global Village: Can Exegesis Serve Inter-Religious Harmony?

It can hardly be doubted that

changing patterns of mobility have shattered older conceptions of the religious history of the world which viewed the faiths as confined, culturally and geographically, within particular boundaries. Personal contact between men and women from different cultures and faiths, at work or in a neighbourhood, is becoming increasingly commonplace. But with the techno-logical revolutions in travel and communications the meaning of neighbourliness now has a global application . . .

The world 'is becoming a "global village" ' where 'personal contact between persons of different religious and cultural affiliations' is commonplace.[1] A wealth of knowledge has accumulated about the non-Christian faiths; 'the days of religious and cultural isolationism are at an end'.[2] Many believe 'that the future of Christian theology lies in the encounter between Christianity and the other faiths'.[3]

Even more importantly, it seems that 'peace in the world very much depends on peace among the various religions'.[4] A laudable step in the direction of promoting this peace is the Declaration by the 'Parliament of the World's Religions', inaugurated by Hans Küng. In it, the attempt is made to found a global ethic on the kernel values common to different religions.[5] Yet religions can only show the way toward peaceful coexistence if they

eliminate those conflicts which spring from the religions them-selves, dismantling mutual arrogance, mistrust, prejudice, and even hostile images, and thus demonstrating respect for the traditions, holy places, feasts, and rituals of people who believe differently.[6]

It can well be asked whether 'tolerance' should not be recognized both as a 'Christian moral imperative, and a Christian theological necessity'.[7]

What does it entail for an exegete to work in this 'global village'? Is it the task of biblical study to promote inter-faith harmony – and how?

Should biblical study produce inter-faith harmony?

Such a demand is vigorously raised by R.S. Sugirtharajah in the well-received collection of articles by Third World scholars, *Voices from the Margin*.[8] He stresses 'the need for biblical scholars to be sensitive to the people of other faiths' (1995, 306). Some of the biblical materials are to be 're-read' 'in the light of the multi-faith context'; one has to 'reformulate the message', 'investing the text with new meanings and nuances' (307).

In this vision, 'the goal of biblical interpretation is not only understanding of the biblical text, but ultimately enacting it'. The primary concern of an interpreter lies both 'in transforming social inequalities' and 'also in bringing racial and religious harmony among peoples of different faiths' (317).

Sugirtharajah does not reckon with much help from traditional exegesis. He polemically rejects the notion of a division of labour 'between biblical scholarship and theological enterprise', calling it 'the original sin of the historical–critical method' (1991, 436).[9]

Sugirtharajah exemplifies his own 'interfaith hermeneutics' by looking at Paul's 'conversion'. He starts from questions raised by 'conversions' in Indian contexts, e.g.: is one religion superior to the other? Should one leave one's own cultural and social tradition entirely in accepting another faith (1995, 307f.)? He rejects two common exegetical approaches to Paul's Damascus experience: 'the conquest approach' and 'the reorientation approach'. According-ing to the former, Paul is 'conquered by Christ and he is sent to conquer others for Christ'; it 'tends to project a Paul who is deeply dissatisfied with the arid spirituality of his own faith', seeing the Judaism of Paul's day 'as outmoded and legalistic'; Paul's conversion is seen 'from the Christian church's apologetical and propagandistic point of view'. The latter approach (that of Krister Stendahl) 'tries to rehabilitate Paul within Judaism and sees his turning point not as conversion, but as call'; Paul, changing from one Jewish sect to another, 'gets a new understanding of his task'. Even this view is to be rejected (309).

From Sugirtharajah's multi-faith perspective, 'both these approaches are insensitive to the people of other faiths', for both see Paul's experience from a mission point of view and envisage 'confrontation with the people of other faiths'. While one approach 'plans for an open aggressive propaganda of the Christian gospel, the other opts for a soft, covert operation', as 'the prophetic vocation is seen in terms of purifying and castigating evil elements in other faiths' (309f.). Oddly, Sugirtharajah seems to assume that Paul's view must be normative for the interpreter, as if interpreting Paul's self-understanding in a certain way entailed that one must share that self-understanding.

Sugirtharajah himself proposes a 'dialogical approach' which

acknowledges the validity of the . . . religious experiences of all people and rules out any exclusive claim to the truth by one religious tradition. In this approach, every religion is worthy of love and respect. All religions contain liberative as well as oppressive elements and the hermeneutical task is to enlist the liberative aspects to bring harmony and social change to all people (310).

I hope that it will become clear in the course of this book that I agree with this author's basic contention: stressing 'the liberative aspects' in any tradition in order to 'bring harmony and social change to all people' is a worthy hermeneutical task. Yet I find it confusing to posit it as an exegetical task as well. No doubt an exegete should acknowledge 'the validity of the religious experiences of all people' (which has, it is true, far too seldom been the case) – but should he or she therefore expound Paul as acknowledging it too? An exegete has to face the possibility that

Paul may *not* have been willing to regard 'every religion' as 'worthy of love and respect'. One has to face the possibility that Paul did envisage 'confrontation with the people of other faiths' – even if the interpreter herself thinks otherwise. Should this be the case, it has consequences for the hermeneutical task: besides listing the liberative aspects of a tradition one may also have to deal explicitly with its non-liberative aspects in some (self-)critical and thera-peutic way.

A similar concern is palpable in the *Contemporary English Version* of the Bible, published in a great 'Bible Reading Marathon' in New York City in 1995. The translators 'have produced a Bible that cannot be exploited by anti-religious bigots' for anti-Jewish purposes. They have decided that 'the use of the word "Jew" in the exclusive sense as the enemy of Jesus' in the New Testament 'represents a misguided, incorrect and, ultimately, harmful casti-gation of an entire people'. 'Until the scriptures are translated more factually in all editions of the Bible, misinformation and hate will be handed down to future generations and the tides of violence will rise again and again and again.'[10] Unfortunately the incorrect-ness is not a feature of the translations at all. It is there in the original text, say, of John; John uses the word 'Jews' as a word of slander in a way that has proved harmful in history, and the trans-lations (unlike the new one!) are true to history in reproducing this feature. The injustices of the past are not to be corrected by an artificial exegesis or a translation which circumvents the real problem; they must be worked through by way of a frank criticism of the text itself.

The last part of Sugirtharajah's account is intriguing precisely from a multi-faith perspective. He thinks that it was Jesus' procla-mation which caused Paul to rethink his 'former life in Judaism'.[11] Jesus, followed by Paul, 'opened up another aspect of the God of Israel – God as merciful and compassionate', thereby 'reiterating a forgotten (!) aspect of God'. God's mercy was now 'available to the very people who were cut off by the pharisaic interpretation of the law', without any intermediaries such as the law or the temple (312).

It looks as if Sugirtharajah does not reckon with the Pharisees as 'people of an other faith' at all. This is not an isolated case; it is surprising how easily theologians of a liberationist branch fall into the old trap of Christian triumphalism which they in principle abhor.[12] Surely a multi-faith perspective must also be able to accommodate the Pharisees of New Testament times as people who enacted a religion 'worthy of love and respect'. A multi-faith perspective must entail that we do not treat Paul automatically as the solution to our problems. He might be part of the problem!

Sugirtharajah claims that his dialogical approach does not view the people of other faiths in terms of mission and conversion, but 'accepts them unconditionally without the requirement of ritual purity' (313). This claim is self-contradictory. How can 'ritual purity' be denounced, if one wants to approach people of other faiths sympathetically? For most Jewish believers 'ritual purity' was (and is) a profound expression of their spirituality and love for God. For me, to be 'sensitive to the people of other faiths' in biblical study means above all fairness to those 'others' who are spoken of in the biblical texts themselves, especially the Pharisees![13]

My proposal is that one should not try to make Paul more 'multi-faith' than he was, but try to understand the problems he and his opponents were involved in and to assess their positions from a multi-faith stance.[14]

Wesley Ariarajah was Director of the sub-unit for dialogue of the World Council of Churches. He has gone a long way in the direction suggested by Sugirtharajah in a little book called *The Bible and People of Other Faiths*. He stresses the implications of biblical creation faith (1985, 9f.), and those of some universalistic passages in the prophets.[15] The narrow biblical notion of election can only be understood in a context of faith (6). Israelites may 'have thought of their choice among nations as an objective truth', and yet 'the outsider can view it only as a subjective experience'. Again,

the Christian understanding that the new covenant abrogates, supersedes, or 'dates' the earlier ones as 'old' is a curious one . . . Does God go back on the covenants he makes (9)?

This is an important point which will concern us in later chapters. But one should face the possibility that curious ideas may also be found, even in central places, in the Bible![16]

Ariarajah chooses frankly between different New Testament texts. Instead of stressing 'exclusive verses' – 'I am the Way and the Truth . . .' (John 14.6); 'there is no other name by which we can be saved' (Acts 4.12) – he turns to the portrait of Jesus in the Synoptic Gospels (as distinct from the picture given in John). Jesus lived a 'God-centred life', making 'no claim to divinity or to oneness with God'. 'In the Synoptic environment it would be strange if Jesus were to say "I and the Father are one", or "I am the way . . .".' Unlike Paul, Jesus 'claims that he has come not to abolish the Law'. This witness to Jesus 'in some ways stands in contradiction' to that of the exclusive sayings (19–22).

Like the Old Testament statements on election, the exclusive sayings of John or Paul are statements of faith which 'have no meaning outside the community of faith'. They 'continue to be valid for those of us who belong to that tradition of confession'. 'The scriptures witness to the struggle that the community of faith had to go through in order to understand the significance of Jesus' (23, cf. 59f., 68f.) We find different titles and many terms, and claims for Jesus which he would not perhaps have made for himself. This is the 'language of faith and love'. Something similar happened to Buddha, who likewise went through a process of deification after his death (23–26).

Ariarajah finally draws a somewhat idealized picture of Jesus' acceptance of people (31) and claims that interfaith dialogue 'is based on acceptance which is at the heart of the gospel message': 'the ability to accept the other in his or her otherness' (33).

Again, I have great sympathy for the intentions of the Asian expositor. But I cannot believe that he is really focussing on 'the overall teaching' of the Bible (e.g. xiv); the 'central message of the Bible' (33) cannot simply be reduced to the statement that 'God's love is unconditional' (31). In Ariarajah's booklet not a word is said about the Deuteronomic attitude to Canaanite religion, or about the biblical condemnation of idolatry. In Deuteronomy 7, for example, we read: '. . . you must utterly destroy them . . . show no mercy to them . . . you shall break down their altars . . .'[17] At best,

Ariarajah seems to be bringing out 'another attitude' possibly found – or perhaps just implied, on a certain interpretation – in the Bible.[18]

Ariarajah's stress on the struggle of the community of faith, when it attempted to express the significance of Jesus, is attractive. I gladly agree with his vision that 'we cannot ignore our own responsibility to continue that struggle' (69). But I must disagree when he states: 'The insistence on absolute and objective truth comes from certain cultural and philosophical traditions that are alien to the Bible' (27). The book of Deuteronomy for one does not represent an unbiblical philosophy! Alan Race, who likewise comes close to Ariarajah on the hermeneutical level, correctly notes: 'Not even the most detached reader of the New Testament can fail to gain the impression that the overall picture of Christian faith which it presents is intended to be absolute and final.'[19]

It would seem helpful to distinguish between exegesis and application, or between historical reconstruction and contemporary dialogue. If this is a sin (Sugirtharajah), it is a beneficial sin. A critical attitude to the biblical record is demanded on the level of application, if one engages in earnest inter-faith dialogue.

Historical study shows that the biblical authors mostly regarded their own faith as the only true one; other alternatives amounted to idolatry. It is just the unattainable but real ideal of fairness and (relative) objectivity which helps a scholar to do greater justice to an alien tradition. If the strong non-dialogical side of the Bible is suppressed in exegesis, it cannot be dealt with adequately. It is better to admit its existence, to wrestle with it and, if necessary, to criticize it openly.

A differentiated approach

Alan Race, in his book *Christians and Religious Pluralism* (1983), discusses exclusivism, inclusivism and pluralism as the main options open to Christian theology with regard to other faiths.[20] Race himself goes in a pluralist direction,[21] but he admits that central parts of the Bible do bear an exclusivist stamp. 'The negative evaluation of other faiths' which Acts 4.12 or John 14.6 suggest 'is hard to ignore', and 'what the New Testament indicates, the church has endorsed through the ages'.[22] The tradition of exclusivism has a firm foundation in the Bible.

However, today it is impossible to avoid theology's reckoning with the results of historical enquiry into the biblical witness. Hendrik Kraemer, the classic proponent of Christian exclusivism, unrealistically claimed that 'the Bible in its direct, intense realism presents no theology'! Race is quite correct in replying that 'the theological nature of the New Testament . . . is manifested in the plurality of theologies it presents', especially in the area of christology. Historical scholarship has also 'highlighted the conditioned character of the biblical knowledge'; 'this has the effect of making the Christian claim to absoluteness in the exclusivist sense appear arbitrary'.[23]

'Inclusivism' accepts the spiritual power and depth manifest in other faiths and yet rejects them as not being sufficient for salvation apart from Christ. It is held that '. . . all non-Christian truth belongs ultimately to Christ'.[24] Earnest Hindus are seen as anonymous Christians. In a hidden manner, Christ is present in other faiths which must be made conscious of this presence by Christian missions. A major problem with inclusivism is, as Race (e.g. 68f.) points out, its pre-judging the issue of religious truth;[25] but at least it represents a step in the direction of a more open dialogue. Does it have a right to appeal to the Bible?

Among biblical authors, Luke has often been viewed as a precursor of inclusivism. The case is made by Race:

> The central ideas of Luke, mainly that Jesus is the culmination of God's providential activity in history, reappear in later inclusivist theories, and are to some extent a foundation for them (41).

> The inclusivist aspect which strikes a 'balance between uniqueness and continuity' (52) is seen in the Areopagus speech (Acts 17.22–31),[26] where the Lukan Paul

> acknowledges the authenticity of the worship of the men of Athens at their altar 'to an unknown God', but goes on to proclaim his identity in terms of the man Jesus.

> Paul therefore includes the impressive spiritual life of the men of Athens in the Christian way of salvation . . . By being so included, their religion was simultaneously brought to completion and perfected (39f.).

Race (40) thinks that Acts provides a contrast 'to the less generous Paul of the Epistles or the more exclusivist "feel" of the New Testament as a whole'.

Acts 17.23 ('What therefore you worship as unknown, this I proclaim to you') is used e.g. by Raimundo Panikkar who holds that 'Christ is present in Hinduism' and that the work of Christian missions is therefore to disclose 'the hidden Christ of Hinduism'.[27] The Areopagus speech is probably the biblical text 'most often quoted by the proponents of a positive view toward other religions'.[28] But Luke is also regarded as 'inclusivist in relation to his own Jewish (!) religious past'; he is concerned to show that the prophecies had been completed in the life of Jesus. This providential ordering of human affairs extends back to the creation of Adam.[29]

The Areopagus speech and inclusivism

Actually Luke's attitude to paganism in the Areopagus speech can be construed in opposing ways. This is in essence what his Paul says to the Athenians:

> I see how extremely pious you are . . . [23] For as I went through the city and looked carefully at the objects of your worship, I found among them an altar with the inscription, 'To an unknown god.' What therefore you worship as unknown, this I proclaim to you. [24] The God who made the world and everything in it . . . does not live in shrines made by human hands, [25] nor is he served by human hands, as though he needed anything . . . [26] From one ancestor he made all nations . . . [27] so that they would search for God and perhaps grope for him and find him – though indeed he is not far from each one of us. [28] 'For in him we live and move and have our being'; as even some of your own poets have said, 'For we too are his offspring.' [29] Since we

are God's offspring, we ought not to think that the deity is like gold, or silver, or stone, an image formed by the art and imagination of mortals.

[30] While God has overlooked the times of human ignorance, now he commands all people everywhere to repent, [31] because he has fixed a day on which he will have the world judged in righteousness by a man whom he has appointed, and of this he has given assurance to all by raising him from the dead.

On Race's inclusivist reading, 'the men of Athens had been Christians without knowing the fact'.[30] 'The apostle's words signify not a judgment upon the lost state of the Gentiles, but rather a fulfilment of their unconscious longings.'[31] But on another interpretation (Kraemer) the speech 'lays bare man's idolatry and ignorance, in spite of God's perennial nearness and also in spite of the fact that man is inescapably related to Him'.[32]

A problem for the inclusivist reading is the narrative framework of the speech. In v.16, Paul's reaction to the 'idols' is described in strong words: he was 'deeply distressed to see that the city was full of idols'.[33] An exclusivist interpreter can dwell on the verse with satisfaction: Paul's soul 'was irritated, embittered, incensed'. 'The pagan world, it is felt, is in the grip of powers alien and antagonistic to God'; for Kraemer the verse shows that it is 'quite absurd' to search in the New Testament for a 'sympathetic and understanding approach' to other religions.[34] But if this is Luke's view, are all the nice things in Paul's eloquent speech then mere tactics?

A related problem is, how should one assess the conclusion of the speech (vv.30–31)? Kraemer writes: 'With a rash leap, Paul comes to the real point which he has at heart. He summons toward "metanoia", towards a radical break with this ignorance . . .'[35] For all the sympathy for the Gentiles, they are guilty of idolatry and have to repent of it. An inclusivist interpretation on the other hand points to the curiously mitigated form in which the Christian message is presented 'with the tenderest pedagogical care'.[36] The repentance 'is naturally to be understood in its Christian sense. It is suggested, however, that repentance consists ultimately of recalling that knowledge of God which, by virtue of his nature, belongs to man.'[37] The motif of ignorance 'ascribes as little guilt as possible to the heathen'.[38] But on the other hand Luke's claim that the period before Christ was a time of ignorance introduces a strong tension into the speech. This claim 'tends to deny even the theoretical possibility of the gentiles' knowledge of God before Christ' and actually contradicts elements of Luke's own argument: God saw to it that people 'might feel after him and find him' (Acts 17.26). Luke 'does appeal to human experience in general', but finally he 'crushes that appeal under the weight of his system'.[39]

If one takes seriously the narrative setting in which Luke's Paul is addressing an audience of 'most pious' philosophers, one cannot but wonder why they actually ought to repent. For Paul's message of the 'new' god, as set forth in the speech, is a very familiar one for them: they already know that God is not gold, silver or stone, and that he does not live in shrines. Paul is criticizing popular Greek religion in terms which contemporary philosophers accepted. The demand to repent seems to by-pass this audience altogether. The new point that the unknown God has ordered a man to be their judge – by raising him from the dead! – seems irrelevant to the thrust of the speech. But precisely this seemingly alien element in the speech is the culminating point aimed at by Luke, as the narrative context confirms: the whole Areopagus episode serves to elaborate the message Paul had first proclaimed in the market-place where 'he was telling the good news about Jesus and the resurrection' (v.18).[40] It was because of this preaching that he was taken to the Areopagus in the first place!

Luke tries to be inclusive – to treat the men of Athens as 'anonymous Christians' – but the attempt fails: there is no clear connection between the 'inclusive' body of the speech and its eschatological-christological conclusion. The speech is inherently ambiguous, even counter-productive. Luke combines the gentle wish for contact with an exclusive attitude to 'idolatry' and with the conviction (stated but not argued) that the risen Jesus is crucial. Luke tries to have the best of both worlds. This is another way of stating, with Martin Dibelius, that the speech is a Stoic creation, slightly Christianized through the concluding verses. In its basic 'inclusive' ideas it is totally alien to the rest of the New Testament.[41]

Luke is indeed trying to show that 'Jesus is the culmination of God's providential activity in history' (Race), but his attempt is less than successful. He has not reached that 'balance between uniqueness and continuity' which might have made him a patron saint for inclusivist theologians. This ambiguity is part of a larger problem in Luke's work. David Seeley has shown that there is a sense in which Jesus seems unnecessary in Lukan soteriology. I shall return to this in the last chapter, asking whether a dialogue can be aided by reading Luke against the grain. But if we simply read Luke's speech in context, the final impression is not that the Athenians have been anonymous Christians, but that they have lived in ignorance; the reference to their spiritual life is used as a point of contact with the missionary purpose of winning them over. On a strictly exegetical level exclusivist theologians do have a point. Nor should we forget that it was Luke who wrote – or preserved – the classic exclusivist statement in Acts 4.12 ('There is salvation in no one else . . .').

The continuity between Judaism and Christianity in Luke

Alan Race finds Lukan 'inclusivism' with regard to Judaism in his concern to show that prophecies are fulfilled in Jesus.[42] Indeed Luke underscores continuity between the old and the new. The opening chapters of his Gospel depict how Christianity grows directly out of Jewish soil, joyfully fulfilling the age-old expectations of God's people concerning a time of peace and bliss. The angel depicts the career of Mary's son in clearly earthly-political terms (Luke 1.32–33). Zechariah, filled with the Holy Spirit, likewise utters a prophecy that God has raised up a mighty saviour for his people, just as he spoke through the prophets (Luke 1.68–75).

It may slowly dawn on the reader as the work proceeds that such promises will never be realized in that concrete form.[43] But Luke never says in so many words that the expectation of an earthly kingdom was a mistake. The restoration of the kingdom to Israel is tacitly assimilated with the spread of the worldwide Christian mission (Acts 1.3–8); the corporate earthly expectation is fused with an individualized, transcendent fulfilment. Jesus reigns on the throne of David when he has been raised to heaven; the people are rescued from their enemies when they know the forgiveness of sins (Luke 1.77) – as if forgiveness had been unknown to the people of the old covenant.

Luke's vagueness is understandable. For had he spelt out that the expectation of an earthly kingdom was a mistake, he would have implied that the angel and the Spirit were in error. And had he made clear that Christian salvation was something other than the redemption expected by Jews on the ground of their prophecies, he would have been in trouble concerning the all-important continuity. Luke would not have appreciated the well-meant suggestion of modern theologians that God had surprises in store when he fulfilled his promises.[44]

Luke has a deep concern for showing that his Christian views are the true interpretation of the Bible. He does not simply 'incorporate' the Jewish heritage into his Christian experience, as an 'inclusivist' reading would have it;[45] he usurps the Jewish past, bending Scripture to serve his own needs. Its peaceful appearance notwithstanding, Luke's work reflects the ideological battle of two religions over the Old Testament heritage. Luke's language, especially in the infancy narratives, suggests a very positive attitude to Judaism, but actually his attitude is quite ambiguous. (A full treatment of this issue in Luke follows in Chapter 3.)

The emphasis on continuity has proved dangerous in history. Unlike old Simeon, Judaism did not consent to be dismissed in peace. Therefore it became an intellectual threat to Christians who had appropriated the Old Testament. In the course of time this threat called for violent means to overcome it, so that after two millennia of fulfilment the prophecy of Zechariah sounds tragically ironic.

We shall have opportunity to dwell on problems of 'fulfilment' later. This discussion of Luke's intrinsic problems was intended to illustrate a possible application of the historical-critical perspective to the issue of inter-faith encounter: equivalents to such encounters in the biblical texts should be scrutinized without closing one's eyes to problematic features in one's own tradition. Exegesis may indeed serve inter-faith harmony – yet not by reading the texts with a 'multi-faith' bias, but by preparing the way for a critical discussion of them from a multi-faith point of view.

Romans 11 and Jewish-Christian dialogue

Let us also cast a brief glance at Romans 11 with its talk of the end-time salvation of 'all Israel' (Rom. 11.25) and the statement that 'the gifts and call of God are irrevocable' (11.29).[46] Increasingly, this passage is taken to have 'massive implications for the dialogue today between Christians and Jews'.[47] This seems, however, to be a too optimistic assessment, one which expresses Christian aspirations much more than Jewish ones. Romans 11 would be a precedent for a uniquely open dialogue between Christians and Jews, if it could be read in terms of a 'two-covenant theology'; i.e., if Paul really suggested that Jews need not convert to Jesus Christ in order to be saved. Even so, we would still be far away from thoroughgoing religious pluralism, since only Jews and Christians would be treated on even terms, not the 'idolaters'. Now a few scholars have taken great efforts to show that Paul's expectation of the salvation of Israel does *not* imply that they will become believers in Jesus as the Messiah; on this reading, for Paul Jesus was only the saviour of Gentiles, whereas Jews had another way to salvation.[48] Surely these scholars have re-read the Bible in the light of the dialogue, showing sensitivity to the people of another faith (Sugirtharajah), but in the process have changed Paul's thought almost beyond recognition.

It remains safe to assume that what Paul expects in Romans 11 is an end-time conversion of Israel to Christ as a solution to his own grave personal problem: how is it possible that his people does not accept his message? This seems an 'inclusivist' point of view, transferred to the eschatological future: you will be saved all right, but that is because God will change you so that you will become like us.[49] Here too the 'truth belongs ultimately to Christ'.[50] The Jews are treated, not as anonymous Christians, but as future Christians. No wonder, then, that Jewish partners in the dialogue have not been too enthusiastic about Romans 11.

Thus, Alan Segal writes that 'as a believing Jew and a twentieth-century humanist', he could have hoped for a different outcome of Paul's meditations in Romans 9–11, an outcome other than the somewhat vague suggestion that Israel will embrace Christianity. Segal frankly states that the theology outlined by Gaston and

Gager[51] – a two-covenant theology which views Judaism and Christianity as two parallel roads to salvation – 'makes more sense for today than does Paul's actual conclusion. It would have been easier for today's Christianity had Paul embraced cultural pluralism more fully.'[52] On the Christian side Gregory Baum notes that here 'we have probably the most generous approach to the Jews in the New Testament' and that 'Romans 9–11 modifies the more negative teaching on the Jews found elsewhere in Paul's writings'; but he too finally admits that even in these chapters, 'Jewish religion has become null and void, and grace is offered to Israel only through conversion to Christ'.[53]

We meet a true two-covenant theology only at the fringe of second-century Christianity. The Jewish-Christian 'Pseudo-Clementine' romance contains the remarkable statement that God accepts the one who has believed either Moses or Jesus.[54] But it is symptomatic that this most distinctly 'dialogical' statement is found in a writing deemed 'heretical' by posterity, one which had no influence on the development of mainstream Christianity.

The contribution of the exegete in the global village

Using a text and trying to understand it are, I insist, two different tasks, both legitimate. Historical exegesis employs the texts as guides to lost worlds. As Wayne Meeks puts it, it belongs to the job of an historian 'to try to protect the integrity of the past, and that often has the effect of emphasizing its strangeness'.[55] The exegete may be needed in the global village as the 'historical conscience' in the dialogue, as one who warns of attempts to make too direct a use of the texts.[56]

Historical biblical scholarship may be able to outline a (very sketchy) picture of 'how it all began'. Having an idea of where we come from may aid us in orientating ourselves to where we are now and where we wish to go, but the yield is bound to be indirect.

An exegete may serve in the 'global village' first by analysing ancient encounters (peaceful and other) of different traditions and visions. I have just tried to illustrate briefly what this might entail; I shall treat relevant texts from Luke and Paul at greater length in Chapters 2 and 4. In between comes Chapter 3 which deals with the reception of one alien tradition in the Bible: the traditional cults, typically called 'idolatry'. In all this I am simply conducting exegetical analyses, though not without a side glance on the issue of dialogue.

Another approach, less often taken by exegetes, is to study in a spirit of fair play the 'alien' reception of the Bible, or of Jewish-Christian tradition, in less familiar contexts, a reception which has often produced unexpected results. Such case studies will be my concern from the fifth chapter on. The chapter on Marcion, whose church remained for centuries a serious rival to Catholicism, will return to themes of the Jewish-Christian dialogue. But today this dialogue is already a matter of course. It is intensely pursued on every side; I shall leave it at that point and turn to less cultivated areas. I shall be looking from an exegetical point of view at the work of four influential figures: 1. the prophet Muhammad and the Qur'an (with a side glance at modern Muslim interpreters wrestling with questions familiar to us from our own history); 2. Isaac la Peyrère, a figure largely forgotten today, but hotly debated in the seventeenth and eighteenth century for his critical views; 3. Joseph Smith, the Mormon prophet, a stunning lay reader of the Bible; and 4. Mohandas Gandhi, the Indian civil rights fighter who appealed to the Bhagavadgita and to the Sermon on the Mount and became an inter-faith saint. This is a random selection; it just happens that at various junctures these figures, for different reasons, have come my way. But what a fascinating company they make!

Looking at the Bible through foreign eyes may help us see some sides in our tradition in a new light.[57] On the other hand, it is helpful to start one's effort to understand an alien tradition by reflecting on familiar elements in it. Both experiences may contribute to the rise and development of a multi-faith vision of some sort, and towards finding a place and a task, however modest, for a biblical scholar in the global village.

2

Saving God's Integrity:
Paul's Struggle in Romans 9–11

Christians engaged in dialogue with Jews often set great hopes in Paul's ruminations in Romans 11 where he states: 'all Israel will be saved'.[1] However, in the opening chapter I suggested that this seems a shaky basis for a genuine dialogue. In what follows I shall try to substantiate this claim in more detail.[2]

Recent interpreters agree: in Romans 9–11 Paul is concerned with the problem of Israel, which is also the problem of the trustworthiness of God's promises.[3] There is also a growing awareness that earlier research focused excessively on Paul's theological ideas.[4] The social context and function of Paul's writing has to be taken seriously. Paul's social experience is reflected throughout the section.

It is also agreed that the chapters are 'as full of problems as a hedgehog is of prickles',[5] but the solutions go in quite different directions. In sketching my own reading of the text and my understanding of the social dynamics behind it, I shall limit my remarks mainly to chapters 9 and 11, which directly address the question of Israel's election.

To me, the internal tensions provide a key to the section.[6] There has been a debate on Paul's theological consistency.[7] Unlike some of my critics,[8] I do not think that inconsistency is a wicked thing; it is simply human.[9]

The amount of exegetical ingenuity needed by those who plead for consistency is noteworthy. In order to get a consistent Paul, interpreters often put forward a whole series of strained interpretations.[10] The price for blameless logic is, then, that the apostle proves a rather bad communicator, as all previous interpreters have got him wrong, in passage after passage. Thus, in a recent book the statement 'all *Israel* will be saved' is taken to mean that *Gentiles* will join Abraham's family; for the author thereby 'the case for finding fundamental contradiction within Romans 9–11 falls to the ground'.[11] To me, it is a weighty argument *against* consistency that so artificial interpretations are needed to rescue it.

Inconsistency should not be reduced to a problem of Paul's psychology; 'conflicting convictions' about the relation of the new to the old are found in early Christianity at large. To Paul goes the credit for really wrestling with the problems.

Romans 9.1–29

In Romans 9–11 Paul explains how the gospel can be taken to represent a triumph for God, even though most of the Jewish people appear to be on the losing side – indeed, to be accursed (*anathema*, 9.3).[12] Paul's concern for the fact that most Jews have rejected his message leads him to raise the worrisome question of the dependability of God's word (9.1ff.). What sort of God does not see to it that his promises to Israel come true?[13] What gain will Israelites have for all the advantages Paul lists in vv.4–5 (sonship, glory, promises . . .), if they remain outside the salvation in Christ? God's integrity is at stake.

Has God's word failed, if Israel stays outside? Paul answers by redefining 'Israel': all those who are 'of Israel' (the empirical people) do *not* really belong to 'Israel' (v.6).[14] Who belongs and who does not is freely decreed by God. He has always freely called some, like Jacob, and not others, like Esau, without any regard to their character or ancestry (9.7–13).

Therefore, the initial question is falsely put. The gospel is *not* being rejected by the elect of God, for the majority of ethnic Israel never belonged to the elect![15] The gospel is being rejected by the non-elect and accepted by the *true* 'Israel'. Everything is as God meant it to be.

Paul goes to great lengths in undergirding the thesis of God's free election. That God can show unexpected mercy is in line with the surprising experience that he has lately called Gentiles to enter his people. But this point alone does not account for the emphasis on the negative side of God's action (9.14–18).[16] God 'hardens whom he wills', too.[17] Astonishingly the Pharaoh, the classical enemy of Israel, here comes to stand for the Jews of Paul's time![18]

Verse 19 shows that Paul senses that a moral problem is involved in his argument. How can human beings be held responsible for their doings if everything is effected by God? All Paul can do is to assert that the Great Potter has the right to create what he wants, even 'vessels of wrath' prepared for destruction (9.22). This would logically imply double predestination.[19] The unbelieving Jews of Paul's time are to be seen as such vessels of wrath.

Paul then shows from Scripture that God always intended also to call Gentiles to be his sons (9.24ff.). At this point it surely seems as if the inclusion of the Gentiles were the point of the whole chapter, the thing in need of justification.[20] But this was not the starting point of chapter 9. It is not the inclusion of Gentiles that could have aroused the suspicion that God does not keep his promises. Such an allegation is due to the apparent exclusion of the majority of Israel. Had the inclusion of Gentiles been the point of the whole chapter, this might account for the emphasis on God's having mercy on whomever he wills. It would not, however, explain the stress placed on the notion that God hardens whom he wills as well, nor the idea that God has in his sovereign freedom prepared vessels of wrath for destruction. It is the *negative* traits in God's dealings that according to Romans 9 cry for an explanation; the salvation of Gentiles is not a sufficient one. Paul's thought has taken a new turn in v.24.

To some extent, this also seems true of vv.27–29. Paul there argues from Scripture that not all Israel will be saved, but only such seed as God has left in it. This idea of a remnant does not entirely agree with the one just presented that all Israel was never elected. Yet Romans 9 gives a clear answer to the question, has God's word failed? No, it has not, for God never promised anything for ethnic Israel. It seems clear that the majority of the Jews will remain outside salvation.[21]

Romans 9.30–10.21

This section introduces a different point of view. Paul explains why Israel, now seen as an ethnic entity after all, has failed to attain righteousness, whereas Gentiles have found it (9.30–33). We now hear nothing about sovereign divine hardening. On the contrary, God has held out his hands toward Israel all day long, patiently inviting her to salvation, but Israel remains stubborn (10.21).[22] Clinging to works, she has refused to obey God and accept his action in Christ with faith. Thus she has stumbled over the stumbling stone, Christ (9.32f.).

Romans 11

In Romans 11 Paul continues to talk of Israel in the ethnic sense. He now asserts that God cannot have rejected his people (11.1f.). This is rather surprising after chapter 9, but it continues the argument about the remnant. Ethnic Israel has split into the elect remnant and the hardened rest (11.7). This is in keeping with chapter 9 in so far as the contrast between divine election and divine hardening seems definitive. There will always be a remnant, but no happy end is envisaged for the people.

Paul goes on to suggest that the hardening of Israel has a positive purpose in God's plans: it serves to bring salvation to the Gentiles (11.11f.). In v.14 the 'apostle to the Gentiles' (v.13) gives a strange account of his motives. The real purpose of his mission is, he states, to aid the salvation of *Israelites* by making them 'jealous' of Gentile Christians. Still, it is only 'some' that Paul hopes to win in this way. That the idea of 'salvation through jealousy' cannot in reality have been the driving force behind Paul's missionary efforts is beyond doubt. When Paul speaks of his call, he speaks of a task among Gentiles and alludes to Isa. 49.1, a passage concerned with the nations (Gal. 1.15f.). He cannot have grounded his mission on an idiosyncratic reading of Deut 32.21. His use of that verse in Rom. 10–11 (no less than three times: 10.19, 11.11b, 11.14!) shows that he desperately needed something that would make him a beneficiary of Israel as well, Galatians 2 notwithstanding. The notion of jealousy seems to serve an apologetic purpose with regard to Jewish Christians.

Paul then presents the parable of the olive tree,[23] from which some branches have been broken off, and on to which some branches of a wild tree have been grafted (11.17ff.). He says in effect that Israel remains God's people; apostates have been excluded, and believing Gentiles accepted as proselytes. This is basically in keeping with the notion of the remnant, though the image of a tree and branches suggests that only a small minority has fallen away. The present state of things is caused by the unbelief of 'some' (11.17,20): by human failure, not by a divine decree. Gentiles are admonished to remain in faith so that they will not be 'broken off' as well (v.22). Here the idea of divine hardening would be out of place. But God has the power to graft anew those Israelites who have fallen, if only they will give up their unbelief (v.23).

And indeed they will! This is Paul's message in the final section. He discloses a 'mystery': the hardening will not be final. When the full number of the Gentiles has 'come in', *all* Israel – not just a remnant – will be saved, for God's call is irrevocable (11.25ff.). Paul implies that he has received this knowledge as a revelation, probably through a spirit-guided exegesis of Scripture.

Does Israel have a special way to salvation?

But how will the salvation of Israel take place and what is involved in it? The suggestion that Paul here envisages two different roads to salvation, one for Christians and another for Jews, has been much debated. It will be convenient to join the discussion by evaluating the interpretation put forward by John Gager (1983) who acknowledges his debt to Lloyd Gaston.[24]

In Gager's view, the salvation of Israel does not consist, according to Paul, in its conversion to Christianity (261, 263). Paul does not even regard Jesus as the Messiah of the Jews. Instead, Christ now offers Gentiles righteousness and knowledge of God (214). For Jews, justification is still 'through the Torah' (218).

This thesis is vigorously argued and admirable in its ecumenical scope, but it is simply insupportable. Why did Paul call Jesus '(the) Christ' in the first place (even in Rom. 9.5) if he did not regard him as the Messiah of Israel?[25]

Still in Rom. 10.12–13, Paul repeats the main thesis of the letter: there is no difference between Jew and Greek as regards salvation. Both have the same Lord (10.12). Romans 10.8–13 specifies the conditions of salvation[26] for Jew and Greek (v.12). Christ is the Lord of all. Gager never mentions in his book Rom. 1.16, the motto of the epistle: the gospel is 'the power of God for salvation to every one who has faith, to the Jew first . . .'

Assuming that the gospel was not meant to be proclaimed to the Jews at all, Gager plays down Paul's stated intention to save (*sozein*) some of his own people in Rom. 11.14, takes no notice of the phrase 'to win Jews' in I Cor. 9.20, and is unable to come to grips with Peter's 'gospel to the circumcision' (Gal. 2.7). But Paul's argument in Rom. 11.11–12,19,28a,31a makes no sense at all if the gospel about Jesus was not meant to be proclaimed to Jews. If it was not, how could the 'disobedience' of the Jews (v.31) become the chance for the Gentiles to receive salvation? If the gospel was meant for Gentiles only, why was it not preached to them right away? Why does Paul suggest that Israel's 'fall' had to occur first?

According to Gager, Paul's problem in Romans 9–11 is 'Israel's refusal to recognize and to accept the obvious continuity between God's promise to Abraham and his act of redemption in Christ' (223), its 'failure to recognize Paul's gospel to and about Gentiles as fully at one with God's righteousness' (250). This is why they stumbled, failing to see that righteousness rests on faith (252), both for the circumcised and the uncircumcised.[27] But why should this cognitive failure have to occur first, before Paul's gospel could reach the Gentiles, its only intended addressees? Just how does the 'disobedience of the Jews' provide the 'divinely ordained opportunity for God to show mercy on the Gentiles' (254–5)? Gager is quite vague on these issues.

If Israel was not supposed to believe in Jesus as the Messiah at all, it becomes unclear why Paul should speak of its unbelief (*apistia*), as in Rom. 11.20–23, or of its disobedience (Rom. 11.31). And why does Paul resort to even much stronger language about divine hardening and double predestination (not mentioned by Gager)? Why was Israel 'cut off' (260)? Why should the rejection of Paul's mission to Gentiles (not rejection of Christ!) count as so enormous a problem that the apology of God put forward in Rom. 9 is needed? Why the deep sorrow expressed by Paul in 9.1–2, 10.1? And what should Israel be made jealous of (Rom. 11.11ff.), if Gentiles do not possess anything that is not available to Israel as well? A lot of Paul's statements make little sense if it was not Israel's failure to believe in Jesus as the Christ that was his problem.

Gager puts forward a forced exegesis of a number of crucial passages.[28] Paul's negative comments on the Torah are eliminated through the interpretation that they apply to the Torah if imposed on Gentiles. But it is impossible to read, for example, all 'under the law' passages, including those in Gal. 3–4, from such a point of view. On the other hand, Gager does admit that *Paul himself had given up the law and Israel's covenant* (234). This is indeed the only feasible way to interpret Gal. 2.18–21 or Phil. 3.7–8. Gager even speaks of Paul's 'apostolic apostasy' (244) – but no one else was, in his opinion, supposed to emulate the apostle in this regard (247). The rejection of the law was Paul's personal decision, made necessary by his special mission among Gentiles.

This, however, is not the case. Paul was not the only Jewish Christian to neglect parts of the Torah. The same position was taken – before Paul – by the 'Hellenists' and by the congregation in Antioch. How could not only Barnabas but even Peter 'live like Gentiles' in Antioch (Gal. 2.14) if 'tearing down' the ritual law was a Pauline idiosyncrasy?[29]

The 'mystery' of Romans 11 is a tenuous basis for an assertion which would nullify everything that Paul writes elsewhere (including Romans 10) about the significance of Jesus for all humanity,[30] to the Jew first (!) and also to the Greek. Still in the olive tree parable Paul stated that the broken-off branches would be 'grafted back in precisely when they no longer persisted in their lack of belief, i.e. when they too came to faith in Jesus Christ'.[31] In v.26 he must mean: all Israel will be saved, for all Israel will – somehow or other – embrace faith in Christ.

But how? Some scholars who allow that Paul does regard Jesus also as the Messiah of the Jews, and that 'Christ alone' consistently remains the centre of his soteriology, contend that Israel's 'special way' to salvation consists in its having 'a special eschatological destiny'.[32] Israel's conversion is not the result of Christian mission.[33]

On this understanding, too, Rom. 11.25–27 would be a singular passage in Paul. Still in 11.14 Paul expresses his hope that he could save 'some' of his kinsmen. Perhaps one should not take the modest *tinas* (some) literally any more than *tines* in Rom. 3.3 or 11.17. Romans 11.14 is immediately followed by verse 15, in which Paul makes a connection between his bringing – indirectly, through 'jealousy' – Jews to salvation and the eschatological 'acceptance' of Israel, which amounts to 'life from the dead'. If 11.25–26 is interpreted in the light of v.12 (*to pleroma auton*, 'their full inclusion' in v.12 corresponds to the *pleroma ton ethnon*, the full number of Gentiles, in v.25) and vv.14–15, it seems quite possible that Paul expected the final conversion of Israel to take place in the course of his – and others' – proclamation of the gospel. While a miracle is necessary, it is perhaps not worked through a *deus ex machina* but through the agency of God's apostles.[34]

Paul may even have deliberately expressed himself vaguely. It is not clear that he is referring to the parousia in his quotation from Isaiah (Isa. 59.20f.; 27.9): 'the Deliverer will come from Zion, he will banish ungodliness from Jacob . . .' (Rom. 11.26f.). After all, the returning Christ should come from Heaven, not Zion. Paul may simply be referring to Jesus' 'first' coming; then the future tense only indicates that this was a future event for Isaiah, not for Paul.[35] But this issue can be left undecided.

God cannot, according to this passage, reject his chosen people. Instead, Paul has rejected the thrust of his earlier argument. Ethnic Israel, or at least its majority, will be saved.

Paul's theological and social problems as the background of Romans 9–11

Romans 9–11 contains two main intellectual problems: the discrepancy between predestination and human freedom, and the election or non-election of ethnic Israel. Both problems are rooted in Paul's social experience in his mission fields; this seems to colour the section more strongly than the the situation in Rome. The latter plays some part, but does not seem crucial.

The problem of predestination versus free will is no Pauline peculiarity. It is paralleled in the Old Testament (Pharaoh, Isaiah's task: Isa. 6.9f.), in Qumran, in the Gospels (Mark's parable theory, Mark 4.11f., God's concealing things from the wise and revealing them to the 'babes' in Q, Matthew and Luke, Luke 10.21f. par.) and in the Qur'an (see Chapter 7 below). The talk of negative predestination has a social function. The idea crops up in settings where the religious majority does not accept the message preached by a minority. It consoles the minority when they fail to convert others, and justifies the situation for them. The tension between divine hardening and that human freedom which is presupposed in preaching is seldom felt.[36]

Elsewhere (II Cor. 4.3–4) Paul occasionally attributes the blinding of the unbelievers not to God, but to the 'god of this aeon'. This shows how far he is from possessing a 'systematic' doctrine of hardening: the introduction of Satan into Romans 9 would have destroyed the argument based on God's sovereignty. The problem of unbelief remains the same; the solutions vary.

The problem of different views on Israel is more distinctly Pauline. Romans 11 differs sharply from the harsh judgment in I Thessalonians (2.14–16)[37] and from the writing off of Israel in Galatians, but it differs equally sharply from the notion that ethnic Israel was never elected, put forward in Romans 9.

The reader of Galatians indeed gets the impression that the people of Israel never had a special relationship to God.[38] Righteousness cannot be gained through the law (Gal. 2.21), and this was always so (Gal. 3.21). The law which gives Jews their identity was only an interim episode in God's plan (Gal. 3.15–25). Galatians 3.19–20 indicates that it may not even stem directly from God. In Gal. 4 Paul goes so far as to construct an analogy between the law and the demonic 'elements of the world', putting observance of the Torah in parallel to pagan worship. In no way does Paul in Gal. 3–4 reflect on God's faithfulness to Israel.[39] Rather, he makes the polemical point that only Christians are children of Abraham (Gal. 3.7ff.).

In Gal. 4.21–31 Paul attacks the old covenant aggressively. The Sinai covenant gives birth to slaves (vv.24–25). Non-Christian Jews are descendants of the slave woman Hagar! It is only the Christians that are 'children of the promise, like Isaac'. This corresponds exactly to Rom. 9.8. Galatians 4.30 even states that the Jews are to be 'driven out'. The rejection of the Jews is spelt out in plain words.[40]

The thrust of Galatians corresponds closely to Romans 9 (except for the ideas of predestination and hardening, of which there is no trace),[41] whereas the parable of the olive tree would be totally out of place in Galatians.[42] Galatians suggests that, like Gentiles, Jews too must take a new step to find righteousness with God (Gal. 2.15ff.); they too must become 'a new creation' (Gal. 6.15). In I Corinthians 10.32, too, Paul speaks of 'God's church' as a third entity alongside Jews and Greeks. If we were to invent an image for Paul's usual 'ecclesiology', we might devise a third tree on to which both Christ-believing Jews and Gentiles, taken from two other trees, are 'grafted'. That would correspond to Paul's missionary practice.

Paul's practice implies that Jews ought to accept Jesus as the Christ and undergo a new initiation rite, baptism. In effect, then, clinging to God's ancient covenant with Israel is not enough. Even a Jew has to join a new group, distinct from the synagogue (though he need not therefore leave the synagogue yet). He must also be prepared to sacrifice some of his Torah observance; Paul speaks of his accommodation to it among Jews 'as if' he were a Jew! Although Paul holds that God gave the Torah as a guide to life, in practice it has come to an end: parts of the divine commands no longer need to be observed, at least not when Jews and Gentiles come together in Paul's communities.[43]

No matter how conservative were the utterances which Paul was, at times, able to make, this attitude of assimilation was bound to cast doubts on his loyalty to the covenant in the eyes of most Jews. He certainly did perceive himself as a loyal Jew, but he could not move many others to share this perception.[44] For the average Jewish perception, selectivity regarding the Torah meant apostasy.[45]

Paul thus finds himself in a difficult situation. He is committed both to his old tradition and to his new experience, trying to do justice to both. God has acted decisively at the Exodus and at Sinai, establishing his covenant and giving the Torah; however, he has also acted decisively in Jesus, making salvation available to all, but also conditional on faith in Jesus. Paul tries to have the best of both worlds.[46] In Romans 9 he presupposes that salvation is to be found in Christ alone, views unbelieving Israel as condemned and non-elect and resorts to an extreme theology of predestination to account for this situation. But in Romans 11 he verbally pleads for classic covenantal theology, although he tacitly lets this fuse with his conviction of salvation in Christ.

From the viewpoint of a non-Christian Jew, Paul's statement of the salvation of all Israel is not as generous as many Christians think. In effect he is saying: you will be saved, since eventually you will become like us. This 'mystery' assures, as Rosemary Ruether saw, 'the ultimate vindication of the church'. Jews 'must admit finally that it is not through Torah, but through faith in Jesus as the Christ, that they are intended to be saved'.[47] It is *Paul's mission* that will be justified in the near future.

It is indeed a question of self-legitimation. It is the tension between a novel liberal practice and the pressure towards a more conservative ideology that gets Paul into difficulty. His practice, the abandonment of circumcision and food laws, amounts to a break with sacred tradition; but his legitimating theory in Romans stresses continuity, so that he can even assert that it is he who truly establishes the law (Rom. 3.31).

A somewhat similar tension is also found in Qumran. A member of the Qumran sect, too, had to take a new step to enter the community; he had to believe in the new things revealed to the Teacher.[48] On the other hand, the rest of the people had fallen away[49] while the sectarians had remained faithful. Does one then remain in the covenant from which others have turned away, or does one take a new step? In any case, despite the novelty, Qumran stuck strictly to the central visible symbols of the old covenant. The sect spiritualized circumcision (1QS 5.1–5), but it certainly did not stop exercising it, and no one thought of accepting Gentiles as members. Therefore, the Jewish identity of the sect was not in doubt. Paul's case was different.

Some Qumran passages suggest 'that eschatological Israel would be formed by the conversion of the rest of Israel to the way of the sect',[50] especially 1QSa 1.1–6: 'This is the rule for all the congregation of Israel in the last days, when they shall join [the Community to wa]lk according to . . . when they come . . .'[51] If so, the sect expected its final vindication before the majority, much as Paul does in Romans 11.[52]

A singular section

In an overall account of early Christian religion, Romans 9–11
would not primarily belong to a section on 'soteriology'. Its appropriate context would be a chapter on the identity of the new sect
and the battles, external and internal, connected with it. The same
chapter would deal with the Torah and Jewish 'identity markers'
as well as the Christian appropriation of Scripture by projecting
new ideas into the old texts.

No 'doctrines' can be deduced from Romans 9–11, neither a
doctrine of predestination nor one of Israel's salvation. Both
Romans 9 and Romans 11 are singular passages in Paul's letters,
though in opposite ways: Romans 9 is 'too' negative and Romans
11 'too' positive about the situation of Israel. Neither passage can
be taken as such as a summary of what Paul 'really' thought when
dictating Romans.

To the singularity of 9.6–23 belongs the fact that 'faith' is not
mentioned at all in the section.[53] The opposite of 'works' in 9.12
is, rather, 'he who calls'. Nor would a mention of 'faith' fit into
that passage; it would damage it. Where *any* human activity is
excluded, even faith disappears from the picture, and rightly so.

One does well to distinguish between Paul's inmost aim – what
he 'really' has in mind – and his way of arguing his case.
Undoubtedly Paul has Jewish *Christians* in mind all the time when
he speaks of God's merciful election. The shape of his argument
prevents him, however, from spelling this out; otherwise the argument which rests on God's total sovereignty would be under-
mined. Paul's omission of any mention of faith here may indicate
that somehow he sensed the tension. In 9.6ff Paul speaks as if
humans are saved simply by God's free, indeed arbitrary action:
their destinies are decreed by God even before they are born.
Romans 9.14 shows that Paul is not insensitive to this issue.
Predestination to damnation is envisaged in 9.6–18.

Compared with the general tenor of his letters, Paul here goes
'too far', as the argument leaves no room for faith. In 11.25–36 the
argument would logically lead 'too far' in the opposite direction: to
the idea of *apokatastasis* (the 'restoration' of all, an idea which was
actually found there by many older commentators).[54] The

difference between the roughly parallel statements Gal. 3.22 and Rom. 11.32b is instructive. The former belongs to a context where 'justification by faith' is set forth: Scripture has consigned all under sin in order that what was promised might be given to 'those who believe'. The latter is about God's sovereign mercy: God has consigned all men to disobedience, that he may have 'mercy upon *all*'. It is difficult to emphasize human faith and divine omnipotence simultaneously.

With all its tensions, Romans 9–11 vividly illustrates how central and how difficult the questions of identity and continuity were. It shows a prominent member of the new sect in a struggle to legitimate his mission and to assert his and his group's identity in terms of the old values.[55] In the tree parable, Paul talks as if the church were a mainstream synagogue, with some new proselytes, from which a few apostates have been expelled. The social reality was quite different! Here a sectarian attempts to claim mainstream status for his group.

On the history of influence

It is intriguing to contemplate how the 'doctrine' of double predestination arose by accident, as it were, as Paul once went to extremes in trying to distinguish the empirical from the true Israel. The consequences, when Paul's statements were taken at face value, are worth noting.

For some, the abstract 'doctrine' of predestination became a source of courage but also 'a fearful doctrine'.[56] It armed an Augustine 'against feeling' in his relentless dealings with dissenters: he could let Donatists burn, predestined as they were for hellfire anyway.[57] For others, the haunting question 'Am I predestined to hell?' presented itself.[58] The 'peculiar existential importance' of the notion of a 'calling' in Calvinism 'was linked with anxieties occasioned by the Calvinist doctrine of predestination',[59] derived from Romans 9.[60] To overcome such anxiety, there was a 'psychological pressure to demonstrate one's election' by exhibiting the signs of election – including 'active involvement in the affairs of the world'.[61] The general later Protestant attitude towards work and secular activism may be taken as the residue of

this anxiety over predestination.[62] Moreover, 'the notion of predestination is easily secularized into that of "fate" or "destiny"';
the fact that 'a secularized America was still able to think of itself as
singled out among nations' is to be 'traced to America's Puritan
past'[63] and thus, in part at least, to Paul's occasional assertions in
Romans 9.

The 'suppression' of Romans 11 in Christianity has been
much criticized of late. But is it not unrealistic to expect that an
unrepeated and rather vague suggestion of a happy end should
have undone all the negative comments about Israel made by Paul
himself and others? Paul might have provided an important
corrective for Jewish-Christian relations, if only he had stated
clearly what many of his recent interpreters take him to mean: the
ongoing validity of the Jewish covenant. If only he had written: 'I
have changed my mind, I am sorry for some of the things I have
said!' It might have helped if Paul had asked Tertius to cancel a
page or two he had just dictated (Romans 9). He did nothing of the
sort, leaving the task of making sense of the whole to his interpreters. Small wonder that the optimistic vision was read in the
light of the more typical statements of the apostle.

Anyway, Romans 11 did have some practical influence on
Christian attitudes towards Jews and even on post-Constantinian
legislation. Care had to be taken that the Jews were not *totally*
destroyed, for then how could their predicted conversion and, consequently, the parousia take place?[64] Christians debated just how
many Jews it was necessary to have left,[65] but Paul's mystery seems
to have saved the lives of some. A few Christians even pleaded for
clemency with regard to the Jews' end-time salvation.[66]

The promise of Israel's salvation was interpreted by some as a
stimulus for missionizing Jews. Others, like Spener, anticipated
small missionary success, the conversion being a miracle of God.
The founder of Pietism paid attention to Paul's parable of the olive
tree and his warning of Gentile arrogance. Such thoughts were in
their time a step towards religious tolerance,[67] though the main
reason for a positive attitude to the Jews was still the assurance that
one day they would convert.

These are some of the fruits, beneficial and harmful, that have
grown from the seeds of Paul's message to Roman Christians. An

assessment of the influence of texts on the life of people could provide the bridge from a historical account of early Christianity to theological or philosophical evaluation.

Toward a personal appreciation

Historical scholarship cannot produce normative results. There is no direct bridge from 'what it meant' to 'what it means'. What Paul meant need not be what we have to say. What historical scholarship can do for today is to give incentives for constructive thinking in new situations.

Rather than taking any of Paul's statements as direct answers to our questions it might be better to see his struggle as a potential example in our situation as well, when embracing cultural pluralism is imperative. Paul is wrestling with his sacred tradition in the light of his new experience (positively, the living together of different ethnic groups in his church; negatively, the rejection of his message by most Jews). We, too, try to make sense of our traditions in the light of our experience which includes the necessity of a critical approach to all traditions, and an awareness of the terrible things that have happened and are happening in the world, partly because of some of our own traditions.

The man

was no plaster saint. Nor did he find lasting and real solutions to many of the problems he encountered. Possibly he did not even see the implications of some of them. He was a man of his time and place, with a particular . . . religious background, facing a specific . . . social situation. He was also deeply human . . . and the roots of his attitudes and actions were deep and tangled, as are most people's. . . . He hurt some, yet consoled and sustained many. He was caught in compromises inevitable in public life. But fundamentally he was a man of vision and action, who asked many of the profoundest questions that face humankind as it struggles to live in community. It was his confrontation out of a real humanity which marks his true stature and which makes his struggles and glimpses of truth of enduring significance. As a man of his time who asked the deepest questions, even though he could not answer them, he became a man for all times and places.

Originally, this was not said of Paul. It is the conclusion to an outstanding biography of Mahatma Gandhi by Judith Brown.[68] But with very little modification her words can be applied to Paul as well. In a new situation, Paul's work – like Gandhi's – in trying to unite different communities must be carried on critically. His views must be treated selectively; they must be adapted and enhanced. As a man of his time who asked some of the deepest questions, Paul, too, could be seen as a man for all times and places.

3

Co-existence and Conflict: Early Christian
Attitudes to Adherents of Traditional Cults

When nascent Christianity spread in the Greco-Roman world, it was *not* moving into a vacuum. Converts to it 'were *not* abandoning a static or dying religious culture'.[1] The religious landscape was governed by flourishing traditional cults. The festivals of the gods were great joyful occasions with processions, music, sacrifices and banqueting; they were also matters of civic self-respect which supported a city's identity.[2] 'At the level of the procession, the impact of a pagan cult can still be sensed in the journeys of the Christian images through the cities of southern Spain during Holy Week.'[3]

The early Christians had a simple name for the adherents to these cults: they were 'idolaters'; their festivals were acts of 'idolatry'.

The Hebrew Bible ascribes to Gentile worshippers the naive belief that the image *is* the deity. Second Isaiah abounds in contemptuous descriptions of the process of making a god. A man uses the wood from a tree as fuel; the rest of it he makes into a god and falls down to it, he worships it and prays to it. Strict prohibition of idolatry which must be violently opposed is a central part of Yahweh's covenant with Israel.

The polemic continued in post-biblical Judaism.[4] Even that great intellectual, Philo of Alexandria, can require the penalty of death for someone who bids us to 'fraternize with the multitude, resort to their temples, and join their libations and sacrifices'.[5] Apart from the temple cults proper, this condemned activity 'might also include joining the various clubs and associations in the cities, since many of these arranged gatherings in localities connected with temples'.[6] Philo 'regards the images of pagan gods as shadows', and yet he 'is not unconcerned about the way they should be treated. He thinks they have a seductive power through their beauty.'[7]

Strict boundaries were thus drawn between the Jewish religious community and outsiders, between order and chaos. To be sure, these boundaries did not necessarily coincide with the borderline between salvation and perdition. Many Jews held that righteous Gentiles who followed some basic religious and moral rules would eventually find mercy before Israel's God. But even this 'covenant of Noah' was not at all a thesis of universal salvation. Its 'inclusivism' is of a very limited type, for it 'explicitly excludes idolaters (and therefore most of the human race)'.[8]

The standard Jewish attitude to 'idolatry' was taken over by Christians. To be sure, Christian contempt for image-worship converged with that of many philosophers, the earliest of them contemporaries of Second Isaiah. But Christians (like Jews) connected idolatry with other wicked things: it brought its practitioners into contact with demons, and it led – automatically as it were – to all kinds of depravity.

Paul

Paul praises his Greek converts in Thessalonica for having turned 'from idols' to serve the living and true God. In Romans 1 he presents an utterly black picture of the 'idolaters'. Those who have changed God's glory for human or animal images are the victims of 'degrading passions', 'filled with every kind of wickedness, evil, covetousness, malice, envy, murder, strife' etc. (the vice list includes some twenty items).

Many commentators still take Paul's tirades at face value, speaking of 'the manifest decadence of the pagan world'[9] or of 'the grossest form of superstition and immorality' (C.H. Dodd).[10] Hendrik Kraemer, the leading representative of the 'exclusivist' position on other religions, was able to quote Dodd on Paul's 'dark picture' of 'demonic perversion': '. . . at every turn the traveller in the Graeco-Roman world met with frank idolatry and its moral accompaniments. This was what Paul saw.'[11] Kraemer added sinister shades to the picture: 'For us, living in a time in which by the satanic folly of Nazism and what has followed in its wake, we have looked into incredible abysses of human depravity, Paul's realism seems quite sober.'[12] But Robin Lane Fox points out that it 'is quite untrue that pagans lived in unfettered sexuality before Christianity came' (although the Christians did create a different code in this regard). Even in the pagan Greek world sexuality was 'governed by the profound restraints of honour and shame'.[13]

Actually Paul's attack on Gentiles in Romans 1 is part of his argumentative strategy which aims at the conclusion that the whole world is 'under sin' and needs Jesus Christ as its redeemer. When he was not arguing for this theological conclusion, Paul had a greater sense of shading in his picture of the Gentile world.

Paul's First Letter to the Corinthians reveals that the relation of his Greek converts to the traditional cults was a practical problem. Is it possible to participate in pagan religious events? In particular there was the issue of food. What can be eaten, where, and with whom? This letter also reveals a broad-minded attitude on Paul's part which one might not expect after reading the opening of Romans.

In I Corinthians 10 Paul makes some clear-cut decisions.

1. Participation in a pagan cult is impossible (10.14–22). The intensity of the argument suggests that some people in the Christian community did attend pagan religious occasions, possibly in the sanctuary of Demeter and Kore which stood not far from the agora.[14] Paul warns them severely: 'Do not become idolaters!' 'You cannot drink the cup of the Lord and the cup of demons. You cannot partake of the table of the Lord and the table of demons.' Here pagan gods are not just pieces of wood and stone; their worship involves the frightening world of evil spirits.

2. Meat sacrificed to a pagan god cannot be eaten at the god's table. Yet when the meat is later sold in the market-place, it is allowed (10.25–26).

3. It is even permitted to accept a pagan host's invitation and to 'eat whatever is set before you'. Eating 'idol meat' in such a context does not matter. If, however, one of the dinner companions points to the origin of the meat and thus makes the eating a matter of conscience, one should abstain from eating the meat (10.27–11.1).[15]

All these issues must have been debated in Corinth. Chapter 8

shows that Paul's own position is less clear than the points just
mentioned suggest. Here the case is that of a Christian causing
offence to his 'weaker' brethren by eating in the 'idol's house'
(v.10) – something we would not expect to happen at all if we only
read chapter 10.[16]

Paul is answering a question raised by an 'enlightened' party,
the 'strong' ones. He concedes that the inquirers have 'knowledge',
but knowledge has the effect of 'puffing up'. Paul agrees that pagan
gods do not really exist (not a word on demons here). Sacrificial
meat is just ordinary meat and can, in itself, be freely eaten. This is
exactly what the strong had thought. The problem is, for Paul, that
some other Christians with a 'weak conscience' still regard the
gods as somehow real. The temptation to eat 'idol meat' is, for
them, a temptation to apostasy. Therefore, the strong should
abstain from eating 'idol meat', if they are observed by the weak.

In principle Paul agrees with the strong: there is nothing wrong
in eating even in a temple (when one is not watched by the
'weak').[17] Since Paul is so adamant about the 'table of demons'
(I Cor. 10), he may have something other than religious festivals
proper in mind here, probably meals with a predominantly social
character: meals of trade guilds or some family events. The
problem is that drawing a line between religious and social
occasions is extremely difficult in practice. If social events took
place in 'the idol's house', some sacrifices and libations were
inevitable.

Paul's solution seems somewhat vague; even his own mind
seems divided. Intellectually he sides with the strong; but he
shares some of the sentiments of the weak, even some of their fear
of demons. He actually wavers, as Jewish thought did in general,
on the issue of the nature of pagan gods: are they mere figments of
the imagination or are they evil demons?

The issue of meat points to social stratification in the congregation. The 'weak' brethren so sensitive to 'idol meat' are probably
those who are weak in social terms as well (1.26f.).[18] Meat was
seldom available to common people in antiquity. In practice they
could only eat meat when it was publicly distributed at the
festivals; perhaps also at some of the common meals of the trade
guilds, which also had a religious character.[19]

The situation was different for those whose social standing was 'higher' – and there were some such people in the Corinthian congregation. Invitations to meals with religious overtones were part of their routine communication with their peers. Restrictions on the eating of sacrificial meat were restrictions on social relations.[20] Christians of a higher social standing were more integrated in society than were rank-and-file Christians.[21] Erastus, 'the city treasurer' of Corinth (*ho oikonomos tes poleos*), would surely have been bound to give up his public office right away if he had turned down all invitations which implied eating 'idol meat'.[22] Yet this man joins Paul in sending the Roman Christians greetings from Corinth (Rom. 16.23).

The issue was not a Corinthian speciality. Romans 14–15 reflects a conflict in Rome between the 'strong' and the 'weak'. Sacrificial meat or wine is not explicitly mentioned, but it is a fair assumption that those who ate no meat or drank no wine did so in order to avoid contact with idols.

Paul's view, as well as that of the 'strong', seems to be rooted in the attitude adopted early on in the mixed congregation of Syrian Antioch toward Jewish food laws. This view, in turn, had its roots in the views of the 'Hellenist' group around Stephen which had to leave Jerusalem because of its liberal views, after Stephen had been killed (see Acts 6–8 and 11). The congregation in Antioch, the first Christian community to accept Gentiles, was founded by members of this group. A free attitude toward food was part of the Hellenist legacy.

What we find in Paul, then, is a combination of freedom, personal counselling, ambivalence – and prejudice. Except in Romans 1, Paul's attitude to the adherents of other cults was more positive than his attitude to the cults themselves. A Christian may freely eat with unbelieving friends, but 'to take part in idolatrous ritual is another matter'.[23] And in the final analysis the internal cohesion of the Christian group was much more important than contact with outsiders. Such contacts were to be abandoned in the name of inner-Christian love if they jeopardized the unity of the congregation.

Still, within the early church Paul's was 'an attitude of extraordinary liberalism', as regards the eating of sacrificial meat. After his time the church almost totally abandoned his subtle reasoning and preferred to retreat 'into a narrow religious shell'.[24] 'Nothing is more striking than that Luke can make Paul himself part-author' of the so-called Apostolic Decree.[25] Luke claims that a decree which, among other things, flatly forbids the consumption of 'idol meat', was promulgated at the 'Apostolic Council' in Jerusalem in order to regulate the relations of Jewish and Gentile Christians. Paul's account of the Jerusalem meeting does not mention such a decision at all, and his basic sympathy toward those who did eat idol meat is in disagreement with it. It is likely that the decree was only issued after Paul's time. Then, however, it became very influential.

Long ago, the classical scholar Eduard Meyer pointed out that the decree brought about a rupture in the relations between Christians and pagans; in everyday life this rupture was even more acute than the one caused by Jewish food laws, since often enough families and close personal relations were involved. Meyer wrote that 'Christians would have been spared a great many persecutions, if Paul's more liberal view had prevailed'.[26]

Revelation

The Book of Revelation, composed in Asia Minor toward the end of the first century, pronounces a fierce judgment on the 'idolaters'. They are classed together with 'dogs, sorcerers, fornicators, murderers, everyone who loves and practises falsehood' (22.15, cf. 9.20–21) or with 'all liars' (21.8). The people thus branded are identical with the 'dwellers on earth' – an expression used throughout as a disparaging phrase by the author, meaning all non-Christians of the world. John expects that eventually those Christians who keep their faith intact will receive 'power over the Gentiles' and 'rule them with an iron rod'.

For one prominent recent scholar of the Revelation of John, the book's world of vision is 'cosmopolitan'[27] and its ultimate goal 'the liberation of all humanity' from oppressive and destructive powers, represented by the power of Rome.[28] The salvation envisaged does not, then, belong to Christians alone. But it is daring to suggest that the multitude of those who have 'washed their robes in the blood of the Lamb' (Rev. 7.9–17) consists of all those, Christian or non-Christian, who have suffered violence,[29] and it is very hard to see that Revelation's 'outcries for judgment and justice' 'rise up not only on behalf of Christians but also on behalf of the whole earth';[30] how would this fit with the thorough-going negative use of 'the dwellers on the earth' in Revelation?

The question is also being discussed whether John implies a conversion of the nations of the world to the one true God.[31] Even if this were the case (which is very uncertain), this would be a kind of eschatological inclusivism like Paul's in Romans 11 (see Chapter 2 above): all those will be saved who will repent and thus join us.

John also attacks some fellow Christians called 'Nicolaitans', followers of someone called Nicolaus.[32] John charges them in Pergamum and Thyatira with eating 'idol meat' (2.14, 20). The backdrop of his criticism is constituted by the Apostolic Decree: 'no other burden' will be laid on the faithful (2.24). In view of the social circumstances in Thyatira, a prosperous trade centre, commentators recognize the relevance of guild-membership to this issue. Some Christians seem to have been members of trade guilds; they were likely to be involved in social events which took place in pagan temples and included meals. The parallelism with the situation in Corinth in Paul's time is obvious.

The Nicolaitans are also supposed to practise fornication or adultery. The context bristles with Old Testament allusions; the Christian prophetess opposed by John is called Jezebel, after a pagan queen known for favouring the cult of Baal. 'Fornication' is a standing Old Testament metaphor to describe Israel's apostasy from Yahweh, and the word is probably also used in this sense here. John would hardly have praised the Thyatirans for their love, faith, service and endurance (as he also does), if the congregation had tolerated actual promiscuity. 'Fornication', then, seems simply another name for eating 'idol meat'.

In patristic tradition, the Nicolaitans are said to have traced their ideas back to one Nicolaus of Antioch. He was one of the seven leaders of the 'Hellenist' wing of the Jerusalem church around Stephen. A historical connection is possible; in fact it makes excellent sense, if a free attitude towards food was part of the 'Hellenist' legacy.

In the light of I Corinthians, Paul might well have approved of the Nicolaitans. For him, the issue of 'idol meat' was a problem of personal counselling. For John, by contrast, eating or not eating was a question of life and death in the ideological battle between Christ and the Beast. – The battle is indeed mainly ideological at this stage for, contrary to common opinion, there is no real evidence for a widespread persecution of the Christians at the end of the first century; the persecutions depicted in the book of Revelation are located in the expectations of the author.[33]

John's counsel to the congregations is that of social separation.[34] 'Come out of her [the fallen Babylon], my people, lest you take part in her sins, lest you share in her plagues . . .' (18.4). Probably the Christian life-style as John understood it was 'incompatible with ordinary participation in the economic and social life of the cities'. John's strict position on 'idol meat' does not seem 'compatible with continued membership in a guild'.[35] It tends 'toward the formation of separate Christian trade associations and burial societies (or toward the congregations taking on these functions)'. Even more: it tends 'toward the establishment of Christians as a third race', preparing (paradoxically enough) for the formation of a Christian state.[36]

Thus, John's group 'sets up high boundaries between itself and the rest of the world' and 'holds to a concomitant "separatist" definition of the church', seeing 'Greco-Roman society as demonic'. The group attacked by him, the Nicolaitans, is 'less concerned with sharp boundaries and exclusive self-definition and seems to have little conflict with . . . Greco-Roman urban institutions'.[37] However, we have no information concerning the attitude of the Nicolaitans to actual pagan cults or to religious festivals.

The conflict with the world thus goes hand in hand with an inner-Christian conflict over life-style. The tendency toward separation takes over; coexistence increasingly yields to conflict. The Nicolaitans, who have undeservedly had to bear the stigma of licentious libertines, belong to those who are best suited to be models for inter-religious openness among early Christians.

Gnostic Christians

From the second century on, Gnostics[38] are the only Christians known to have eaten sacrificial meat.[39] Justin Martyr complains that many nominal Christians actually eat food offered to idols and claim that they have no harm from it (*Dial.* 35.1); to him, however, they are not real Christians (35.6). Irenaeus (*Adv.haer.* I. 6.3) says that some Gnostics eat idol meat without scruples and are even 'the first to arrive' at pagan festival parties and also enjoy the spectacle of fights in the circus. Unfortunately we are dependent here on polemical second-hand sources; the Nag Hammadi texts are silent on 'idol meat'. In any case the new finds have changed our view of Gnostic morality: isolated cases there may have been, but no generalizations about supposed Gnostic libertinism are possible any longer.[40]

A certain affinity between the strong in Corinth, the Nicolaitans and the later Gnostics is obvious. The followers of Valentinus and Basilides included Christians of a relatively high social standing. Many Gnostics were on a high intellectual level. Gnostic Christians included people who seldom found their way to the catholic church. Their attitude to sacrificial meat is a sign of a greater integration into society.[41]

Unfortunately it is very difficult to establish what the attitude of the various Gnostic groups to their pagan neighbours was actually like.[42] Some Valentinians, at least, seem to have made a strict separation between Christian truth and pagan religion. A fragment from the Valentinian Heracleon (frag. 21) reads: 'One is not allowed to pray as the Greeks who believe in material things and worship wood and stone.'[43] Yet this could be taken as an intellectual person's criticism of popular practice, paralleled in Greek philosophers. If what we have here is a tension between an open-minded attitude to everyday social contacts on one hand and polemic against the cult on the other, then this reminds one of the similar tension found in Paul. On the other hand, there are hints that some Gnostics themselves fostered a cult of images, even owning statues of gods.[44] They may have reinterpreted the significance of these statues. According to Irenaeus, the Carpocratian disciples of Marcellina in Rome had, along with busts of philosophers, even images of Jesus which they crowned and observed 'like the heathen' (*Adv.haer.* I. 25.6).[45] This practice surely points, at the very least, to tolerance of the standard use of cultic images.[46]

Pagan reasons for suspecting or hating Christians

The author of Luke-Acts tries to establish a positive contact with the Hellenistic moral-philosophical tradition. Much of Luke's work serves as a political apology: the Christians are harmless, and this is time and again confirmed by Roman authorities. But for Luke, too, 'image-worship' and 'idol meat' constitute an insuperable boundary, as we saw (see p. 11 above). Luke tells how Paul, visiting Athens, 'was deeply distressed to see that the city was full of idols'. Nevertheless Luke lets Paul use this observation as a point of contact, as he starts his preaching with a reference to an (alleged) altar to 'the unknown god'. This God has overlooked the ignorance of the Greeks, but now he commands 'all people everywhere to repent'.

Luke's apology does not seem to have been a great success in the pagan world. Pagan authors agree that *odium humani generis*, hatred for humankind, was a general reason for pagan distrust of Christians.[47] Exclusivity and isolation were likely to cause suspicion and misunderstanding. But was it a case of total *mis*-understanding?

The 'First Letter of Peter', written by an unknown author toward the end of the century, documents an attempt at peaceful coexistence in a climate of slander and suspicion. The opponents of the Christians are private slanderers; state authorities are not regarded as cruel or corrupt in the letter. Trials of Christians are presupposed. They have to suffer because of false accusations (financially and perhaps physically), but death penalties are not yet in evidence (4.12–17).[48]

Christians are maligned by their neighbours as evil-doers, yet through the honourable conduct of the Christians the neighbours may eventually glorify God (2.12, cf. 3.16).[49] Astonishingly, Christians have got the reputation of being murderers, thieves, criminals and mischief-makers (4.15).[50]

Actually, it is a question of mutual slander. Pagans are lumped together by the author as evil-doers (4.3–4). He tells his readers:

> You have already spent enough time in doing what the Gentiles like to do, living in licentiousness, passions, drunkenness, revels, carousing, and *lawless idolatry*. They are surprised that you no longer join them in the same excesses of dissipation, and so they blaspheme.

Again the connection suggested between licentiousness and idolatry is noteworthy. Moreover, what arouses suspicion is the Christians' abandonment of some activities in which they had previously joined their pagan neighbours. It is natural to think of organized feasts and guild meals as those activities in which 'you no longer join them'.[51] Christians have withdrawn from their previous social contacts; this has created suspicion. The result is mutual vilification.

In a number of passages, other Christian writings also contrast the Christian way of life with pagan conduct, or with the Christians' previous pagan life in harsh words.[52] Here is one example:

> You must no longer live as the Gentiles live, in the futility of their minds . . . They have lost all sensitivity and have abandoned themselves to licentiousness, greedy to practise every kind of impurity . . . (Eph. 4.17–19).

If this attitude was at all reflected in the Christians' actual relations with their pagan neighbours, it is no great wonder if the latter sensed that they were not loved. So it happens that 'both sides attribute the same vices to each other: it is the other one who is 'full of hatred'' '.[53]

Even today, many of the people who attend religious services in our societies 'find that the traditional rituals provide them with a link with tradition and give them a sense of security . . . In rather the same way, many of the pagans of late antiquity loved to worship the ancestral gods, as generations had done before them. The old rituals gave them a sense of identity . . .' People 'would feel obscurely threatened if a new cult set out to abolish the faith of their fathers'.[54]

And then there was the anger of the gods.[55] The gods could show their anger by bringing natural disasters and diseases on whole areas, if they were not content with the worship given to them; however, they could be appeased through proper rites. It was the fear of this anger which 'impelled people to persecute Christian "atheists", dangerous groups who refused to honour the gods'.[56]

The Christians must have made a negative impression in the city of Rome. Otherwise Nero could not have made them scapegoats for the fire. The Neronian persecution, for its part, increased the negative publicity, branding the Christians as dangerous out-siders.[57]

Contrary to a common view, the imperial cult seems *not* to have been a central issue in either official or unofficial attitudes towards Christians. This is confirmed by the correspondence of Pliny, governor of Pontus and Bithynia around 112 CE, with the Emperor Trajan.[58] It is useful to distinguish between 'hard' and 'soft' forms of the imperial cult.[59] The 'hard' form entailed sacrificing before the image of the emperor and cursing Christ, but this was not at all the rule.

> It occurred more seldom than we think, and it was not the Roman authorities who were mainly responsible for it, but the local pagan population; the authorities only became active after a denunciation from their side. John regards the 'soft' cult of the emperor as much more dangerous, i.e. when someone joined a festive multitude or participated in a social guild meal with religious overtones.[60]

The sacrifices in connection with the imperial cult were 'for the most part made *on behalf of* the image of the emperor, not to it'.[61] '. . . the cult attached itself to the lively, traditional religious-ness . . .'[62] It was not the Roman authorities who were mainly responsible for the trials of Christians, but the local population; the authorities only became active after a denunciation from the people's side. The problem was that Christians 'could not sacrifice to *any* god on behalf of the emperor'.[63] *That* put them on a collision course with local religious activity.

Thus the persecutions of Christians were a tragic consequence of their increasingly strained relations with their pagan neighbours, the adherents of traditional cults.

Jewish and Christian inability to understand other cults

The tragedy bore in itself the seeds of victory, but it was a victory for a price. With this statement we are moving towards a 'theo-ethical' evaluation of the historical findings. Bishop Richard Hanson states that 'it must not be denied that one of the great reasons for Christianity prevailing over its rivals was its intolerance'; 'it paid the price for this strength by the intolerance which it continued to show when it had won'.[64] Or, as Karen Armstrong puts it: 'Today we have become so familiar with the intolerance that has unfortunately been a characteristic of mono-theism, that we may not appreciate that this hostility towards other gods was a new religious attitude. Paganism was an essentially tolerant faith . . .'[65] Of course there were other reasons for the spread of Christianity which 'was also due to faults in pagan society. In cities of growing social divisions, Christianity offered unworldly equality. It preached, and at its best it practised, love in a world of widespread brutality.'[66] But the intolerance cannot be eliminated from the picture either.

The Bible misrepresents the cults in which images are used;[67] some of the cult-critical philosophers do the same. The connection which was perceived to exist between statue and god was different in different cases.[68] It could be very close, but normally no full identity should be posited; it is not the material object itself which is worshipped.[69] Jon Levenson notes that 'the polemical misrepresentation of Canaanite and other "pagan" religion in the Hebrew Bible parallels the polemical misrepresentation of Pharisaism (or Judaism) in the New Testament' – an insight especially valuable as it comes from a perceptive Jewish scholar.[70]

John Strong gives a differentiated account. According to him, there is 1. 'the thoroughgoing image-worshipper' for whom 'the image may well be divine – that is, there may be a permanent and intimate relationship between the god and the image, in which the deity can always be found';[71] 2. 'the devotee who views the god as somehow present in the image, but only for the duration of a ritual'; and 3. 'the person who thinks that images are helpful foci for veneration, but that ultimately they are only reflections and reminders of the deity's characteristics'; 'such individuals do not actually worship the image but worship before the image'. As Karen Armstrong puts it: 'Despite the bad press it has in the Bible, there is nothing wrong with idolatry *per se*: it only becomes objectionable or naïve if the image . . . is confused with the ineffable reality to which it refers.'[72]

Wilfred Cantwell Smith deplores the 'Christian (and Jewish) failure to understand . . . what is going on in the spiritual life of communities served by images', actually 'a failure to recognize that anything at all was going on spiritually'. This error 'has done untold damage on the human scene through the centuries'.[73]

Smith is writing in the context of inter-religious dialogue. His appreciation of the 'spiritual life of communities served by images' stems from his experience in India, where the closest present-day analogies to image-worship in the Greco-Roman world can probably be found. Smith concludes that 'we had good reason to dismiss "idolatry" as a concept'. 'As an interpretation of others' religious life' 'it has been intellectually wrong, and morally wrong'.[74]

Smith notes, however, that while the Christians' vision of other communities has been limited, their 'discernment regarding matters within their own group' has been quite sharp. Thus, they have also used the term 'idolatry' metaphorically to connote spiritual phenomena in their own community: putting one's faith in material wealth or worldly fame for instance has been called a form of 'idolatry'.[75]

Smith finds such metaphorical usage helpful, but he turns the tables on traditional Christianity. He states that 'exclusive claims' for one's own religion are also 'idolatry' in the bad sense.[76] To identify one's own conception of God with the 'ultimate mystery' (as Jews, Christians and Muslims have so often done) is an error analogous to that of identifying the image with the transcendent reality which the image is meant to represent.[77] 'We Christians have substantially been idolaters, insofar as we have mistaken for God, or as universally final, the particular forms of Christian life or thought.'[78]

The theologian Tom Driver agrees: Christians speak

> of the religions of others as idolatries, a usage in line with the Old Testament, where 'idol' is a word to name the icons employed by persons who worship gods other than the God of Israel . . . in high contrast to Yahweh . . . of whom no image can be made. But of course images of Yahweh *are* made, if not 'graven' in stone[79] then 'writ' in concepts and metaphors that become sacrosanct – for example, the surety on the part of many Christians that it is proper to call God Father but improper to say Mother.[80]

Driver sums up: 'Idolatry is the insistence that there is only one way, one norm, one truth. It is the refusal to be corrected or informed by the "other".'[81]

Paradoxically, then, strictly monotheistic or monolatrous polemic against the others' 'idolatry' can be seen as an expression of one's own 'idolatry' in a metaphorical sense. Since Old Testament times such polemic has gone hand in hand with an attitude which approves of wiping out the others' 'idolatry' even with violent means, whenever one has the power to do so. This is evident in the so-called Deuteronomic history, which now governs the Old Testament story. Bernard Lang comments: 'In order to strengthen . . . the boundary between Jew and non-Jew', its authors rewrote the history of Israel. This they did in the spirit of intolerant monolatry, publishing 'their fantasies about a military powerful people who would annihilate polytheistic nations that threatened its unique religion'.[82]

Unfortunately, Christians who used the book much later took it for history. Worse, they even took the story of the conquest of Canaan for a model to be acted on. For instance, the Puritan emigrants applied the Deuteronomic fantasies literally to the indigenous, supposedly 'idolatrous' cultures in America.[83]

Closer to home, 'idolatry was associated with popery – with images, with the miracle of the mass'.[84] Milton, for example, explicitly compared Catholicism with Old Testament idolatry and insisted that it was right to hate the enemies of the church.[85] The sentiment of the time was that 'all papists are idolaters, properly equated with heathen: they must not be tolerated'.[86] It became 'a common Anglican practice' to replace images in churches with the Ten Commandments in English on church walls.[87]

As for early Christianity, Lane Fox has this to say:

> Pagans had been intolerant of the Jews and Christians . . . Yet the rise of Christianity induced a much sharper rise in religious intolerance and the open coercion of religious belief. Christians were quick to mobilize force against the pagan cults and against their own unorthodox Christian brethren . . . The change from pagan to Christian brought a lasting change in people's view of themselves and others: to study it is to realize how we, still, live with its effects.[88]

Indeed we live with the effects of these old religious conflicts. As was noted in Chapter 1, it is probably true to say that there can be no peace in the world without peace between religions. But a necessary precondition for such peace is a readiness for critical self-examination on the part of the religions. In this process it is helpful to remember that in earliest Christianity there were – along with the polemics – also some attempts towards peaceful co-existence with adherents of traditional cults.

4

The Redemption of Israel: A Salvation-Historical Problem in Luke-Acts

The author of Luke-Acts strongly emphasizes the continuity between Israel and the church; this has given him the reputation of an 'inclusivist' theologian in the eyes of many.[1] Nonetheless, he also depicts a fatal crisis within Israel. Many Jews have accepted Christ. They constitute the nucleus of God's true people into which believing Gentiles have been included. For these Jews and Gentiles God's promises to Israel have been fulfilled. But, according to the common view, 'the unbelieving portion of the people (of Israel) is rejected for all times'.[2]

This common view has been challenged by some.[3] Mussner reads Luke-Acts in the light of Romans 11 and finds the idea of Israel's end-time restoration spelt out in Acts 1.6 and 3.20. The 'establishing' of Israel belongs together with 'God's continuing covenant with Israel'. 'Jesus is and continues to be the previously described Messiah' who is 'for the Jews, even if Israel in its majority is still not able to see that'.[4]

The most sophisticated attempt to overthrow the scholarly consensus stems from Robert C. Tannehill's literary analysis of Luke's narrative. In the birth stories 'we find very strong emphasis on the view that Jesus means redemption for . . . the Jewish people' (Luke 1.32–33, 54–55, 68–69, 71, 74). The salvation in view is specified as 'the redemption of Jerusalem'. Yet such expectations are not fulfilled in Luke's narrative: it ends by stating that the Jews are blind and deaf and will remain so, while Gentiles will hear and receive salvation (Acts 28.26–28). Readers aware of the outcome of the Jewish-Roman war would sense the disappointment strongly.[5]

Tannehill correctly rejects two possible explanations for this discrepancy. First, Luke 1–2 cannot be excluded from consideration as a piece of evidence not fully integrated into Luke-Acts as a whole. Second, it cannot be assumed that any of the characters who voice the hope of Israel's redemption in 'political' terms in the birth narratives are unreliable witnesses who do not represent the narrator's real point of view.[6] After all, these witnesses include not only the mother of the Lord, who is, for Luke, the paradigm of a believer, but also an angel of God. Furthermore, to attribute a mistaken point of view to Zechariah in his *Benedictus* is to disregard the explicit remark that he was filled with the Holy Spirit.

Tannehill thinks that Luke views the recent history of the Jewish people as tragic, dominated as it is by Jewish rejection of Christ (75). The promise of a kingdom free of oppressors is as valid as ever – if only Israel would accept its Messiah. Towards the end of Acts, Paul insists that he is on trial 'for the hope of Israel' (26.6–7). In rejecting Paul, his opponents 'are rejecting the fulfilment of their own hope' (78).

For Tannehill, the sombre statements at the end of Acts (28.25–28) cannot be Luke's last word on the Jewish people. 'It is hard to imagine' that Luke, 'for whom the fulfilment of scriptural prophecy is a central article of faith, would ever admit that a primary aspect of prophecy, emphasized in his own work, is finally void' (83). A complete disappearance of the hope for the restoration of the people of Israel 'would leave him with an unresolvable theological problem. Salvation for Israel has been presented as a major aspect of God's purpose, certified by Scripture, but the final outcome would be the opposite.' Therefore Acts 3.19–21, supported by Luke 13.34–35, must refer to 'a lingering hope' for 'salvation through conversion' which Luke still holds (85).

I think that Tannehill has put his finger on a real problem, although his solution is unviable. The remarks that follow are an attempt to show why, and they pave the way for a different explanation.

The birth narrative

In the birth narrative, the 'national-political' statements on the career of Jesus are linked with different statements which tend to obscure the political meaning or move the message to a different level. Thus the messianic promise concerning David's throne and an eternal reign over Jacob's house (Luke 1.32–33) is surpassed by the statement on the manner of the conception and the divine sonship of Jesus (1.34–35). The assurance that 'with God nothing is impossible' (v.37) is not given with reference to the acquisition of David's throne but in view of the manner of the conception.[7]

In Zechariah's *Benedictus*, the political message is unmistakable. God has prepared redemption for his people (v.68) through the 'horn of salvation' in the 'house of David' (v.69). This fulfils the words of the prophets (v.70) and reinforces God's covenant mercy (v.72) and his oath to Abraham. This redemption is specified as 'salvation from our enemies and from the hand of all who hate us' (v.71). As a result, we may serve God without fear, being delivered from the hand of our enemies (v.74). A great national accomplishment is expected of Jesus the Messiah!

Verses 76–77, however, introduce another meaning for 'salvation'. It no longer consists in freedom from oppressors but '*in the forgiveness of sins*' (v.77). Two different views of 'salvation' are fused.[8] But it is not said in so many words that the latter vision would supersede the political one.

In 2.10–11 the language is again suggestive of national deliverance: a saviour, the lord Christ, is born for the people in the city of David. However, the angels' song (v.14) introduces a restriction: there will indeed be peace on earth, but only among those with whom God is pleased (*en anthropois eudokias*). This indicates a division within Israel.

In 2.25 the 'consolation' of Israel which evokes passages from Second Isaiah (esp. Isa. 40.1; 49.13) has clear political-messianic overtones, and 2.38 reintroduces the notion of redemption (*lytrosis*), this time of Jerusalem. But surrounded by the glimpses of the national vision is the canticle of Simeon. It praises the salvation of the Lord which has been prepared not just 'for glory to thy people Israel' but also as a 'light for revelation to the Gentiles' (2.30–32). It is difficult to conceive of the light to the Gentiles simply as the political redemption of Israel. Simeon moves on to predict a division within Israel: many will fall, others will rise (2.34). The effects of the work of the Saviour will not be the same for all Israel.[9] This must mean that the work will *not* take place in the political sphere.

Luke does not state that there is progress in the vision of salvation in Luke 1–2. He makes no corrections, say, to the *Benedictus*. The national vision does not simply yield to a more spiritual or more comprehensive conception, but both views are juxtaposed.[10]

The vision of the Twelve before Pentecost

The political vision recurs on the lips of Jesus' followers later on in the Gospel. In 19.11, drawing near to Jerusalem, they suppose that 'the kingdom of God was to appear immediately'. Luke does nothing to deny the justification of such an expectation, connected with the city of Jerusalem; he is only concerned to show that the kingdom will not appear very soon. In the parable of the pounds that follows, the 'nobleman' goes away to receive kingly power. In due time, however, he will return; then his citizens who did not want him to be king (v.14) will be cruelly punished (v.27). Jerusalem and the kingdom of God do belong together, but the kingdom will bring no joy to those Jews who have rejected Jesus: they will be 'slain'. Instead of a 'lingering hope' for the restoration of Israel, Luke confronts us with eschatological genocide.[11]

The next passage describes Jesus' entry into Jerusalem. Strikingly enough, at the very moment when the eventual political content of his christology could have been clarified, Luke has carefully stripped the account of this-wordly restoration overtones. The cry that 'the kingdom of our father David is coming' (Mark 11.10) is omitted by Luke, who replaces it with a variation of the angels' other-worldly song (Luke 19.38b; cf. 2.14).

The eschatological speech in Luke 21.7–28 ends with the promise of 'redemption' (*apolytrosis*) in v.28. Some interpreters find here the idea of a restoration of Israel and Jerusalem.[12] Yet the text speaks of 'your' redemption, and the speech is addressed to Jesus' ('Christian') disciples.[13] The promise of redemption to the addressees would seem to equal the earlier promise that 'by your endurance you will gain your lives' (21.19). So the hope of redemption seems thoroughly individualized.[14] The faithful can 'raise their heads' in hope. As for Jerusalem, the speech only speaks of preordained vengeance (21.22) and slaughter (21.24). Not a single word indicates that after the sack of the city,

Jerusalem would experience a reversal of its fortune with the Parousia.

Nevertheless, the political hope of Jesus' followers surfaces again in Luke 24.21. Obviously, what Jesus accomplished in his lifetime did not meet the hope that he would be 'the one to redeem Israel'. In his answer the risen Jesus refers to Scripture: all that the prophets have spoken *is* actually being fulfilled. Yet Jesus does not correct the followers' political understanding of his task. The lesson is repeated in 24.44ff. The predictions that must be fulfilled include the suffering and resurrection of Christ and the preaching of repentance and forgiveness to all nations. All this seems to fuse with the 'redemption of Israel'. At least no hint is given to the effect that the two notions of salvation are contradictory.

Indeed, after this exegetical lecture by the risen Christ, and even after additional weeks of instruction concerning the kingdom (Acts 1.3), the disciples still regard the notion of a 'kingdom for Israel' as self-evident! 'Lord, will you at this time restore the kingdom to Israel?' (Acts 1.6). Even more startling is the fact that Jesus does not find the question stupid at all. The only mistake is the timing, which is corrected (1.7): it is not for the disciples to know times fixed by the Father. Jesus does not touch the issue of the 'kingdom for Israel'. Yet, on the face of it, v.8 suggests that the kingdom will be restored when God so wills; in the meantime the disciples are to devote themselves to mission.

Once more, then, the two horizons are fused. The restoration of the kingdom to Israel is assimilated with the spread of the Christian mission.[15] But there is no outright correction of the political view,[16] nor will Luke ever state, say, that at last the disciples realized what Jesus' message was all about. Soon enough they will simply go about proclaiming it. But no moment of awakening from national dreams is singled out.

It is true that here Luke mainly wishes to account for the delay of the Parousia. He lets the disciples formulate a question which can be so answered that *that* problem is solved. The destiny of Israel is not the main issue. Thus it is striking how self-evidently Luke's 'Israel language' crops up. The beginning of Jesus' answer (v.7) stems from the eschatological discourse (Mark 13.32, omitted in Luke 21) and thus suggests that the restoration of Israel belongs with the Parousia. The question of Israel's kingdom is not rejected – it will just gradually drop out of sight as the narrative proceeds.

Here Luke had a splendid chance to remove all misconceptions and make clear the apolitical character of salvation. He fails to take the opportunity, leaving it open to the reader to imagine that Jesus' return (v.11) will bring about the restoration.

The speeches in Acts

In his Pentecost address, Peter mentions God's oath to David: one of his descendants will be set on his throne (Acts 2.30). The reader recalls the angel's word in Luke 1.32–33. Yet instead of depicting a political restoration, Peter claims that the oath applies to the resurrection of Jesus (v.31). But again Luke feels no need to pronounce that a false interpretation is being corrected. The prediction and its Christian application fuse, as if such an assimilation were the most natural thing in the world. In 2.39 Peter confirms that 'this promise' is 'to you and to your children'. This statement serves as an argument for the exhortation to repent and be baptized.[17] As in the *Benedictus*, the fulfilment of Israel's political hopes narrows down to the forgiveness of the sins of individuals who are exhorted to be saved from their 'crooked generation' (40). Thus a division will occur within Israel. On the other hand, v.39 also envisages Gentiles as fellow participants in the promise, so that nothing is left of a promise to Israel alone.

In Peter's second speech (Acts 3.12–26) the addressees are defined as 'the people' and 'Israelites' (v.12). God has fulfilled what all the prophets proclaimed: Christ had to suffer (v.18). The hearers are exhorted to repent (v.19). This is a condition for the coming of 'times of refreshment' and the sending of the Christ appointed 'for you' (v.20) – events which seem to coincide with the refreshment. This is not the restoration of 'all', but the establishing of all that God spoke through the prophets. In the light of such passages as Luke 24.44ff. or Acts 2.30–31, it cannot be taken for granted that Luke is thinking here of a 'kingdom for Israel'.[18]

To be sure, v.20 seems to indicate that God has preordained the sending of Christ to Israel in the Parousia. Yet the goal of the predictions is soon afterwards (v.22) regarded as the *historical* appearance of Jesus, the 'first' coming. Verse 23 goes on to state that whoever does not listen to Jesus 'shall be destroyed from the people'. A Jew who is not converted to Jesus ceases to belong to the people of God![19]

All prophets have predicted the time at hand (v.24). The promise concerning Abraham's seed is fulfilled in God's raising up Jesus and sending him to the men of Israel (v.26). The promised blessing will be realized when the listeners turn away from their wickedness.

It is clear from Peter's speech that the covenantal promise to Abraham and all the predictions of the prophets have come true in the sending and resurrection of Jesus. God has already sent Jesus to the Jews once (v.26). Verse 20 suggests that he is intent on doing it a second time, in 'times of refreshment', if only the men of Israel will repent for their sins (v.19, cf. v.26b). That repentance is identical with accepting Jesus as the Messiah (22f.). The blessing will only reach that part of Israel which accepts Jesus and is not 'cut off' (v.23).

But then it is quite unlikely that an actual 'kingdom for Israel', which is liberated from its national enemies, is in view.[20] Peter is saying no more than that the faithful, that is, the faithful in Israel along with those who will hear the message later, will enjoy blessings – both now and in the Parousia.[21] No national privilege is held out for Israel.

Paul's speech in Pisidian Antioch (Acts 13.16–41) is addressed to 'men of Israel', 'sons of the family of Abraham', and to the God-fearers (v.16, 26). After an account of God's mighty works among his elect people, Paul mentions David, of whose seed God brought Jesus as a saviour for Israel (v.23). The fulfilment of the promise given to the fathers (vv.32–33) has taken place in the resurrection of Jesus. In it, God's 'holy and sure blessings of David', promised to Israel ('you'), have come true (v.34).[22] To receive this blessing equals the forgiveness of sins and justification (vv.38–39). The resurrection of Jesus grants such forgiveness as could not be provided by the law. Adherence to the new message is called staying 'in the grace of God' (v.43). The implication is that grace is absent among non-Christian Jews.

Once more, the tacit reinterpretation of the promise could

hardly be more drastic. Evocative old words are used in the service
of a novel message.[23] The covenant with the fathers may be eternal
and the promise to David holy and sure, but anyone who does not
accept the new message is threatened with a menacing deed of God
– the rejection of Israel on the acceptance of the Gentiles (v.41).

The outcome is that Paul and Barnabas solemnly leave the men
of Israel who have judged themselves unworthy of eternal life
(v.46), and turn to the Gentiles in order to 'bring salvation to the
uttermost parts of the earth' (v.47). Salvation in Christ (vv.26, 47)
is equated with 'eternal life' (v.48) – an eschatological goal which
has no national Jewish ring about it. To this eternal life the men of
Israel are invited, but they thrust it away (v.46). By contrast, a
number of Gentiles have been 'ordained' to this very same life
(v.48). So there is no difference, as regards the eschatological goal,
between Jews and Gentiles. Anyone who believes in Christ goes on
to eternal life; *everyone* who believes is justified (v.39). Anyone
who does not believe is excluded.

In Acts 15.14 James affirms Peter's account: in the house of
Cornelius God 'first visited the Gentiles, to take out of them a
people for his name'. Here Gentiles (i.e., those chosen among
them) are called 'people' (*laos*) – a name which so far in Luke's
narrative has always denoted Israel. Israel and the church of Jews
and Gentiles fuse together. The word 'visited' recalls Zechariah's
psalm: 'Praised be the Lord God of Israel, for he has visited and
redeemed his people' (Luke 1.68; cf. 1.78). Just as Zechariah went
on to praise the raising of the horn of salvation from the 'house of
David' (Luke 1.69), so James proceeds to speak of the rebuilding of
David's dwelling (Acts 15.16). Both refer to the fulfilment of the
words spoken through the prophets in the events to which they
testify (Luke 1.70; Acts 15.15). Acts 15.14–18 has indeed the
appearance of a tacit reinterpretation of the *Benedictus*. The
prophecies concerning David's dwelling apply to the events of
which Peter has just spoken (v.15). On the other hand, its rebuilding is a prerequisite for the Gentiles to seek the Lord (v.17). The
rebuilding thus denotes the gathering of the faithful in Israel
around Jesus.[24] A concrete restoration of Israel's kingdom cannot
be meant, for the 'rest of men' would hardly start seeking the Lord
after the Parousia.

On the same occasion, Peter states that Jews and Gentiles will be saved in the very same manner (v.11), by having their hearts cleansed by God through faith (v.9). There is no difference whatsoever. This has been planned by God from of old (v.18). The passage thus does not favour the view that the end of the days might bring with it some special blessing for the nation of Israel.

Towards the end of Acts Paul insists that he is on trial for the hope of *Israel* (Acts 26.6–7).[25] By now it is no surprise that the Jewish hope of (general) resurrection and the Christian claim that the resurrection (of an individual) has occurred fuse together;[26] Jesus' raising comes to be seen as the fulfilment of God's promise to the fathers (v.6). Luke adds the nuance that it is what the 'twelve tribes' have been hoping for 'as they earnestly worship night and day' (v.7). The last phrase recalls Anna and her speech to those who waited for the 'redemption of Jerusalem' (Luke 2.38). 'Israel language' is evocatively used, but there is no hint of a 'kingdom for Israel' beyond participation in the same 'light' that is reaching the Gentiles (Acts 26.23) in the resurrection of Christ.[27]

Jesus' inaugural sermon

In the programmatic section Luke 4.16–30, the salvation brought by Jesus (v.18), described in healing and social terms, is something that concerns individuals. Otherwise it could not be fulfilled 'to-day' when Jesus speaks in Nazareth (nor even when Luke writes about the scene). Later Jesus uses the same sort of language with reference to his present activity (7.22). The Nazareth story also prefigures the Jewish rejection of Jesus' message and its orientation towards the Gentiles. And it is Jesus himself who provokes the anger of his kinsmen by starting to blame them and their ancestors (although they have said only nice things about his sermon!) and setting up the Gentiles as a positive example, so that the Nazarenes finally try to kill him (v.23–30). Jesus' first public confrontation with his people does not anticipate a glorious future for Israel. That this fits with Luke's view is confirmed by his account of the rejection of the Jews in Acts.[28]

The statements on the rejection of the Jews in Acts

Tannehill is forced to explain away the significance of those passages in Acts where the rejection of the Jews is made clear. He states (1988, 83) that Acts 13.46 cannot mean that 'Paul will never again preach to Jews, for as soon as he reaches the next town, he begins his mission by preaching in the synagogue to Jews' (14.1). On the other hand, the preaching to Gentiles cannot be a consequence of the Jewish rejection of the message in Antioch, for it has been announced in Scripture long ago (84). Therefore, Paul's turning to Gentiles means no more than the end of his preaching to a Jewish assembly in the Antioch synagogue (89). But this is too trifling an interpretation of a scene to which 'the narrator has given a great deal of space' (89); quite clearly it has a programmatic significance. Paul's repeated visits to synagogues even after the Antioch scene are needed for literary reasons: the Jews get more opportunities to reject God's word (which they repeatedly do). Luke's message must be sought in what Paul says rather than in what he does.[29]

Nor is it possible to evade the hard message of the closing scene of Acts. It is a counsel of despair to claim that 'nothing prevents us from understanding the announcement in 28.28 as applying to Rome, leaving open the possibility of preaching to Jews elsewhere'.[30]

Jesus on Jerusalem

Tannehill then stakes everything on Luke 13.34–35:

> Jerusalem, Jerusalem, the city that kills the prophets . . . How often have I desired to gather your children together as a hen gathers her brood under her wings, and you were not willing! See, your house is left to you. And I tell you, you will not see me until the time comes when you say, 'Blessed is the one who comes in the name of the Lord.'

Tannehill finds here 'a possible time limit' to God's judgment on Jerusalem because of the possibility that the Jews will finally accept their messianic king.[31] It is true that 'blessed' in v.35b sounds joyful. But for the Gospel's readers the reference of Jesus' coming to be seen by the Jerusalemites 'can only refer prophetically to the events of 19.37ff.'.[32] Any hopes for the people of Jerusalem seem to be extinguished at the latest in Luke 19.41–44. There Jesus has only harsh words of judgment left for Jerusalem which did not know the time of its 'visitation'. The wording recalls Luke 7.16. God visited Israel in the historical career of Jesus; Jerusalem failed to realize this and will be judged. The word 'visitation' also reminds one of the Benedictus (Luke 1.68, 78). God 'visited and redeemed his people' when Jesus was fulfilling his mission in Israel – or rather God would have done it, had Jerusalem realized that the day of visitation was at hand.[33]

Evaluation

Our findings can be summarized as follows. Time and again, statements which at first seem to suggest a special hope of redemption for the Jewish people, for Israel *qua* Israel, tacitly fuse with or yield to a more individualized and spiritualized view of salvation.[34] Encounter with the Messiah will divide Israel in two.[35] 'Israel language' is used to indicate that the Messiah will bring salvation to Gentiles as well.[36] Jews who do not accept Jesus will be excluded from God's people and damned.[37]

The striking thing in all this is that Luke presents nothing that comes close to an analysis or a critique of the 'Jewish expectation' of the Messiah. This is what causes the 'inclusivist' impression. He never sets out to discuss the relation between the old and the new, apart from sweeping statements about the promises being fulfilled. He never once states that the old expectation was somehow false – e.g. that it was too narrowly conceived in national or political terms. To be sure, such a critique of the Jewish view is sometimes attributed to him by modern expositors, but then they must read a great deal into the text and overlook passages where Luke produces massive assimilations of the old expectation and of the new conception of the reign of Jesus.

Yet another place where Luke could have openly confronted different views of the work of the Messiah, had he wished to do so, is the temptation story (Luke 4.1–13).[38] To him Jesus' second temptation (Luke 4.5–8) cannot mean a differentiation of his task from the political task of the Davidic Messiah. For to criticize a political view of the Messiah's task would amount to criticizing the messianology of Zechariah – and he spoke in the Holy Spirit. If Luke let the devil propose a similar view, he would in effect imply that the *Benedictus* contains 'Satanic verses'!

Tannehill, then, has a point, although his overall interpretation fails to convince. He does justice to one of Luke's concerns: Luke's need to create the impression that full continuity exists between the old biblical religion and his Christianity. But Tannehill reads Luke's narrative with the eyes of a modern critic. So it does not escape him that Luke's case for the fulfilment of the promises given to the fathers actually amounts to admitting that 'a primary aspect of prophecy . . . is finally void' (1985, 83). Tannehill is quite correct in stating that Luke would never admit this. Such a concession would indeed 'leave him with an unresolvable theological problem' (84). But it does not follow that Luke therefore holds out a special hope for Israel. Too many indications point in a different direction: he simply evades the issue, fusing the expectation of national salvation with the salvation in Christ of the individual or of the new community which consists of Jews and Gentiles.[39] He indulges in his soteriology in assimilation procedures analogous to those which Kari Syreeni has isolated in Matthew's treatment of the law: 'the implicit, non-analytical placing together of divergent things'.[40] The unresolvable theological problem remains.

Tannehill finds in Luke a 'passionate concern . . . that God's salvation be realized comprehensively – for both Jews and Gentiles' (1988, 101). But he fails to realize Luke's deep need of legitimation. Luke must be able to show that his Christian views are the true interpretation of the Bible. Rather than being really 'comprehensive', this concern might be termed sectarian. It is always important for a new sect to legitimate its ideology by claiming that it is *its* message that really stands in continuity with the old values of the community. 'Quite often in a sect the theological or ideological claim to be the legitimate people of God contradicts the actual situation of this sect.' 'Luke's manner of viewing the Christian congregations is that of a sect member . . .'[41]

Luke's 'conservative biblical' imagery in the birth narrative is part of his legitimating strategy. He creates a suggestive 'biblical' atmosphere and lures the reader into thinking that precisely such promises as are uttered by the angel and such expectations as are voiced by the pious 'biblical' characters have indeed come true in Jesus. I am not suggesting that he is following a conscious strategy. But it is revealing that he does not introduce the topic of Jesus' resurrection in open speech in the birth narrative. Had he done so, say, in 1.32–33, readers might have felt the hiatus between the expectation and its actual 'fulfilment'. It is very important for Luke's 'fulfilment theology' that the expectation is first described in classical biblical language, even though he time and again 'slips' into assimilations already in the birth narrative itself.

For a proper evaluation of Luke's achievement in his socio-historical setting it ought to be compared to other reinterpretations of Jewish Messianic traditions. One thinks first of all of Philo. A proper comparison cannot be attempted here, but a few hints are apposite.

According to Richard D. Hecht's acute analysis, the issue of the Messiah is quite complex in Philo. There are texts where Philo describes political processes that seem to culminate in the messianic era. They are, however, contradicted by others where Philo 'seemingly allegorizes the process, making it into a spiritualized experience within the individual' (Hecht 1987, 148). Often enough, he turns 'the messianic designators into symbols for the Logos or how virtue is stimulated in the human soul'.[42] One text where this happens is *De Confusione Linguarum* 62–63; there Philo argues that 'Rising' (Zech. 6.12) would be a strange title for a (messianic) human being and must therefore refer to the Logos.[43] But there is one lengthy text (*De Praemiis et Poenis* 79–172) where a messianic 'scenario is descriptive of events that take place in the world' (149). Still, even here Philo 'presents a thoroughly dehistoricized description of the messianic drama when compared to other contemporary visions'. The battle fought is bloodless; the enemies conquered are unnamed abstractions. The unexpected liberation of the exiles arises because of their mass conversion to virtue. Philo presents an individualistic soteriology; his view that only those Jews who maintain their 'nobility' (*Praem.Poen* 171) will participate in the future salvation recalls the division within Israel envisaged by Luke. Hecht argues that the messianic imagery, pale as it is, reflects the ideas of 'popular messianists' in Philo's environment. Through his 'ever-present spiritualization of history', Philo 'neutralizes' the messianism of the community. His real message, intended for those who understand, is the identification of the Messianic figure with the Logos (161–162).

Philo's treatment of the expectation of the Messiah and the Messianic age is reminiscent, at several points, of Luke. Philo, too, uses messianic words and images in an abstract and spiritualized sense, without making it clear that a reinterpretation is taking place. The same could be said of another much later Jewish current: modern Hasidism.[44] How close the resemblance to Luke actually is in these cases remains to be studied.

Philo, however, does not try to impose his elitist view on those less enlightened. He does not make the masses culpable for not adopting a spiritualized view of the messianic expectation. (They will forfeit salvation, though, if they do not walk in the way of 'nobility'.) His nonconformist thinking has not had much effect on Jewish history either. Philo showed himself to be a loyal (prominent) member of his Jewish community in the turmoils of first-century Alexandria. Things were different with Luke, who was active in a quite different social context. In his view, such Jews as do not acknowledge Jesus to be the Messiah are indeed culpable. Luke's view has had a tremendous impact on Christian thought and, consequently, on the life of Jews in Christendom.[45] Therefore, his view deserves discussion from the viewpoint of 'content criticism' more urgently than does Philo's.

Luke's language suggests a very positive attitude to Judaism. In reality, however, his attitude is quite ambiguous. Lloyd Gaston argues that in his 'exaggerated continuity'[46] he is anti-Jewish in driving a wedge between the good Old Testament religion and the bad contemporary Jews.[47] He is not trying to win sympathy for the allegedly tragic fate of the Jews. The real tragic victims are Jesus, Stephen and Paul; the Jews get only what they deserve.[48] Therefore, 'the paradox remains that Luke-Acts is one of the most pro-Jewish and one of the most anti-Jewish writings in the New Testament'.[49]

What a disqualification of the Jewish religion Luke actually presents! Many times over he lets the salvation promised to Israel in the Bible blend together with the new gift of forgiveness. Was forgiveness, then, something new that could not be provided by Judaism? How could mere forgiveness of sins really be the fulfilment of the promise to David? Had David not been forgiven for his sins? Was grace a novelty that only came along with the gospel? Disguised in inclusivist clothing, Luke actually presents an exclusivist thesis: outside Christ, no salvation.

Indeed, Luke expects that Jews should convert to Jesus. Jervell writes: 'Conversion means a share in the messianic salvation and a share in the covenant of Abraham . . . To be sure, the listeners, as Jews, are already the sons of the covenant of Abraham . . . and thus salvation means a ratification of this covenant for those who have been converted and have not been excluded from the people.'[50] Note the anomaly from a Jewish point of view: to get the age-old covenant ratified you need to convert to something novel! Your Jewishness as such, then, is good for nothing.

Luke does have a salvation-historical problem which is not solvable in 'objectifying' terms. If God's old promises are fulfilled in Jesus, their content has been changed to such an extent as to be in effect nullified. Luke's vague use of the old language is an indirect indication of this dilemma. In this, Luke shares the problems of all Christian theologies of 'fulfilment' in which the old vocabulary is made to serve a novel cause.[51]

5

Attacking the Book, Not the People:
Marcion and the Jewish Roots
of Christianity

Marcion is known for his attempt to separate Christianity radically from Judaism: far from being an organic continuation or a crowning fulfilment of Judaism, Christianity was something quite new. Marcion has got the reputation of being the arch-enemy of the Jews. Henry Chadwick is quite representative in stating that 'in Marcion's evaluation of the Old Testament there lurks a constant overtone of anti-Semitism'.[1]

Adolf von Harnack was attracted to Marcion, whom he considered a reformer comparable to Paul and Luther.[2] Usually, however, Marcion is mentioned as a warning example in the history of theology. Anyone with doubts about the authority of the Old Testament is counted in 'the same group as the arch-heretic Marcion'.[3] A generation ago, John Bright warned of a latent 'neo-Marcionism' in our churches: 'If the Old Testament is accorded only the auxiliary, pedagogical function of preparing men's minds to the reception of the gospel, then the door is thrown open to Marcionism . . .'[4] Nowadays it is claimed that 'any "Marcionism" in Christian theology and exposition necessarily leads to Anti-Judaism'.[5]

I shall argue that a reappraisal of Marcion – and of the modern 'Marcionism' of Harnack and others – is called for in the framework of inter-faith dialogue.

Marcion, a wealthy ship-owner from the Black Sea region, joined the Roman congregation and donated a large sum of money to it.[6] Inner-Christian diversity flourished in Rome at that time;[7] problems arose, however, when Marcion insisted that the leaders of the congregation meet to discuss his interpretation of the faith in AD 144.[8] The result was that Marcion left Rome (and that his money was returned); he now founded a church of his own. Down to the fourth century, this church was a most formidable rival of the catholic church. There are many indications that in the second century it was one of most important forms of Christianity.[9]

For an 'orthodox' bishop the 'wolf from Pontus' was the first-born of Satan. By contrast, the Marcionite church saw its founder in heaven on the left side of Christ (the right side being reserved for his mentor, Paul).[10]

Marcion produced a revised edition of Paul's letters and Luke's Gospel and wrote a work called *Antitheses*. None of his writings have been preserved; all our information is gathered from the polemical writings of his opponents. The most important source is the thorough refutation written by Tertullian.[11]

The outline of Marcion's thought-world

Marcion was neither a philosopher nor a systematic theologian, but a 'biblical theologian' who pondered on texts.[12] His thought-world is based on a literal understanding of the Bible, although his final conclusions differ drastically from any biblical lines of thought. Marcion subjected the Bible (i.e., what Christians now call the 'Old Testament') to a rigorous criticism in the light of his understanding of Paul's letters and his experience of life. To be sure, the allegorical interpretation of passages which were offensive if taken literally can be construed as an implicit criticism of the Old Testament, and this was routinely done in most Christian circles and even in some Jewish ones. Marcion, however, rejecting allegory, was explicit in his criticisms.

According to Marcion, the Old Testament god cannot be identical with the Father of Jesus. The Old Testament speaks of a creator whose foremost quality is 'righteousness' according to the principle of retaliation ('an eye for an eye'). This god is not good. He is not bad either; he is just a strict ruler.[13] The imperfection of the creator is shared by his creation which he formed from matter. Therefore, according to the principle of justice, most people face judgment and perdition.

But in the fifteenth year of the emperor Tiberius (*Adv.Marc.*

1.19.2) an alien God, pure goodness, appeared in this world. He came in the form of his Son, 'in the likeness of flesh'. He could not possibly be a real human being, since the humans made by the creator are imperfect; docetism has a central place in Marcion's thought. This God taught people goodness; he taught them to overcome the law of righteousness with love. The god of the Old Testament represented the law; the new 'alien God' represents the gospel, and faith means the acceptance of his offer of goodness.[14] For instance, the new God taught 'a new degree of forbearance' (*novam patientiam*) by refuting the law of retaliation (*Adv.Marc.* 4.16.2) – something which Tertullian does not understand at all.[15]

The creator did not recognize this God, but had him crucified and sent him to Hades. There Christ continued his work. He literally redeemed, i.e. bought free from the power of death, people who belonged to the creator.[16] In Hades a stunning version of the 'justification of the ungodly' took place. The impious of the Old Testament – Cain, the Sodomites, the Egyptians – believed and were redeemed. But the pious from Noah and Abraham on were too closely bound with their creator to be able to receive Christ's invitation. They thought that their god was once more tempting them with error, and they did not respond to Jesus.[17]

Marcion's hostility to matter – 'a deduction based on human experience'[18] – took expression in asceticism. Baptized Marcionites seem not to have married.[19] Fasting was abundant; strict dietary regulations were observed; no wine was consumed at the Lord's Supper. Christian writers routinely accuse their adversaries of immorality, but no such accusation is raised against Marcion.[20] In his church, high morality combined with readiness for martyrdom.

The much-debated issue whether or not Marcion was a Gnostic is largely a question of definition. Gnosticism was not a monolith; in fact grave doubts have arisen regarding the usefulness of the very category 'Gnosticism'.[21] Marcion's notion of an inferior creator god and his criticism of the Old Testament come close to views found in sources commonly included under the category 'Gnosticism', but many other views of his differ from such views.[22] There is no divine spark in man; he is not akin to the Redeemer. Redemption reaches him vertically from above. Marcion empha- sizes faith more than knowledge as the mode of redemption.

Salvation does not consist in the return of the dispersed elements to the divinity, but in freedom from the creator's law.[23] Even Marcion's docetism is incomplete: Christ suffers and dies.[24] His christology does not have much in common with 'Gnostic' redemptive myths.

Stephen Wilson conjectures that Marcion began as a 'Paulinist', but 'with a brand of Paulinism already open to gnostic influence'.[25] Marcion's pupil Apelles developed his doctrine in the direction of full-blown Gnosticism. For him, the good God is the only basic principle of reality; the demiurge and the Old Testament god are angelic beings.

Christian Gnostics conceded a relative right to the faith of the church, regarding themselves as Christians of a higher order; we might call this a kind of inner-Christian inclusivism. By contrast, Marcion 'made an exclusive claim to truth'[26] and tried to convert others to his views.

Marcion's criticism of the Bible

For 'orthodox' expositors the Old Testament was important as a collection of (alleged) predictions and promises about Jesus. Marcion read the Old Testament in a literal way. He did not explain away difficulties through allegorical devices, being in this regard a more sober exegete than his opponents;[27] his suspicion of allegory was indeed 'a mark of uniqueness in that age'.[28] Marcion does not assume interpolations or corruption in the Old Testament either. For all his contempt of the book he regards it as trustworthy as an historical account, and Jews can really expect the Messiah promised for them in Scripture.[29]

Marcion pointed out one contrast after another between the old god and the new one. The Old Testament god is 'a judge, fierce and warlike' (*Adv.Marc.* 1.6.1). 'Joshua conquered the holy land with violence and cruelty; but Christ prohibits all violence and preaches mercy and peace . . .'[30] 'The prophet of the creator' stopped the sun so that it would not set before the people had revenged their enemies (Josh. 10.12ff.); the Lord says, 'do not let the sun go down on your anger' (Eph. 4.26).[31] The prophet of the creator stretched out his arms towards God in order to kill many in war; the Lord stretched out his hands (on the cross) to save people.[32] Marcion even pays attention to what might be called the human rights of the Canaanites in his ironical comment: 'Good indeed is the god of the law who envied the Canaanites to give to the Israelites their land, houses they had not built and olive trees and fig trees they had not planted.'[33]

The creator commanded the Israelites to leave Egypt with shoes on feet, staff in hand, a sack on shoulders, and to take with them the gold and silver of Egypt; Christ sent his disciples into the world without shoes, knapsack, extra clothes or money.[34]

Marcion seized on every opportunity to point to a contrast – or to construct one. Christ said: 'let the children come to me'. By contrast, the prophet of the creator invited bears from the forest to tear up children.[35] The only answer Tertullian has to this is that the boys were already capable of judgment: 'so then, being a just God, he did not spare even boys when disrespectful . . .'[36]

The god of the Old Testament acts in a self-contradictory manner. He prohibits work on the Sabbath, but tells the Israelites around Jericho to carry the ark even on a Sabbath.[37] He forbids images and tells Moses to make a bronze serpent. He requires sacrifices and rejects them; he elects people and repents. Even worse than his capriciousness and lack of foresight is his confession that he creates evil (Isa. 45.7);[38] he sends disasters and repents of them. Drawing on Isa. 45.7, Marcion 'interpreted with reference to the creator the evil tree that creates evil fruit and assumed that there had to be another God to correspond with the good tree' (*Adv.Marc.* 1.2.2). God is ignorant too: he had to ask, 'Adam, where art thou?'[39]

Of course Marcion was very one-sided in his criticisms. He took up the dark sides of the Old Testament, paying no attention to such parts which are quite different[40] – say, the wonderful treasure of wisdom materials which has been collected by John Eaton.[41] Tertullian, though singularly weak in his answers to the criticisms just mentioned, is able to present (*Adv.Marc.* 4.14) a wealth of material in which the creator shows his concern for the poor, or demands love for enemies (4.16). But to Marcion goes the credit that he did not explain away the problems; he 'acutely perceived the wretched humanity of the Old Testament God'.[42] Structurally, his reaction to the Old Testament resembles the reaction of radical feminist interpreters to a Bible experienced as a hopelessly patriarchal book. Nor should one underestimate the impression gained of the Bible by the best authority on its use in seventeenth-century England: 'If one reads the Bible straight through, the remarkable tolerance of the gospels comes as a shock.'[43]

Marcion read the Old Testament with common sense. He exposed ruthlessly a problem which lay dormant in the basics of Christianity: the new religion had adopted an old book, the contents of which partly militated against its own teachings. To be sure, the problem was implicit in the basics of Judaism as well.

The problem of continuity

The key to the deep contrast between the old and the new was derived from Paul, especially from Galatians.[44] If the resulting picture of Paul is one-sided this is no wonder, for Galatians *is* one-sided, especially when compared to Romans. Even in modern scholarship the nature of one's overall picture of Paul's thought depends heavily on whether Galatians is read in the light of Romans, or vice versa. In Galatians Paul speaks in a negative tone of the Old Testament law and he even obliquely suggests that it may not stem from God (Gal. 3.19–20). Marcel Simon correctly notes on these verses that 'we are not really very far here from Marcion's radical solution'; Marcion 'did no more than push the apostle's thought to its logical conclusion'.[45] In Romans Paul is at pains to see more continuity between the old and the new, although there is still a great deal of ambiguity.

Even though Paul could thus underline continuity and undoubtedly wanted to remain a Jew, he did state that Christ had put an end to the law. He even stopped observing consistently the food regulations of the law which were fundamental to a Jewish identity. Marcion needed to do no more than draw the logical conclusion: an order that loses its validity cannot be divine. Marcion's conclusion paralleled the inference which Paul's Jewish contemporaries drew from Paul's practice (cf. Acts 21): an apostate.

One of the oddest things in Paul's view of the law was the

connection he established between the law and sin: the law increases and even engenders sin. Marcion got directly from Paul the idea that the most doubtful thing about the law is the fact that it was given in order to arouse and to let grow exuberantly the sin which did not exist prior to it.[46]

Harnack found that the step which Marcion took in a radical direction was actually smaller than the one taken by Paul; in effect, Paul had already put an end to the Jewish god's order of salvation.[47] In Harnack's thought this assessment is connected with the notion, typical of his age, that Judaism was a religion of externals. Yet the assessment remains sound, although our evaluation of Judaism has rightly undergone a revolution; only, it can no longer be deemed a compliment to Paul! A Jewish scholar, reflecting on Paul's talk of the curse of the law and of the slavery of the Jews under it, notes that Paul has in effect 'somewhat demonized the God of Israel'.[48]

Judaism underlined the covenant which God had, in his mercy, made with Israel. It was the grateful response of humans that they wanted to observe the law given to them by this gracious God. If now obedience to the covenant law was replaced by faith in Jesus as the Messiah, the faith of the fathers was null and void. The right relationship to God could only be based either on God's hoary covenant to which belonged the observance of the Mosaic law, or else on God's alleged new action in Jesus whose followers gave up the law. It was logically impossible to combine both convictions, even though Paul attempted something to that effect. For example, in Gal. 3.15–18, a key passage on the promise to Abraham, there is nothing that 'could be interpreted as the history of a corporate people of God created by the power of that promise'.[49] Paul could jump from Abraham to the Christ event and omit the history of God's covenant with Israel as if there had been no 'salvation history' at all. Paul is not thinking of Abraham as an ancestor of the people of God, but as an exemplary individual who received promises which aimed far to the future, so that the promise given to Abraham remains somewhat 'docetic', since it could be realized only after the coming of the Christ.[50]

However, Paul's problem is found in other ancient sources as well.[51] Mark and Matthew let Jesus abolish Old Testament commands without considering the problem that in the Old Testament these commands are given by God himself (actually the evangelists almost suggest that they were traditions of men). The Epistle to the Hebrews states that the law of the 'old covenant' which has now been abolished was 'weak' and 'useless' – without pausing to ask why God could have given such a law in the first place. John Gager notes that the Jewishness of Hebrews 'reduces itself to his background and culture. Take away that background and culture, and we are well on the way toward Marcion.'[52]

The Fourth Gospel had gone a long way in Marcion's direction: all 'shepherds' prior to Jesus had been 'thieves and robbers' (John 10.8) – apparently even Moses.[53]

Of course, Marcion's idea of two gods was strange. But the inevitable logical conclusion from the thoughts of Paul and others was almost as offensive: the one and only God had, contrary to his own affirmations, changed his mind. Christians were ridiculed on this score by Celsus:

> Who is wrong? Moses or Jesus? Or when the Father sent Jesus had he forgotten what commands he gave to Moses? or did he condemn his own laws and change his mind, and send his messenger for quite the opposite purpose?[54]

The same issue is raised, as we saw in Chapter 1, in the inter-religious dialogue today.[55]

It was clear to Marcion that God could not display such instability. This was equally clear to his critics,[56] who resorted to an artificial usurpation of the Old Testament. The 'orthodox' compromise cut the Gordian knot with violence: God has not changed his mind;[57] his plan had been misunderstood.

Every opportunity was taken by the Fathers to deny any dichotomy between law and gospel in Paul's teaching.[58] The patristic exegesis of Pauline passages which attribute the increase of sin to the law is very revealing. 'On no account may any increase of sin be attributed to the coming of the Mosaic law; that would be to fall into the heresy of Marcion.' Romans 5.20 ('law came in, in order that the trespass be multiplied'), for example, is said to speak of the 'natural law' or, better still, of 'the law in my members'.[59]

Yet it could hardly be denied that parts of the law (at least its 'ritual' parts) had been abolished. Admitting this, Tertullian resorted in his refutation of Marcion to the explanation that this was all right; in fact one ought to have known that it had to happen, for the Creator had of old taught this very thing by his prophets! The pertinent prophecies (*Adv.Marc.* 1.20.4–6) included Isa. 43.19 ('the old things have passed away, and behold they are new things which I now make'); Jer. 31.31ff. (a new covenant); Jer. 4.3–4 ('renew for yourself a new fallow; be circumcised in the foreskins of your heart'), and even Isa. 1.14 ('your new moons and sabbaths, and the great day, I cannot abide: your appointed days and your fasting, and your feast days, my soul hates'!).[60] Therefore, 'by exchanging the obligations and burdens of the law for the freedom of the gospel', the apostles 'were doing as the psalm advised, "Let us break their bonds asunder and cast their yoke from us" (Ps. 2.3)!' (*Adv.Marc.* 3.22.3). It does not bother Tertullian that, in the context of the Psalm, this 'advice to the apostles' is presented as the counsel of the kings of the earth 'against the Lord and his anointed'.

Christ 'has been foretold of all down the ages' (*Adv.Marc.* 3.1.2); 'with God nothing is unexpected!' (*Adv.Marc.* 3.2.3). His work of salvation 'required preparatory work in order to be credible (!)' (3.2.4).[61] But in the law Christ was preached 'under a figure, which is why not all the Jews were capable of recognizing him' (5.13.15).[62] Indeed, the reason for the giving of the burdens of the law was the sinfulness of the Jews; we shall return to this.

If Marcion presented a radical solution, he 'did not create or invent the problem'.[63] The problem of continuity and discontinuity was inherent in the basics of Christianity.

Marcion's new Bible

Marcion wanted to replace the Old Testament with the authentic basic documents of Christianity which were Paul's ten letters[64] and what Paul had occasionally called 'my gospel'. Marcion took this to be a reference to a written Gospel; his choice fell on that of Luke.

In itself Luke's Gospel, which stresses continuity, does not fit well with Marcion's view; in Paul's letters, too, continuity is the other side of the coin. Both the Gospel and the letters therefore had to be purified from Judaizing additions supposedly made by the apostles of the creator god. The opening chapters of Galatians showed that there had been heated battles about Paul's gospel in the early church; why should they not have left traces in the extant letters of Paul? But even after this revision on Marcion's part, Tertullian has an easy task in showing the impossibility of his position on this score, as he demonstrates page after page the Jewish context of Jesus' activity.[65]

Marcion omitted a great deal from the texts of Luke and Paul (and made some minor verbal changes); but he made hardly any additions. This testifies to the sincerity of his intentions. If one aims at reconstructing the original wording, it is natural to limit oneself to excising the alleged additions. Additions would undermine the credibility of the enterprise.[66]

Of course Marcion's method was arbitrary; his only criterion of authenticity was the suitability or otherwise of the contents. Still, he was attempting to act as a philologist keen on reconstructing original documents. Unlike John, he did not appeal to the Spirit, nor did he claim to have found hidden documents as some Old Testament authors did (II Kings 22). As an editor of sources Marcion leaves a more conservative impression than Matthew or Luke (not to mention John!), who not only omitted material from Mark, but also 'created' new passages. Luke in particular seems to have proceeded much more freely than Marcion.[67]

Marcion's work was of the greatest influence on the development of the church's canon, which took place essentially as a reaction to Marcion's new canon. A discussion of this issue is beyond my present concern.[68]

Marcion and the Jews[69]

For Marcion Judaism was an inferior religion. No doubt this is a condescending view. But can it be regarded as anti-Jewish? Unlike so many 'orthodox' church fathers, Marcion does *not* blame the Jews for killing Jesus. After all, the death of Jesus was to be blamed on the imprudent creator![70]

Tertullian complains indeed that Marcion has formed 'an

alliance with the Jewish error' (*Adv.Marc.* 3.6.2),[71] the heretic 'borrowing poison from the Jew' (3.8.1); 'for from the Jew the heretic has accepted guidance . . . , the blind borrowing from the blind, and has fallen into the same ditch' (3.7.1). For Marcion conceded to the Jews that Jesus could not have been the Messiah awaited by them; their Messiah was to be a warrior and a liberator. Isaiah's Christ, called Emmanuel, would 'take up the strength of Damascus and the spoils of Samaria against the kings of the Assyrians' (Isa. 8.4; *Adv.Marc.* 3.12.1). Marcion believed that this Jewish Messiah would still come to establish a temporary earthly kingdom for his people (3.6.1–2), regathering them out of dispersion (3.21.1). 'Your Christ promises the Jews their former estate, after the restitution of their country, and, when life has run its course, refreshment with those beneath the earth, in Abraham's bosom' (3.24.1).[72] It had not been predicted that he would suffer and die on the cross. On the other hand, Christians were warned of this Messiah of the creator by Jesus (4.39, on Luke 21.8.)

So can Marcion really be regarded as an enemy of the Jews? No, the tables should rather be turned on his 'orthodox' opponents: *they* seem a lot more anti-Jewish. Marcion only acted as an involuntary catalyst. He forced Tertullian and others to pose with new seriousness the question: if, as is agreed, parts of the law are to be abandoned, how can one take seriously the God who gave this obviously inferior law? Tertullian's answer is representative and clear: the blame is transferred from God to the people who cling to this law.[73]

The law of retaliation had to be given because 'to that stiff-necked people, devoid of faith in God, it seemed a tiresome thing, or even beyond credence' to expect vengeance from God. When the law 'places restraint upon certain foods', it is 'advice on the exercise of self-restraint, and observe how a bridle was put upon that gluttony which, while it was eating the bread of angels, hankered after the cucumbers and pumpkins of the Egyptians . . . Nor should anyone find fault with the burdensome expense of sacrifices and the troublesome scrupulosities of services and oblations', for 'when the people were prone to idolatry and transgression, God was content to attach them to his own religion by the same sort of observances in which this world's superstition was engaged' (*Adv.Marc.* 2.18.1–3). The law has made all manner of regulations in order 'to tame the people's hardness, and smooth down with exacting obligations their faith as yet unpractised in obedience' (2.19.1).

Even if God visited the fathers' sins upon the children, 'it was Israel's hardness which demanded remedies of that sort, to cause them to obey the divine law at least through consideration for their posterity . . .' (*Adv.Marc.* 2.15.1). Tertullian ominously finds here a prediction of what Matthew attributes to the Jewish people when in his passion narrative he makes them cry, 'His blood be on our heads and on our children' (Matt. 27.25). The visitation of the fathers' sins upon the children in the law, writes Tertullian, 'applies . . . to those who were, at a time then future, going of their own will to call down this judgment upon themselves . . . So then God's foresight in its fullness passed censure upon this which he heard long before it was spoken' (2.15.3).

Marcion's criticism 'focusses almost exclusively on the god and the scriptures of Judaism and says little of Jews as such'. It was not in Marcion, but rather among his Christian opponents that 'the focus shifted from the god of the Jews to the Jews themselves'.[74] 'Marcion's claim about Jesus triggered a new and heightened emphasis on the clarity of the prophecies and the guilt of the Jews'; 'Jesus was "he who should have been recognized".'[75] 'Jesus was "retrieved" from Marcion for traditional Christianity . . . by means of the anti-Judaic myth.'[76]

Catholic Christianity wrenched the Scripture from the Jews, reinterpreting it to fit its own experience. Covenantal symbols were appropriated by way of spiritualized and ethical interpretations: actual circumcision was replaced with that of the heart; observance of the law with obedience to moral commands. Precisely because it was asserted that the Old Testament already spoke of Jesus – an inclusivist claim, if you like – the continuing existence of Judaism as a religion with rival claims to Scripture was felt to be a threat. In the course of time, the threat was repressed even with violent means. Such is the danger inherent in an inclusivism which bends sacred traditions of others to serve its own ends.

For all his contempt for the Old Testament, Marcion did grant the Jews the right to expect their own Messiah and his earthly kingdom. He conceded to them their rites and symbols, as long as Christians did not start to observe them. Marcion's condescending attitude notwithstanding, this seems closer than, say, Romans 11 to a two-covenant theology; or perhaps we might detect here some modest – but very modest – germs of a tolerant attitude to other faiths. At least, 'at no point does Marcion's opposition to the "judaizing" of Paul's gospel become opposition to the *Jews*'.[77] John Gager is right in pointing out that 'Marcion's anti-Judaism, like that of the Nag Hammadi documents but unlike that in the Gospel of John, focuses almost exclusively on the god and the scriptures of Judaism and says little of Jews as such'.[78]

Paul redefined the Jewish symbols; his attitude to the Jewish people oscillated. Catholic Christianity took the symbols and attacked the people. Marcion 'attacked the symbols but left the people alone'. Stephen Wilson rightly notes that it is worth a moment's reflection 'whether the Marcionite position, had it pre-vailed, would have led to the same sad consequences as the view of its opponents'.[79]

Consider a nineteenth-century parallel. It has been pointed out that 'the same Harnack who frankly denied any importance of the Old Testament to the Christian faith' also stated that 'to write anti-semitism on the banners of Evangelical Christianity is a sad scandal'. On the other hand, the same Adolf Stöcker, the Berlin court preacher who delivered antisemitic speeches to large audiences, was a conservative theologian who saw the importance of the Old Testament 'in the traditional scheme of prediction and fulfilment'.[80] This is no paradox at all. The German scholar who calls attention to the phenomenon correctly notes: 'The apparent contrast disappears with the insight that reading the Old Testament as part of the Christian canon . . . denies the claim of current Judaism to any right of its own to the text.'[81]

The challenge of Marcion: the Old Testament in the church

Harnack presented a famous assessment of the church's relation to the Old Testament in his book on Marcion:

To reject the Old Testament in the second century was a mistake which the Church rightly repudiated; to retain it in the sixteenth century was a fate which the Reformation could not yet avoid; but to continue to keep it in Protestantism as a canonical document after the nineteenth century is the consequence of religious and ecclesiastical paralysis.[82]

Harnack's main point in this much-criticized dictum is generally missed.[83] He was referring to the sad influence of parts of the Old Testament in Christian history. Allegorical interpretation had once helped to side-step the most questionable parts, but the 'Scripture alone' principle of the Reformation elevated the literal meaning of Old Testament to a pedestal. The patristic 'inclusivism' in doctrine (the Christian appropriation the Old Testament) now backfired, when what might be called the sub-Christian – or sub-Jewish, for that matter – contents of parts of the Old Testament broke through. Harnack writes:

If Marcion had reappeared at the time of the Huguenots and Cromwell, he would have met at the very centre of Christianity the warlike god of Israel whom he abhorred.[84]

While the churches

are afraid of the consequences of a break with the tradition, they do not see or they disregard the much more fatal consequences which continually follow from the preservation of the Old Testament as a holy and therefore inerrant scripture.[85]

What Harnack wished – and here he differed from his hero, Marcion – was *not* a rejection of the Old Testament, but simply an elimination of its canonical status and a critical sifting of its contents.[86] His proposal would have meant, for Christianity, the placement of the Old Testament among the books which are 'good and useful to read', where Luther placed the Apocrypha.

Thus Harnack's suggestion is not very radical at all. Clearly the effective history of the Old Testament, especially in post-Reformation Christendom, shows how dangerous the book has been as part of the Christian canon.[87] An early eighteenth-century critic observed 'with cheerful cynism' that

> whenever pillage or shedding of blood are to be justified or encouraged by a sermon, or men are to be exhorted to battle, to the sacking of a city or the devastation of a country, by a pathetic discourse, the text is always taken from the Old Testament.[88]

To take a random example: in a sermon charging his people to attack the native inhabitants of New England, the preacher Cotton Mather explicitly equates the Indians with Ammon and Amalek, the ancient adversaries of Israel; they are 'an indigenous population who will be displaced and disinherited by divine decision to make way for the new Israel'. In a splendid study of war in the Hebrew Bible, the Jewish scholar Susan Niditch writes:

> Mather is in a lengthy tradition of Christian preaching on war when he treats the enemy as Amalek and the fighting as justified crusade . . . This ongoing identification between contemporary situations and the warring scenes of the Hebrew Bible is a burden the tradition must guiltily bear. The particular violence of the Hebrew Scriptures has inspired violence, has served as a model of and model for persecution, subjugation and extermination for millennia beyond its own reality.[89]

To be sure, this is not the only ideology of war in the Hebrew Bible; but it is there at a central place.[90] It is possible to sympathize with the efforts of various Israelites to come to terms with war, as analysed by Niditch,[91] even when one abhors some of the results. However, this sympathy is possible precisely because one is thinking of these efforts as human ones, not as divine words.

Not surprisingly, a native American of today feels forced to 'read the Exodus stories with Canaanite eyes'; the Canaanites are for him or her the obvious characters to identify with in these stories.[92] Likewise, we find Palestinian Christians desperately wrestling with the issue that the Bible which is 'usually viewed as a source of strength', now 'appears to offer to the Palestinians slavery rather than freedom, injustice rather than justice, and death to their national and political life'.[93] Prominent rabbis in present-day Israel 'interpret the ancient commandments to annihilate the Canaanites and the people of Amalek as applicable to the Arabs today. Israel's wars against these peoples are holy wars, and the Israel Defence Forces are sanctified holy warriors'.[94] The story of Joshua, seen as a paradigm of successful wars, 'plays a prominent part in Israeli education'.[95] For Palestinians, God's character is at stake: 'God's integrity has been questioned'.[96] We recall that Marcion was appalled at the creator's treatment of the Canaanites of old.

The tree is known by its fruits. Marcion applied this principle to the Old Testament god. Modern scholars of the effective history of the Bible are beginning to apply it to the book.[97] One no longer concludes that there must be two or more gods; what one does conclude, inevitably, is that holy books can be dangerous – a curse as well as a blessing.

The example of Marcion and Harnack reminds us of the urgency of moral (or 'ideological') criticism of the Bible. We have to be explicit in our criticism of the Old Testament – and of the New! For the New Testament in its canonical status can be just as dangerous as the Old Testament. There are 'sub-Christian' – or 'sub-Jewish' – features in the New Testament as well.

If foreign peoples are demonized in parts of the Old Testament, the same tradition of destructive intolerance continues in those parts of the New Testament which declare non-Christian Jews 'children of the devil' and the 'synagogue of Satan'. Christian anti-semitism must partly be traced back to the canonical lectionary use of the New Testament in the liturgies of churches, 'whereby day by day, week by week, year by year, century by century, the New Testament is read as "the word of God" without omission or comment'.[98]

> Most of the documents of the New Testament originated in a context of polemic . . . The church, by defining these documents as Scripture, has, in a sense, frozen that moment of bitter separation and ensured its preservation for the last two millennia, if not for all eternity . . . There is a tragicomic irony

here, that a tradition which sets such great store on love and reconciliation should have canonized literature deriving, in part, from a situation of hatred and strife.[99]

Nevertheless, it is probably unrealistic to think that the church could still change the contents of its canon. Certainly Marcion should not be followed in his attempt to purge the New Testament by way of a fictitious reconstruction of its original message. It will not do to manipulate New Testament translations 'in order to reduce emphasis upon the Jews, Judaism, and the Pharisees'.[100] We have to go the more difficult way of coming to terms with our canon as it is, with all the fruits it has borne. What can be changed – and has long been in a process of change – is our attitude to the texts. We have to be critical and consciously selective.[101] Selectivity and reinterpretation is honest, if we admit what we are doing and do not hide behind the smoke screen of '*the* Bible' or the 'Word of God'. This proposal entails a reappraisal and vindication of Marcion.[102]

A scrutiny of the encounter between Marcionism and its opponents helps to appreciate a position which lost in the church, but which might just as well have won. A sympathetic assessment of Marcion's case may make us see problems, logical and moral, in what became our classic tradition. To me the problems are of such magnitude that they make 'absoluteness' seem impossible and strongly tip the scales in favour of religious pluralism. But Marcion's frank criticism of the Hebrew Bible, now viewed as a 'foreign' tradition, raises another question too: may not an honest discussion of problems in the others' tradition turn out helpful to the others in *their* coping with life in the global village?

6

Jesus Between Christianity and Islam: Muhammad's Portrait of the Jewish Prophet

One of the Christian intellectuals who have recently converted to Islam is the theologian Rosalyn Kendrick, now called Ruqayyah Waris Maqsood. Describing her spiritual journey, she tells how in her youth she studied Christian theology at university.

> There, however I became very impatient with the intricate maze of doctrinal axioms I was supposed to accept by faith (because they did not fit in with 'reasons') in order to grasp the meaning of the Holy Trinity . . . In fact, I discovered that the doctrine of the Trinity was to be found nowhere in the Bible, and was not formally accepted by the church until the fourth century CE.

Ruqayyah Maqsood tells what happened decades later:

> I think it was when I finally admitted to myself that God did not need any 'sacrifice' to make him more merciful than he already is, that I realized that I had become a Muslim.[1]

According to her, Christian converts to Islam usually feel

> that they are 'coming home' to something they have always known to be true in their hearts. They do not regard themselves as blasphemous renegades, turning their backs on all the Christian values they used to hold dear, nor do they feel that they are forsaking the love of their first religion for the entice-ments of a new one. On the contrary, most of what was incom-prehensible in Christianity falls neatly into place, and there is often a 'flash of light' experience . . . that can be compared to any Christian 'born again' experience.[2]

If converts can thus 'feel at home' in Islam, this may be so because Islam, in the words of Hans Küng, 'poses a challenge to Christians . . . as a reminder of their own past'.[3]

The roots of Islam lie deep in the Jewish-Christian soil. Contacts with Jews and Christians had a great significance for Muhammad's religious development. Through them biblical material as well as post-biblical popular traditions, Jewish and Christian, flowed into the Qur'an, often in an altered form. Consequently, Jesus has a prominent position in the Qur'an. His portrait is drawn throughout with sympathetic colours.

To speak of the Qur'an as an expression of Muhammad's experience and thought is bound to offend Muslims. Indeed, a conflict between (any) religious faith and the Western academic approach can indeed hardly be avoided. For the academy, there is no going back on the historical insights of the last two centuries. Christian theologians have had to learn (slowly and painfully) to cope with the historical treatment of their Scripture. When a biblical scholar tries to reconstruct the teaching of Jesus, he or she cannot stop to ask the average Christian – let alone some teaching authorities – what they think of the issue. On the contrary, the critic may try to persuade the ordinary believer and even the authorities to take another look at the evidence and perhaps rethink. Critics may be forgiven if they apply the same methods to other Scriptures too, provided that the standards are really the same (which is not always the case). Even if my view of the Qur'an remains incurably heretical, it is precisely critical study of it that has taught me to esteem Islam and its Prophet to a degree which has been a surprise to me.

Jesus in the Qur'an[4]

Jesus is often called the son of Mary in the Qur'an. He is born virginally after an angel has promised Mary 'a boy most pure'. Mary is accused of unchastity, but the child speaks in its cradle and testifies to her innocence (19.16–36).

The Qur'an tells more of Jesus' birth than of his later mission. Apparently it was the former that had attracted the simple Christians from whom Muhammad heard of Jesus. There are many similarities with apocryphal 'infancy gospels', e.g. that Jesus breathed life into clay birds he had created and caused them to fly. He healed the blind and the leper and broughtthe dead to life (3.49; 5.110)

God taught Jesus 'the Book, the Wisdom, the Torah and the Gospel' (3.48) and 'confirmed him with the Holy Spirit' (2.87). His teaching as summarized in the Qur'an would be appropriate in the mouth of any prophet: 'Fear God and obey me. Assuredly God is my Lord and your Lord; therefore serve Him; this is a straight path' (43.63–64). Jesus made lawful certain things that had been forbidden to the children of Israel (3.50), perhaps the consumption of forbidden food; he also predicted Muhammad's coming (61.6).

Jesus was a righteous man (3.46), 'high honoured in this world and the next' (3.45), displaying the basic Muslim virtues: prayer, almsgiving and piety toward his mother (19.31–32). Nevertheless, his mission met with opposition. He was accused of 'sorcery manifest' (5.110; 61.6). The Jews (!) tried to crucify him. Their arrogant claims that they had succeeded are sharply denied. The Jews did not crucify Jesus; 'only a likeness of that was shown to them' (4.157). This difficult verse is later interpreted with the aid of a Gnostic theory:[5] God substituted someone else for Jesus (e.g. Judas Iscariot); the substitute was crucified and killed. God rescued Jesus and 'raised him up to Him' (4.158).

The Qur'an refutes the claim that Jesus is 'God's son' – meaning, in Muhammad's ears, the son of God and Mary – let alone God himself. Muhammad likewise denies that God could consist of three persons (5.73; 4.171); in his view, the Christian Trinity seems to comprise God, Jesus and Mary (5.116). The worst possible sin is to put something beside God. The Christians are guilty of this sin of 'association'.

Jesus, like Muhammad himself, was a prophet (19.30) and a messenger (3.49), as many others had been. He was a servant of God (4.172), even though he is also called God's Word (3.45; 4.171) and Spirit (4.171).

Traditional evaluation

This portrait has always aroused special interest among Christian readers. From the days of John the Damascene down to the begin-

ning of our century Islam was treated polemically in the Christian
West. Nonetheless, some Christian features which had escaped
Muslim readers were also discovered in the Qur'an (one could
speak of a kind of polemical inclusivism). It was claimed that
Muhammad involuntarily teaches the divinity of Christ in calling
him 'Spirit' and 'Word'.[6]

The legacy of mediaeval polemics survives in a modified form in
studies which look for points of contact for Christian mission
in the Qur'an. 'To help our Moslem brethren to answer (the)
question ["What think ye of Christ?"], we must . . . lead them up
to higher truth by admitting all the truth which they possess.'[7]
Scholars of this brand have searched for 'traces of Christian truths
of faith' in the Qur'anic picture of Jesus, as 'points of contact for
. . . the proclamation of Christian doctrine to Mohammedans'.[8]

Naturally, there are analogies to this missionary literature on the
Islamic side. One critic blames the Gospels for having 'distorted
the beautiful picture of Jesus'. According to the Qur'an he was
'dutiful towards his mother'; the Qur'an thus refutes the less
respectful biblical accounts (Mark 3.31ff. par; John 2.4). 'The
Quran has exalted him so the Christians should be thankful . . .'[9]
We even find an express analogy to the Christian search for points
of contact:

> The recognition [of British churches] that 'the death of Jesus
> Christ on the Cross may seem a scandal and affront to divine
> justice' is a welcome announcement. This raises the possibility
> that *if the reality of these questions is expounded to our Christian
> brethren with love in the best manner possible, they would give up
> their wrong tenets* and will recognize that the belief that Jesus
> died an accursed death on the cross and that an innocent one
> was punished for the sins of the guilty would not only 'seem' but
> would truly be a scandal and affront to divine justice.[10]

Since the last century, a genetic-historical comparison of
the Qur'an with Christian tradition has been in vogue. Western
scholars have diligently traced the roots of many Qur'anic notions.
Jewish and Jewish-Christian, Manichaean and Gnostic, Nestorian
and Monophysite influences have been unearthed.[11] Many valuable

results have been gained. Yet source analysis is only part of the historical task. The Qur'an is not just the sum of its 'sources' (nor is any other text). One-sided concentration on sources can delude one to overlook Muhammad's creative contribution.

Recently a dialogical approach has gained momentum. The common ground is emphasized, the goal being 'a fraternal understanding between the children of Abraham'.[12] This approach is reflected in the document *Nostra aetate* of the Second Vatican Council in which Christians and Muslims are admonished to strive for mutual understanding and to promote together social justice, morality and peace and freedom for all people (ch. 3). Dialogical aspirations have been voiced on the Islamic side as well, and a Muslim scholar has suggested, on the basis of an assessment of the picture of Jesus in the Qur'an, that in the end Islam and Christianity may be seen as 'basically identical'. 'The bone of contention between the two religions lies in the interpretation of the "symbolism" which occurred in the prophet's utterances, rather than in the essence of the faith which is found in the New Testament and in the Qur'an in full compatibility.'[13]

The dangers of this approach are superficiality and anachronism. It is easy to read the Qur'an with a Christian bias. Paradoxically, certain 'inclusivist' claims from the old polemical literature are repeated in the dialogue. It is claimed that the Qur'an denies neither the divinity of Jesus nor the Christian doctrine of the Logos.[14] The problem with this approach is that the Qur'an is not being expounded by the Qur'an.

I regard the dialogue as vitally important, and in the present it takes a tremendous effort to keep it going. But – as indicated in Chapter 1 – I do not think that this concern should affect our exegesis directly. The dialogue belongs to another stage in the work. Even here exegesis has the task of an 'historical conscience'.[15]

The portrait of Jesus in the Qur'an: interpretation

Actually such titles as 'word' and 'spirit' do not represent anything like the Christian Logos theology. They occur in a context where the alleged tritheism of the Christians and the deification of Jesus is attacked:

People of the Book, go not beyond the bounds in your religion . . . The Messiah, Jesus son of Mary, was only the messenger of God, and his word that he uttered to Mary, and a spirit from Him. So believe in God and his messengers, and say not, Three.' Refrain; better is it for you. God is only One God. Glory be to Him – that He should have a son! (4.171).

Elsewhere it is stated: 'Truly, the likeness of Jesus, in God's sight, is as Adam's likeness; He created him of dust, then said He unto him, "Be," and he was' (3.59). Jesus can be called God's word, since his birth was due to God's creative command, 'Be!' Correspondingly, the designation 'spirit' suggests that God gave life to Jesus by 'breathing his spirit' in Mary – another expression used in the Qur'an also of the creation of Adam.

Undoubtedly, the designation 'word' comes from Christians, in the last analysis from the prologue to the Gospel of John (which, for its part, draws on pre-Christian traditions). But it is equally clear that the Christian content of the term has not been adopted. Muhammad has reinterpreted a traditional term, filtering it through his own experience and perception. Actually, the meaning of 'word' has been almost reversed: in the Qur'an the term emphasizes Jesus' position as a human being created by God.

Muhammad accepts the virgin birth of Jesus, but denies that it has anything to do with his divinity. It is a sign of God's omnipotence.[16] 'God creates what He will. When He decrees a thing He does but say to it "Be," and it is' (3.47). And when the Qur'an mentions Jesus' miracles it does not omit to add that Jesus worked them 'by the leave of God' (3.49; 5.110) – that is, not by his own power.

This portrait of Jesus consistently reflects Muhammad's own experience and views. What he heard of Jesus was interpreted, consciously or unconsciously, in the light of his own experience and of his strict monotheism. Like the earlier messengers[17] Jesus, too, became a model of Muhammad. Like all other men of God he, too, proclaimed God's unchanging message for his time and place. Jesus had received from God a book, 'the Gospel'. No doubt Muhammad thought that Jesus had received this book in similar moments of inspiration as the Qur'an was sent down to himself. In praying, giving alms and being gentle towards his mother, Jesus displayed the basic virtues of a Muslim.

The story of Jesus must have been a source of comfort for Muhammad. If he himself was accused of fraud or regarded as possessed, Jesus had met with similar accusations. Faced with opposition it was good to recall Jesus, who was rescued by God from an ignominious death on the cross. Jesus' disciples are called 'helpers unto God' (3.52; 61.14). The same term is used of those inhabitants of Medina who first joined Muhammad. Jesus' disciples are even called 'the surrendered', *muslim* (3.52; 5.111). Jesus with his disciples is portrayed in the same colours as Muhammad with his adherents.

On the other hand, Muhammad took a consciously polemical attitude toward the Christians' dogmatic claims about Jesus. It was clear to him that the Christians must have falsified Jesus' pure monotheism, in spite of Jesus' explicit prohibition.

At first, Muhammad had conceived of his message as a reform of Judaism and Christianity. As it became clear, however, that the 'people of the Book' were not inclined to accept the message, he connected it with Abraham's original religion, which was older than both Judaism and Christianity and was envisaged by Muhammad as purely ethical monotheism. Jesus had proclaimed the same message, but it had been falsified by Christians. Muhammad now preached a return to the original message.

Thus Jesus is allotted a place in a long chain of messengers which ends with Muhammad, 'the seal of prophecy'.[18] But Jesus is not his most prominent precursor; even more attention is paid both to Abraham and to Moses. Still, Jesus is the messenger who is closest in time to Muhammad and has also predicted the coming of the latter.

The Qur'an thus presents a fairly coherent account of Jesus, filtered through Muhammad's own experience.

The portrait of Jesus in the Qur'an and Christian theology

From the point of view of Western scholarship, the portrait of Jesus in the Qur'an presupposes and modifies such Christian notions as existed in Muhammad's environment.[19] Earlier the differences between the Qur'anic picture of Jesus and Christian (Chalcedonian) christology used to be emphasized. What has been less clear in this connection is the fact that there are also remarkable differences between the christological definitions of the patristic councils and the various New Testament portraits of Christ. As far as I know, the epilogue of my 1971 book *Das koranische Jesusbild* was the first attempt to employ those parts of the New Testament which exhibit a low christology in a comparison between the Qur'an and the Bible.[20] Again, this is an issue on which the historical conscience is badly needed.

Ruqayyah Maqsood is right about the Trinity: the idea is missing in the Bible. Nowhere in the New Testament is Jesus fully identified with God. When he is called the Son, he always remains subjected to God. The Gospel of John goes farthest in the direction of an identification in that it has Jesus state 'I and the Father are one' and refer to the glory which he had with God even before the creation of the world (John 17.5). Yet it is clear to modern scholars that this Gospel has moved far beyond older christological views.[21] In many other layers of the New Testament Jesus is clearly portrayed as a man chosen and employed by God for a certain purpose, and elevated by him to a new position. The view of Jesus as God's chosen servant finds its clearest expression in the speeches attributed to Peter and Paul in Acts, but all three Synoptic Gospels, too, abstain from deifying Jesus.

In the speeches of Acts it is stated that Jesus was 'his (God's) Messiah', whom he had appointed (Acts 3.18, 20), 'his Anointed' (4.26), God's 'servant' (3.13) or 'holy servant' (4.27), 'the Holy and Righteous One' (3.14) raised up by God (3.26). The terms God's 'son' and 'Messiah' are both defined in Luke's Gospel with the aid of the expression 'the chosen one' (Luke 9.35; 23.35). Jesus of Nazareth was 'a man attested to you by God with deeds of power, wonders and signs that God did through him' (Acts 2.22); he was 'anointed' by God 'with the Holy Spirit and power' and 'went about doing good and healing all who were oppressed by the devil, for God was with him' (10.38). Such God-centred statements remind one of the Qur'anic statement that Jesus worked his signs (a key word in the Qur'an!) 'by the leave of God'.

Jesus died according to God's plan. No saving significance is attributed to his death in Luke-Acts. Quite in accordance with Ruqayya Maqsood's experience, no sacrifice is required 'to make God more merciful than he is'.[22] It was God who raised him and made him 'Lord and Messiah' (Acts 2.36). Thereby God made Jesus his 'son': 'what God promised to our ancestors, he has fulfilled . . . by raising Jesus; as also it is written in the second psalm, "You are my Son, today I have begotten you"' (13.32–33).

Those Christians whose voice is heard in these formulae would have agreed with Muhammad that Jesus was a man, not God, even though they held that he had a unique task and afterwards a unique position of honour (a view which Muhammad would not have shared). The term 'God's son' suggests no 'metaphysical' or 'physical', but rather something like an 'adoptionist' relationship: God made Jesus his 'son'.

It is not clear whether Luke has access to old christological traditions or whether his 'adoptionism' reflects his own point of view. If the latter is the case, it is all the more remarkable that a Gentile Christian author could, at the end of the first century, present so 'low' a christology. By no means, however, can Luke be regarded as the inventor of the theocentric christology.

Paul already cites an old formula according to which Jesus 'was declared (or appointed) to be Son of God with power . . . by resurrection from the dead' (Rom. 1.4). According to Paul, Jesus will carry out his task as 'God's son' in the (near) future: the Christians 'wait for God's Son from heaven, whom he raised from the dead – Jesus who rescues us from the wrath that is coming' (I Thess. 1.10). After having conquered the inimical spirit powers which now reign in the world Jesus will surrender his reign and be subjected to God 'so that God may be all in all' (I Cor. 15.28).

In the first Christians' view, Jesus' mission and person was placed into a God-centred eschatological perspective. Jesus had a role to play in God's plan for the future of the world; he carried out his God-given task as the chosen one. But the original eschatological expectation could not be upheld in generation after generation. The interpretation of Jesus' mission was separated from the eschatological framework; typically, futurist eschatology plays a very minor role precisely in the Gospel of John. There the emphasis lies wholly on the speculations concerning the person of

Jesus; the 'Jewish prophet', to take up the title of Maurice Casey's Cadbury lectures, is being transformed into a 'Gentile God'.[23] Another scholar speaks of 'a definition of Jesus' divinity that is well on the way to ditheism', a doctrine of two gods.[24]

It is this process of deification that is so adamantly opposed by Muhammad.[25] As the church has thrust aside the Qur'anic portrait of Jesus, it has also repressed an aspect of itself. Muhammad's monotheistic picture of Jesus reminds one of the very first phase when the 'Jesus movement' was still a Jewish sect with Jewish monotheistic convictions and a more or less adoptionist christology.

No doubt there have been historical links between earliest Christianity and Islam.[26] One thinks here of that branch of Jewish Christianity which after the rebellions against the Romans (66–70 and 132–135 CE) was isolated from the mainstream and stuck close to the old views.[27] These Christians honoured Jesus as God's servant, the last prophet and the authoritative interpreter of the law; they held fast to the law (or most of it) and engaged in polemics against Paul.

The sources are sparse and beset with problems,[28] but we do get a glimpse of a combination of low and high christology which reminds us of the Qur'an.[29] Eusebius mentions in his *Church History* two different groups of Jewish Christian 'Ebionites'. One of them seems to have regarded Jesus as a simple man who was declared righteous because of his highly moral life.[30] The other group accepted the virgin birth of Jesus but denied his pre-existence as Logos. As we saw, the same configuration occurs in the Qur'an.[31]

Altogether a number of Jewish Christian (and other Christian) elements can be traced in the Qur'an. 'Even if we could never scientifically verify a genetic connection, the traditional-historical parallels are inescapable.'[32]

In this light it is not at all surprising that someone like Ruqayya Maqsood can feel that she has come home through her conversion to Islam. It is also with good reason that Hans Küng claims that Islam entails a challenge to Christians, 'a reminder of their own past'. Küng emphasizes that he can himself fully understand and accept 'the Hellenistic development of Christology'. Nevertheless, he asks whether a Christian can really require that a Muslim (or a Jew for that matter) should accept the decisions of the Hellenistic councils from Nicaea to Chalcedon.[33]

Others have drawn more radical conclusions. John Hick takes up the early 'adoptionist' christology and suggests that later incarnational theology should be understood as a myth in the sense of poetical or metaphorical truth. The talk of incarnation can be understood as a poetical way of underlining the significance of the man Jesus. If Christians seized on the 'adoptionist' component of their christological heritage, quite new possibilities might arise for a dialogue between Christians and people of other faiths. A Muslim group engaged in such a dialogue states indeed that 'Islam could tolerate any metaphorical interpretation' of the title 'Son of God'.[34]

Comparing the interpretative processes

If we look not just at the contents of the two scriptures, but at the interpretative processes involved, a number of interesting similarities emerge. Take the Johannine portrait of Jesus. In itself, this picture is poles apart from the Qur'anic one. John represents a full-blown christology 'from above': the Logos who took part in the creation, the Son who was with the Father before all time, visits the world of humans and returns to the glory of the Father. The contrast with the Qur'anic prophet could not be sharper. And yet the two different images of Jesus have come into being in rather similar processes. The Fourth Gospel too represents a free reinterpretation of Jesus' message in the light of later experiences and reflections, e.g. in John 17.5 where Jesus reflects on the glory he had in the Father's presence before the world existed. In the Synoptic Gospels the idea of Jesus' pre-existence is not attested.

Both John and Muhammad resorted to conceptual models known to them from their environment when interpreting the significance of Jesus in the light of their own conviction: John fell back on Jewish speculations concerning the pre-existent Wisdom of God; Muhammad leaned on the Jewish or Christian categories of prophet and messenger. On a certain level, scholarly assessments of what John did remind one of Muhammad's contribution: John 'may have access to excellent traditions' (an advantage which Muhammad did not have, to be sure) 'but he recasts them radically to suit his interpretation of the meaning of Christ';[35] the life story of Jesus is largely 'emptied of all real content', as 'it seems to be almost a projection of the present back into the past'.[36]

It is easy to notice that some later experiences are reflected e.g. in John 9: the parents of the man born blind (now cured by Jesus) 'were afraid of the Jews; for the Jews had already agreed that any-one who confessed Jesus to be the Messiah would be put out of the synagogue' (John 9.22). Such a decision is incomprehensible in an account of Jesus' life, but can be understood as a reflection of later events.

Christians have always objected that Muhammad falsely applied biblical prophecies to himself. Yet precisely the same kind of thing happened when early Christians read the Old Testament, searching for prophecies about Jesus, claiming that 'all (!) the prophets, as many as have spoken . . . predicted these days' (Acts 3.24). Every serious New Testament scholar agrees with Joseph Fitzmyer's point:

> . . . the modern reader will look in vain for the passages in the Old Testament to which the Lucan Christ refers when he speaks of 'what pertained to himself in every part of Scripture' . . . especially to himself as the 'Messiah' who was 'bound to suffer' . . . Luke has his own way of reading the Old Testament and here puts it on the lips of Christ himself.[37]

Later Muslims have searched for indications of Muhammad's proclamation in the Bible: apart from the Johannine Paraclete, the biblical passages most often invoked are Matt. 23.39, 'Blessed is the one who will come in the name of the Lord' and especially Deut 18.15, 18, 'from among your brothers a prophet like me'. The brothers of the people of Israel are the Arabs, so the promised prophet can only be Muhammad.[38] Further witnesses include Isa. 5.26–30; 9.5; Dan. 2.37–45; Hab. 3.3–7 and other messianic texts. This does not seem any more (or any less) arbitrary than the patristic devices!

Surely the Qur'anic prophets are flat characters, unhistorical stereotypes; but in the New Testament too attention is paid to only one aspect in the mission of Old Testament prophets – their messianic prophecies (alleged or real). On the basis of the New Testament alone we would know next to nothing about the activities of the prophets, with the exception of the miracles of Elijah and Elisha. Especially we would not know of their struggles against social injustice. The New Testament portrait of Isaiah is even more colourless than the Qur'anic portrait of Jesus.

These are random examples. In fact the whole history of the growth of the Bible could be set forth as an account of the development of traditions and their actualizations and reinterpretations in new situations.[39] In the Bible no less than in the Qur'an it is quite usual to present figures of the past as incarnations of the ideals of the writer's own time and environment.

This is very clear in the case of David. Once a bandit chief, then the military founder of a kingdom, in Chronicles he has become a blameless holy king who delivers solemn speeches, the founder of the Temple service. We hear nothing of the colourful events in connection with his rise to power, of his activities among the Philistines, of the case of Bathsheba or of the humiliation caused by Absalom's rebellion.[40] In the New Testament David is first and foremost an inspired psalm singer; in the Qur'an, too, he is a divine messenger who received the Psalter.

Or think of Abraham who was so important that every generation projected its ideals into him or traced its way of worshipping back to him. Early Christians participated in this process of legitimation whereby Paul and James came to opposite conclusions regarding the relationship of faith and works, as they considered the story of Abraham. Paul noticed that Abraham's faith is mentioned in Genesis (Gen. 15.6) before the commandment of circumcision is given (Gen. 17); he concluded that Gentiles can be included in God's people without circumcision. In a sense, Muhammad puts forward a similar argument when he states that Abraham's religion was older than both Judaism and Christianity; it thus presents the authentic model of true religion to which one should return.

In the Qur'an Jesus is 'degraded' to a precursor of Muhammad and testifies to the future coming of the latter. Something very similar happened to John the Baptist in early Christian tradition. It is assumed by scholars that the historical John considered himself to be the last messenger before the end. He can hardly have recognized Jesus as the Messiah. In the New Testament, however, it is one of John's main tasks to witness to Jesus and his mission. In the Fourth Gospel this is his only task: the Baptist has become 'the normative image of the Christian preacher, apostle and missionary, the perfect prototype of the true evangelist'.[41]

If the Qur'an contains polemics against Christians, the New Testament has preserved traces of rivalry between the Christians and the followers of the Baptist, who probably regarded the latter as the crucial eschatological figure. In Luke-Acts and in the Fourth Gospel the Baptist explicitly confesses that he is not the Messiah (Luke 3.15–16; Acts 13.25; John 1.20). This reminds one of the Qur'anic passages in which Jesus denies that he has made himself God (contrary to the claims of his followers).

In the Gospel of Matthew the picture of the Baptist is thoroughly Christianized. His mission very closely resembles that of Jesus. John is not portrayed as preaching about the baptism which he himself administers (as he does, reasonably enough, in the Gospel of Mark). On the contrary, he proclaims the very same message about the kingdom of heaven as does Jesus (Matt. 3.2 = 4.17). This identification of the messages is accomplished by the evangelist 'without a shadow of authority in the tradition and against all historical probability'.[42] At other points, too, identical statements occur in the mouths of John and Jesus: the axe at the root of the tree (3.10b John = 7.19 Jesus); the brood of vipers (3.7 John, cf. 12.34 and 23.33 Jesus). The constant opposition to Jesus by 'the Pharisees and the Sadducees' (a peculiarly Matthaean combination) is projected back on to the mission of John as well. Thus, in his editorial framework for John's preaching of judgment in Matt. 3.7, Matthew (differing from Luke and probably 'Q' as well) makes the Baptist address 'the Pharisees and the Sadducees'. On the whole Matthew speaks of John quite innocently 'as if he and his disciples belonged to the Christians'.[43]

All these features recall Muhammad's treatment of the Jesus traditions. Jesus preaches just like Muhammad, faces a similar front of opposition to Muhammad's, and makes his disciples Muslims. On the other hand, just as Matthew never allows John to interfere with the decisive position of Jesus in the Gospel, so Muhammad makes a clear distinction in rank between Jesus and himself, the 'seal of the prophets'. Both the Baptist in the New Testament and Jesus in the Qur'an point to the greater one who was to come.

Is it a question of genuine dialogue? It would seem that in both cases we have a kind of inclusive vision which tries to assimilate a rival tradition. The rival is reshaped in one's own image and thus, in the end, made harmless. John was a Christian for Matthew; Jesus was a Muslim for Muhammad.

The portrait of Jesus in the New Testament: a challenge for Muslims?

We have been speaking of the challenge which Islam presents to Christianity. Yet every dialogue has two sides. The challenge of Christianity to Islam can be expressed in a question: could Muslims adopt a historical-critical attitude to their own holy Book, as mainstream Christians have done with respect to their scripture? This issue will be addressed later in Chapter 8, but we shall anticipate it briefly with reference to the Qur'anic portrait of Jesus.

Is a historical assessment of the Qur'an, based on a comparison with earlier sources such as the Gospels, conceivable within Islam? To take a concrete example, what about Jesus' death on the cross, a point affirmed by the New Testament and by Western historians of all schools, but denied in the Qur'an? The relevant words (4.157) read: (The Jews said:) ' "We slew the Messiah, Jesus son of Mary, the Messenger of God" – yet they did not slay him, neither crucified him, only a likeness of that was shown to them.'[44] Can a Muslim be convinced by the historical evidence to hold that Jesus actually died?

In fact, Muslim scholars have sensed the problem, and some have suggested that the passage should not be interpreted as a historical statement but as a theological affirmation. Mahmud Ayoub for one perceives the historical problems connected with the Qur'anic passages. He seems to admit that, historically speaking, Jesus did die on the cross. He therefore wants to interpret the Qur'anic passage theologically or symbolically:

. . . the denial of the killing of Jesus is a denial of the power of men to vanquish and destroy the divine Word, which is forever victorious.[45]

For Cyril Glassé, an American Muslim, Jesus' death on the cross is simply a fact. He, too, gives a theological interpretation of the Qur'anic statement: it means that Jesus' death on the cross plays no role in the Islamic perspective.[46]

Such interpretations could be taken as parallels to the view of John Hick and others that Christian talk of incarnation does not amount to a literal truth. So there is an interesting similarity in the ventures of pioneering Christian and Muslim theologians. Some Christian theologians claim that a central Christian doctrine expresses a poetical or metaphorical truth rather than a literal one; some Muslims suggest that a Qur'anic statement contains a theological truth rather than a historical one.[47]

The question is, how far can such paths be pursued? There is a symbolic challenge to Islam in the fact that Ruqayyah Maqsood's book, which tells why she left Christianity for Islam, was published by a Christian publisher – SCM Press.

Symptomatically, the most likely places in the Islamic world where one can expect to find innovative views are not exegetical discussions, but works of fiction. An intriguing picture of Jesus is painted by the Egyptian author, the Nobel-prize winner Naguib Mahfuz, in his novel *The Children of our Quarter*, actually an allegorical narrative about the great monotheistic religions.[48] For Mahfuz, who uses both Qur'anic and biblical material, Jesus was undoubtedly killed. His image of Jesus 'represents an enormous step in the direction of a "Christian" understanding of Jesus in that the crucifixion and death of Jesus . . . occupy an important place in this narrative'.[49] Sympathetic emphasis is also put on the fact that Jesus – called Rifa'a in the narrative – 'absolutely rejects the use of violence' (a feature not always admired by Muslims).[50]

Jesus has of old stood 'between Christianity and Islam' in the sense that his different position in the two religions has been a hindrance to an encounter. Yet today it is also possible to think that he stands between the two (actually between three religions, for Judaism should be included in a 'trialogue') in the opposite sense: in the no man's land, or on the common ground which does not belong to any single party. Jesus was not a Christian, and his vision overlaps only partially with Christianity. Nor was he a Muslim, though Muslims are right in esteeming him and finding points of contact with Islam in his message. He stands in-between.

The more both sides learn to assess their own tradition from a critical perspective – the more one learns to understand it as the outcome of an historical development which cannot be changed but may be reassessed – the better are the chances for a *rapprochement* in a truly ecumenical spirit. The difficulties are formidable: can one relativize something which has traditionally been understood to be absolute? Christians ought to see their christology and Muslims the Qur'an in a rather more relative light. It is probably unrealistic to expect this to happen soon (or at all). But at least for a small minority on both sides, a historical view of Jesus, christology and the Qur'an holds out the hope of new prospects.

7

Arbitrary Allah? Predestination
in the Qur'an[1]

There are striking similarities between the history of Christian theology and that of Muslim theology. One of the common problems has been the question whether the salvation or damnation of humans depends on themselves: can man choose his path and destiny, or has the eternal lot of each person been predestined by God? In classical Muslim thought the emphasis has been laid on the latter alternative; yet certain movements (Qadarites, Mutazilites) have insisted on freedom of the will, which modern Muslim thinkers also tend to emphasize.[2] The majority of Christian theologians have been inclined to attribute freedom of choice (within certain limits) to human beings, but the dissenting minority includes men of the stature of Augustine, Zwingli, Calvin and Luther.[3]

The problem arose on both sides because of the Scriptures. The Qur'an is replete with sentences in which God is said to lead astray or guide to the right path whomever He pleases, e.g.:

> Whomsoever God desires to guide, He expands his breast to Islam; whomsoever He desires to lead astray, He makes his breast narrow, tight . . . (6.125).

> God guides whomsoever He will to a straight path (24.46).

The Bible, too, contains a number of passages in which the obduracy of men is traced back to God himself (cf. Chapter 2 above). On the other hand, both scriptures are flooded with utterances appealing to the will of man. To quote only one verse from the Qur'an:

> The truth is from your Lord; so let whosoever will believe, and let whosoever will disbelieve (18.29).

The question of predestination also arose quite soon in the theological controversies between Christians and Muslims. The anonymous *Dialogue between a Saracene and a Christian* (erroneously attributed to John Damascene) suggests that this is a fundamental point of disagreement between the two faiths: the Christians ascribe *liberum arbitrium* (free will) to man, the 'Saracenes' do not.[4] Down to the present, numerous Christian apologists have perpetuated the claim that with regard to predestination the spirit of the Bible is quite different from that of the Qur'an. One speaks of Allah as a true oriental despot: he is capricious, incalculable and cruel.[5] Hendrik Kraemer, the leading spokesman of Christian exclusivism, spoke of an 'over-heated monotheism', the will of Allah being 'august divine arbitrariness'.[6]

In view of such comparisons one may note that some scholars have used precisely the same kind of language in discussing the 'demonic' features of Yahweh in the Old Testament[7] or the conception of God in some New Testament texts. C.H. Dodd stated that in Romans 9 Paul portrays God as an 'immoral despot' who possesses 'absolute and arbitrary souvereignty',[8] and the predestinarianism of Revelation has invited even sharper comments.[9] As if this were not enough to show the unfairness of the comparisons, we shall shortly find 'predestinarian' passages in the Qur'an which have probably been influenced from the biblical tradition.

I analysed Romans 9 in Chapter 2, concluding that Paul's predestinarian language is an attempt to make sense of his negative social experience. I then referred to Muhammad as a parallel case; I now wish to substantiate that claim.

The first Meccan period[10]

In the surahs from the early days of Muhammad's mission the proclamation of the impending judgment dominates everything. Muhammad appeals to people in a way that presupposes their freedom of choice and responsibility. The virtuous will reach heaven, the scoundrels will land in hell (82.13–14). God sets before man two highways, and man ought to choose the 'steep' one:

The freeing of a slave, or giving food upon a day of hunger to an orphan near of kin or a needy man in misery; then that he become of those who believe and counsel each other to be stead-fast, and counsel each other to be merciful (90.12–17).

The sinners in Hell know that they went there because of their failures:

We were not of those who prayed, and we fed not the needy, and we plunged along with the plungers, and we cried lies to the Day of Doom, till the Certain came to us (74.43–47).

'This is a reminder; so whoever wills shall remember it' (74.54). 'He who turns his back, and disbelieves, God shall chastise him with the greatest chastisement' (88.23–24). Everything depends on man's attitude and actions.

Nothing points to arbitrariness on God's part in these early surahs. To be sure, the notion that man's fortunes and mis-fortunes, his life and death are totally dependent upon God makes its appearance from the start (e.g. 53.43–48).[11] This idea does not, however, imply the notion that man's destiny at the last judgment is predestined.

The second Meccan period

The so-called second Meccan period is a time of transition. The ardent enthusiasm gradually gives way to calmer reflection. The surahs of this period are already affected by disappointments experienced by the Prophet.

Several passages contain a vigorous appeal to the will of the hearer.

Then whosoever follows My guidance shall not go astray, neither shall he be unprosperous; but whosoever turns away from My remembrance, his shall be a life of narrowness . . . (20.123–124).

The truth is from your Lord; so let whosoever will believe, and let whosoever will disbelieve (18.29).

God tries through his messenger to make people repent. God alternates his threats in the Qur'an in order that people may be godfearing (20.113). Moses and Aaron had to speak gently to the godless and arrogant Pharaoh in the hope that 'haply he may be mindful, or perchance fear' (20.44). Not even Pharaoh, the prototype of a hardened man in the biblical tradition, is here regarded as hopelessly incurable in advance. God is all-forgiving 'to him who repents and believes, and does righteousness' (20.82).

Yet the call of the merciful God found almost no echo at all. The Prophet is deeply depressed by the scornful attitude of his hearers; he is almost 'worrying himself to death'. He is encouraged by God: no sign, however compelling in itself, could ever persuade these people (26.4–5). Muhammad need not blame himself; he has performed his task. He cannot make the dead or the deaf hear, nor can he guide the blind out of their error (27.80–81; 43.40). Yet despite his failure he has to cling to the revelation given to him (43.43) and to God's promise that he will show his power over the despisers (vv.42–43). In these contexts no thought is given to the question how the despisers have arrived at their state of unbelief. The words are meant as practical consolation to the proclaimer in trouble.

More austere language is used in 36.5–11:

The sending down of the All-mighty, the All-wise, that thou mayest warn a people whose fathers were never warned, so they are heedless. The Word has been fulfilled concerning most of them, so they do not believe.[12] Surely we have put on their necks fetters up to the chin, so their heads are raised; and We have put before them a barrier and behind them a barrier; and We have covered them, so they do not see. Alike is it to them whether thou hast warned them or thou hast not warned them, they do not believe. Thou only warnest him who follows the Remembrance and who fears the All-merciful in the Unseen; so give him the good tidings of forgiveness and a generous wage.

This colourful description, which draws its imagery from camel training, emphasizes that the possibility of faith has been excluded for some of the hearers by God. This is probably the earliest of those Qur'anic passages in which men's blindness is attributed to

God. But is it traced back to God's 'arbitrary' predestination, or is it seen as a just punishment? What 'word' has been fulfilled (v.7)?[13]

The point that the word has been fulfilled 'concerning *most* of them' does not match the idea of absolute predestination, for what is a predestination which is not valid in all cases? The verb used here typically occurs in passages which refer to punishment.[14] It therefore appears natural to interpret v.6 along these lines: God's threat that he will punish unbelievers has been fulfilled as regards most of the 'heedless'. The fetters, barriers and the cover on their eyes are a punishment for their indifference and anticipate the final punishment of hell. God has made these people unable to accept guidance, but only after they themselves have deserved this destiny. There is no indication of 'arbitrariness'. The passage ends quite naturally with a consolatory note: Muhammad need not worry about these hard-hearted people.

Similar ideas find expression in 18.57:

> And who does greater evil than he who, being reminded of the signs of his Lord, turns away from them and forgets what his hands have forwarded? Surely We have laid veils on their hearts lest they understand it, and in their ears heaviness; and though you call them to the guidance, yet they will not be guided ever.

Accordingly, it is futile to hope that this kind of people would let themselves be guided. The veils on their hearts and the heaviness of the ears are punishment for evil-doers. Intriguingly, the slightly awkward image of veils on the hearts reminds one of Paul's exploitation of the motif of the veil on Moses' face in II Cor. 3.15: 'to this very day whenever Moses is read, a veil lies over their [the Jews'] hearts'; and the sequel 'lest they understand' plus the reference to ears recalls Isa. 6.9–10, a passage used several times in the New Testament about divine hardening. Thus the issue of influence from the biblical tradition is seriously raised; some kind of influence can hardly be denied.[15]

In 18.17 the idea of God leading people astray occurs for the first time. Muhammad inserts into his account of the 'men of the cave'[16] a somewhat disconnected comment: 'whomsoever God guides, he is rightly guided, and whomsoever He leads astray, thou wilt not find for him a protector to direct'. There is no indication in the context that the leading astray will be arbitrary. The phrase concerning guidance seems to be associated with v.13, where it is said of the heroes of the story: 'They were youths who believed in their Lord, and We increased them in guidance.' Obviously the 'leading astray' here is a punishment similar to the covering of eyes (36.9) and the veiling of hearts (18.57). The point is this: whoever is sent astray by God will be completely without protection. By contrast, he who believes in God's signs will find a patron on the day of judgment.

The idea of absolute predestination, even in 'an extreme form in which human responsibility appears to be completely eclipsed', has sometimes been found in 15.60.[17] God says of the family of Lot: 'them we shall deliver all together, excepting his wife – we have decreed, she shall surely be of those that tarry'.[18] Yet one is not allowed to infer that God arbitrarily decrees some people to perish. For it becomes clear from another passage that, according to the Qur'an, Lot's wife had deserved her destiny, having betrayed her husband (66.10). This is a good example of how mis-interpretations occur, when a single verse is divorced from a wider context.

In the surahs of the second Meccan period the error of men is sometimes traced back to Satan (*Iblis*, from the Greek *diabolos*). To the people of ancient Sheba, Satan had 'decked out fair their deeds' and 'barred them from the way' (27.24–25). By making sin seem fair, Satan leads men astray, except for God's servants, for he only has authority over those who let themselves be perverted and follow him (15.39–43). The reponsibility rests with men them-selves. On the day of judgment God will ask them: 'Did I not enjoin you . . . that you should not serve Satan . . . ? . . . did you not understand?' (36.60–62). They must roast in hell because of their unbelief. God will 'assuredly fill Gehenna with thee [Satan], and with whosoever of them follows thee, all together' (38.84). 'Whoso blinds himself to the remembrance of the All-Merciful, to him We assign a Satan for comrade . . .' (43.36). The pious will not let themselves be seduced by Satan.

Satan has no independent authority. His activity is possible only because God permits it to happen. Satan has even been 'perverted' by God himself (15.39); yet the story of Iblis' fall makes abundantly clear that he is perverted because of his own disobedience (15.31). In this case, too, the divine leading astray is the punishment for sin, not its cause.

In a few verses salvation is positively ascribed to God's work. A person who escapes hell says: 'But for my Lord's blessing, I were one of the arraigned' (37.57). It is only because of God's mercy that an unbelieving friend had not led him to damnation. Moses was one of 'those astray', but God gave him wisdom and made him a messenger (26.21). The 'man of the fish' (Jonah) would have been 'cast upon the wilderness, being condemned', had it not been that 'a blessing from his Lord' overtook him and the Lord 'placed him among the righteous' (68.48–50). In such verses the emphasis lies on God's positive election. Man himself is to be blamed, if he is condemned, but salvation is essentially the work of God.

In the surahs from the second Meccan period, then, God figures as a frightening but righteous judge rather than as an arbitrary despot. He may blind a sinner or lead him astray, but in such cases man has certainly deserved his deplorable fate.

The third Meccan period

In the surahs from the third Meccan period the growing tension between the Meccans and the prophet is reflected throughout.

Again, it is not difficult to detect passages which refer to judgment according to one's deeds and clearly presuppose man's free will and responsibility. 'Those who believe and do righteous deeds' will receive their reward (29.7–9). God calls men to the straight path, but those who do not believe, deviate (23.73–74). 'Whoso does righteousness, it is to his own gain, and whoso does evil, it is to his own loss' (41.46). Everybody will get what he longs for:

> Whosoever desires this hasty world, We hasten for him therein what We will unto whomsoever We desire; then We appoint for him Gehenna wherein he shall roast, condemned and rejected. And whosoever desires the world to come and strives after it as

he should, being a believer – those, their striving shall be thanked (17.18–19).

Strikingly enough, it is stated at the beginning that God gives what he wills to whomever he desires, even though the whole passage is based on the idea that a person will be judged exactly according to his own aspirations. Obviously, the clause 'what We will' is, in a context like this, a phrase which rhetorically emphasizes God's omnipotence and has nothing to do with arbitrariness. God calls people in order to forgive their sins (14.10). He is compassionate to those 'who do evil deeds, then repent thereafter and believe' (7.153). God gives long life so that everybody has the opportunity to take warning (35.37), and tries them 'with good things and evil, that haply they should return' (7.168).

As a counterbalance, there are numerous passages that show God actively involved in leading men astray. God sends a man astray, he 'sets a seal' over his hearing and heart and 'places a covering' over his eyes (45.23). How are such passages to be understood?

In many cases the Qur'an explicitly states that those led astray have deserved this fate.

> God confirms those who believe with the firm word, in the present life and in the world to come; and God leads astray the evildoers; and God does what He wills (14.27).

In a context like this, the closing formula which emphasizes the sovereignty of God certainly sounds rhetorical. There is no trace of despotic arbitrariness in it. God simply leads astray the evildoers. Similarly, the phrase 'God leads astray whomsoever He wills' (13.27) is best interpreted by the sequel 'and He guides to Him all who are penitent'. Neither does the clause 'God chooses unto Himself whomsoever He wills' (42.13) refer to an arbitrary election, for the verse goes on: 'and He guides to Himself whosoever turns, penitent'. Such examples point to the conclusion that the 'whomsoever He wills' type of phrase is indeed a rhetorical hyperbole.

The phrase 'who shall guide those whom God has led astray?'

(30.29)[19] is paralleled by the reproach 'the evildoers follow their own caprices, without knowledge'. The statement 'He admits whomsoever He will into his mercy' (42.8) no doubt sounds arbitrary, but it is 'corrected' by the sequel 'and the evildoers shall have neither protector nor helper'. Surah 40 is quite explicit: God does not guide 'him who is prodigal and a liar' (v.28); he leads astray 'the prodigal and the doubter' (v.34) and sets a seal 'on every heart proud, arrogant' (v.35). In 16.93 the clause 'He leads astray whom He wills, and guides whom He wills' is immediately followed by the phrase 'and you will surely be questioned about the things you wrought'. The famous statement 6.125, quoted at the beginning of this chapter, does not imply arbitrariness either, for it ends up with the clause 'so God lays abomination upon those who believe not'.

Upon the 'hearts and hearing and eyes' of the apostates, too, a seal is put by God as a punishment for their having 'preferred the present life over the world to come', for 'God guides not the people of the unbelievers' (16.106–108). Obviously, the fact that apostasy is possible for a believer speaks against the idea of absolute predestination.

Wrong-doers even lead other people astray (6.144; 11.18–19), but the latter cannot be freed from responsibility (34.32). In a few passages Satan again acts in the role of the seducer. He 'decks out fair' to people their sins, so that they do not humble themselves before God (6.43) and 'lures' them 'to bewilderment', so that they do not listen to companions calling them to the right path (6.71). When incitement comes from Satan, one has to seek refuge with God (41.36).

In this period, too, the Prophet, distressed by the hearers' lack of response, receives consolation from the thought that his only task is to warn people; he is not responsible for the unbelief of others. 'God makes to hear whomsoever He wills; thou canst not make those in their tombs to hear – thou art naught but a warner' (35.22–23).

However, the comforting passages now increasingly contain sentences with a predestinarian note.

And what of him, the evil of whose deeds has been decked out

fair to him, so that he thinks it good? God leads astray whomsoever He wills, and whomsoever He wills He guides; so let not
thy soul be wasted in regrets for them; God has knowledge of
the things they work (35.8).

In this case, too, God leads astray the one who has already shown
'evil deeds', for God knows everything about him. The focus is on
the comfort given to the prophet. He need not sigh because of the
blindness of the sinners, for their well-deserved lostness depends
on the will of God.

In 39.36–37, too, the talk of God's leading astray belongs to a
practical context:

Shall not God suffice His servant, though they frighten thee
with those apart from Him? And whomsoever God leads astray,
no guide has he. But whomso God guides, none shall lead him
astray; is not God All-mighty, All-vengeful?

What is focussed upon here is the concrete question concerning
whose side God's power is on, rather than the metaphysical
question of the original source of straying. Muhammad need not
be concerned over the threats of his opponents. Since God himself
has led them astray, they do not have anybody in whom to take
refuge. The prophet, by contrast, cannot be led astray by anybody,
since he is guided by God. It is no wonder that Muhammad a few
verses later makes use of rather 'anthropocentric' language:
'whosoever goes astray, it is only to his own loss; thou art not a
guardian over them' (v.41).

Muhammad cannot force people to believe:

And if thy Lord had willed, whoever is in the earth would have
believed, all of them, all together. Wouldst thou then constrain
the people, until they are believers? It is not for any soul to
believe save by the leave of God; and He lays abomination upon
those who have no understanding (10.99–100).

'Save by the leave of God' no man can believe. In this sense the
fate of man depends on God. But this does not exclude man's

responsibility: 'abomination' (punishment) is laid upon those who do not understand. The function of these sentences, too, is to encourage the prophet in the midst of doubts.

His faith in God working everything gives Muhammad courage to carry out his mission despite all adversities. Clearly his 'social experience' has deeply affected his language. The idea that in the last analysis everything depends on God is not a theoretical answer to the intellectual question of the causes of unbelief; it is a practical source of comfort.

The miserable state of those sent astray is depicted in strong colours in 17.97:

> Whomsoever God guides, he is rightly guided; and whom He leads astray – thou wilt not find for them protectors, apart from Him. And we shall muster them on the Resurrection Day upon their faces, blind, dumb, deaf; their refuge shall be Gehenna, and whensoever it abates We shall increase for them the Blaze.

It is clear from the context that in this case, too, those sent astray have deserved their punishment. The reason for their unbelief is this: they have taken offence at the fact that God has sent a human being as his messenger (v.94) rather than given miraculous signs (vv.90–93). They want to refuse Muhammad the right to call himself God's messenger, but he appeals to God, and God knows who is right (v.96). It is to this appeal that v.97 is linked. In this verse the point is to show how completely helpless Muhammad's opponents will be at the judgment. Whoever is sent astray by God himself will certainly be without a helper. No one else can aid him.

The phrase concerning God's sending astray has here nothing to do with scholastic speculations about the extent to which salvation depends on God or man respectively. The sentence in question is part of a reproachful and warning passage. Muhammad tries to overcome the resistance of his hearers with threats: to be sent astray by God is the most terrible fate one can imagine.

Sometimes Muhammad even threatens his hearers with divinely caused intransigence:

> What think you? If God seizes your hearing and sight, and sets a

seal upon your hearts, who is a god other than God to give it back to you? (6.46)

Hast thou seen him who has taken his caprice to be his god, and God has led him astray out of a knowledge, and set a seal upon his hearing and his heart, and laid a covering on his eyes? Who shall guide him after God? What, will you not remember (45.23)?

A few passages still remain which are usually taken as clear proofs of the arbitrary character of God's actions according to the Qur'an.

And when We desire to destroy a city, We command its men who live at ease, and they commit ungodliness therein, then the Word is realized in them,[20] and We destroy it utterly (17.16).

Does God command the people to sin, in order to get a pretext for destroying the town?[21] Hardly. It is not said that to 'commit ungodliness' is identical with obeying the command. A natural interpretation is that to 'commit ungodliness' is to act against the command, which is then a natural reason for God to take vengeance. The 'men who live at ease' are in the Qur'an people who have always and everywhere opposed the word of God's messengers (e.g. 56.45–46). The implication of 17.16 is that the sinners incur by their conduct the justified punishment of God upon the town. This is explicitly stated in another verse from the same period: 'Thy Lord would never destroy the cities unjustly, while as yet their people were putting things right' (11.117).

The context of 17.16 is that of a serious warning. Man is warned not to go astray (vv.13–15); in v.17 there is a warning which hints at the destruction of former generations by God, who is aware of the sins of his servants. Still, in vv.18–19 man's personal responsibility is vigorously stressed. The word which comes true is the word of judgment upon the affluent.

In the same passage a heavenly book is mentioned, which everyone 'shall find spread wide open' on the last day (v.13). In several connections Muhammad speaks of a book in which all deeds of men, and even the fortunes and misfortunes of all men, are written down (57.22–23 et al.).[22] It is obvious that Muhammad considers the outward course of man's life as predetermined by God. But it does not automatically follow that a person's ethical and religious decisions are predestined as well. There is no compelling reason to see a reference to predestination in the religious sense in the words 'every man – We have fastened to him his bird of omen upon his neck' (17.13). Immediately thereafter Muhammad emphasizes the decisive significance of the deeds recorded in the book for man's eventual fate.

When 'the arbitrary character of Allah's action'[23] or 'the predestination *ad malam partem*'[24] is spoken of, 32.13–14 are often presented as a case in point:

> If We had so willed, We could have given every soul its guidance; but now My Word is realized – 'Assuredly I shall fill Gehenna with jinn and men all together.' So now taste, for that you forgot the encounter of this your day! We indeed have forgotten you. Taste the chastisement of eternity for what you were doing!

Several expressions in this passage speak against 'arbitrariness'. Men must taste punishment 'for what they were doing', because they have forgotten the day of judgment, and that is why God has forgotten them. The first sentence is consonant with Muhammad's general theocentric view: God's initiative is necessary if man is to be rightly guided. God could have brought the resistance of every man to nought, but he wants to judge everyone according to his deeds.

The only point in this section where a slightly predestinarian tone is discernible is God's promise that he will fill Gehenna with jinn and men. Surely this should not be understood too literally, as if God had to take pains to find, by whatever means, a sufficient number of people to fill Gehenna. Nothing indicates that there is anything arbitrary in the selection of those who will fill hell. The whole discussion belongs in the context of a serious warning.[25] The hearers are not inclined to believe in a 'new creation' after death (v.10), and Muhammad attempts to convert them by describing the sinner's fate in terrifying terms. 'Ah, if thou couldst see the guilty hanging their heads before their Lord!' (v.12). Hell will be filled, and on the day of judgment there will be no chance to return to the earth and act uprightly (v.12). It is best to believe in time!

This interpretation is corroborated by 7.18, which speaks of the expulsion of Satan. The word of God which is to be fulfilled is his threat to fill Gehenna with Satan and those who *follow him*.[26]

Thus far, not a single unambiguously predestinarian passage has been found. Yet such passages are not entirely lacking. Very strong language is used in 7.179: [27]

> We have created for Gehenna many jinn and men; they have hearts, but understand not with them; they have eyes, but per-
> ceive not with them; they have ears, but they hear not with them. They are like cattle; nay, rather they are further astray.
> Those – they are the heedless.

Muhammad here draws an extreme inference from his bitter experience. All around him there are the deaf, blind and neglectful people who disregard the truth proclaimed by him. The Prophet reaches the embittered and polemical conclusion that his opponents have even been created for hell.

Yet it is not credible that Muhammad even here consciously ascribes arbitrariness to God. The context is filled with warning admonitions, aimed at producing conversion. Muhammad cites examples from history (v.167 etc.) and affirms that God does not 'leave to waste the wage of those who set aright' (v.170). God performs clear signs so that people will 'haply return' (v.174). Muhammad is enjoined to tell a story to make people reflect (v.176). He bemoans the fate of the unfaithful (v.177). To this warning and exhortatory context is appended the commonplace 'Whomsoever God guides, he is rightly guided; and whom He leads astray – they are the losers' (v.177). The end of this sentence makes clear that the emphasis does not lie on the theoretical question of the cause of the deviation but on the sorrowful fate of those gone astray (cf. also v.186).

This is where the passage concerning those created for hell comes in (v.179). It is immediately followed by an exhortation to call upon God and to pay no attention to 'those who blaspheme His names' (v.180). In the light of the context, the actual emphasis obviously lies on exhortations which appeal to the will of the hearers. The talk of creation for hell contradicts this proclamation as such, but in practice it seems only to add a rhetorical effect to the appeal. One has to scare people to make them repent!

The Qur'an includes a few hints to the effect that some hearers drew their own conclusions from Muhammad's predestinarian language.[28] Their inference was this: if God is as Muhammad presents him, man has in fact no choice.

> The idolaters will say, 'Had God willed, we would not have been idolaters, neither our fathers, nor would we have forbidden aught' (6.148).

An apparently ironical objection to Muhammad's proclamation is presented by the polytheists: in practising idolatry and rejecting Muhammad, they are only doing what God wills. Had the omnipotent God willed something else, they would have done that. Muhammad declines this claim as a mere pretext.

The section 39.53–59 is most illuminating. Muhammad exhorts his hearers to turn unto their Lord before the chastisement comes upon them (v.54) lest someone attempt to say: 'If only God had guided me, I should have been among the godfearing' (v.57). Such a thought is as impossible as is the idea of returning to earth on the day of judgment (v.58). 'Yes indeed! My signs did come to thee, but thou hast cried them lies, and thou hast waxed proud, and become one of the unbelievers' (v.59). The unbeliever cannot take God's omnipotence as an excuse for his unbelief. He cannot accuse God of having denied him guidance. Muhammad's move reminds one of that of Paul in Romans 9.19–21. Paul's imaginary opponent raises the question of theodicy: if God has mercy on whomever he chooses, and hardens whomever he chooses (v.18), 'Why then does he still find fault? For who can resist his will?'. Paul retorts, 'Who are you to argue with God?' No more does Muhammad accept the implication that God is arbitrary.

Finally, reference should again be made to those passages which in a positive way emphasize God's work in man's salvation.

Abraham says: 'If my Lord does not guide me I shall surely be of the people gone astray' (6.77). The righteous exclaim in Paradise: 'Praise belongs to God, who guided us into this; had God not guided us, we had surely never been guided' (7.43).

In the surahs from the third Meccan period there are more predestinarian-sounding verses than in the earlier ones. Yet, despite the strong language of a few sentences, it is hard to maintain that Muhammad regards God as 'arbitrary' in them. A closer examination of the pertinent passages has suggested that it is proper to speak of predestinarian language rather than of a doctrine of predestination. The idea that God is the cause of everything is, for Muhammad, a source of confidence for the believer and a reason for fear for the unbeliever, rather than a metaphysical doctrine. In the surahs from the third period, as in the earlier ones, man's responsibility is vigorously stressed. If one goes astray and lands in hell, he has deserved it.

The Medinan period

The surahs from Muhammad's last period reflect a different historical situation. Having emigrated to Medina, the prophet has become the leader of a theocratic community. The problems posed by the new environment differ from those caused by the scornful opponents at Mecca. Muhammad must address various groups which have adopted different attitudes toward him: believers, the Medinan 'Doubters'[29] whose support fluctuated, Bedouin tribes whose reliability was also questionable, Jews and Christians.

Judgment according to deeds continues to be a fundamental theme. 'Whoso obeys God and His messenger' will enter Paradise, whereas whoever disobeys them will enter the fire (4.13–14). God recompenses doubly every good deed, for 'God shall not wrong so much as the weight of an ant' (4.40). 'The worst of beasts' in God's eyes are 'those who are deaf and dumb and do not understand'. Had God known any good in them, he would have made them hear; but even so these perverted people would have turned away (8.22–23).

It is stressed even more than before that it is the reprobate who are led astray by God. By the Qur'anic similes God leads many astray and guides many, 'but He leads none astray save the ungodly' (2.26).[30]

To the 'Doubters' Muhammad has many harsh words to say. The 'affluent' who did not want to participate in an expedition 'are well-pleased to be with those behind, and a seal has been set upon their hearts, so they understand not' (9.87). The Doubters have forgotten God, and he has forgotten them and cursed them (9.67–68). At Medina Muhammad is constantly confronted with apostasy. He talks a good deal about the severe punishment of renegades (3.106, etc.). It does not occur to him to trace men's apostasy back to God's eternal plan. Theocentric language ('to seal') does occur, but the emphasis is polemical, the words are directed against those who are falling away.

4.88 is quite explicit:

How is it with you, that you are two parties touching the Doubters, and God has overthrown them for what they earned? What, do you desire to guide him whom God has led astray? Whom God leads astray, thou wilt not find for him a way.

Those led astray have deserved to be treated that way. The context is the familiar one: whoever is led astray by God cannot be guided to the right path by anybody; he is beyond all help. By this warning Muhammad tries to prevent his adherents from joining the Doubters who 'wish that you should disbelieve as they disbelieve' (v.89). The talk of God's leading astray has a practical polemical intention. The fact that it has nothing to do with predestinarian speculation becomes abundantly clear from v.89: 'take not to yourselves friends of them, until they emigrate in the way of God!' Obviously, it is quite possible that those led astray will return to the right path. It is up to them.

The decisive significance of God's mercy for man's being a believer is again emphasized. 'God provides whomsoever He will without reckoning' (2.212).

Satan, too, is again referred to a few times as a tempter, but he cannot injure people except 'by the leave of God' (58.10). The renegades have yielded to the spell of Satan, but they will receive a harsh punishment (47.25ff.).

Comforting words to the prophet continue. If people 'surrender themselves', 'they are right guided, but if they turn their backs, thine is only to deliver the message' (3.20). The 'whom he will' type of terminology is found in a reassuring context: 'Thou art not responsible for guiding them; but God guides whomever He will' (2.272).

In the Medinan period, predestinarian language occurs in highly polemical contexts. God has set a seal upon the hearts of unbelievers (2.7) and renegades as a punishment for their impiety. He has led the wrong-doers astray and given guidance to the believers.

Conclusions

It is often thought that Muhammad went through a development from a preacher of free will to a teacher of predestination.[31] My analysis suggests a slightly different line: the 'doctrine of pre-destination' no longer seems to have a central place in the very last phase of the prophet's career. The strongest language is used toward the end of the Meccan time; the Medinan phase tends to weaken the intensity of the 'doctrine'.

However, it seems better not to speak of a doctrine at all, but rather of the development of Muhammad's language. Muhammad is not a philosophical theologian, but a practical proclaimer. As a proclaimer he is anything but a determinist. He has recourse to every possible means to appeal to the will of his hearers: he tries to win them over by way of urging, warning, terrifying, threatening. The idea of man's responsibility and of judgment according to one's deeds is in fact so fundamental that it predominates even where the language has taken on a predestinarian colouring.

The usual view that the idea of predestination predominates in the Qur'an over against the notion of free will is, I must conclude, mistaken. It is based on the simplistic method of detaching Qur'anic sentences from their contexts. In attempting to grasp the book as a whole, I could not escape the strong impression that almost every page is governed by the idea of man's responsibility and God's rightful judgment. The Qur'anic God is not the arbitrary despot as he has been presented by Western scholarship (which has, to be sure, been led astray by orthodox Muslim theology). He is, rather, a strictly impartial judge, the 'God of justice'.[32] Still, a number of passages show that a Muslim should ascribe his salvation not to his own deeds, but to God who has given him guidance. Salvation depends on God; if, however, somebody ends up in hell, he has no one but himself to blame.

This conclusion is the outcome of an examination of the contexts of the 'predestinarian' passages. In them three emphases predominate. Muhammad appeals to God's leading astray in polemical, warning and consoling situations. 1. It is the wrongdoers and renegades who are led astray. 2. God can lead the prophet's hearers irrevocably astray, so that they will be without a helper at the judgment, unless they soon repent. 3. Muhammad need not worry about the hearer's unbelief, for it manifests God's will.

The 'predestinarian' statements are not doctrinal propositions; they serve the needs of proclamation. When Muhammad addresses an audience concerning which he has some hope of success, he never presents them with a theory of divine election and rejection. He appeals to everybody's will. Undoubtedly Paul did the same in his situation.

In summary, it is the social experience of Muhammad that has caused him to resort to predestinarian language. The general theocentricity of his thought, typical of his Arabian environment, is a necessary presupposition for such language, but it is not a sufficient condition for it. It is unlikely that Muhammad would have had recourse to such usage had it not been for his bitter experience with his fellow men. In the predestinarian-sounding passages the prophet is working through this experience, and he utilizes traditions about divine hardening which seem to go back to Christian origins. But even apart from the genetic connection, the parallel to Paul (Rom. 9) and the evangelists (Mark 4.11–12 par.) is obvious.[33]

It is unfair to brand Muhammad's God as arbitrary and use this characterization to set up a contrast between the biblical and the Qur'anic conceptions of God. I hope to have shown that the application to the Qur'an of critical exegetical methods which are orientated on the context (literary and social), developed in biblical study, may serve inter-religious dialogue by removing some obstacles – especially by demolishing unfair contrasts and distorted comparisons. The great monotheistic religions largely share with one another both the strengths and the problems of the notion of the one almighty God.

8

Word of God, Word of Muhammad: Could Historical Criticism of the Qur'an be Pursued by Muslims?

We have discussed the challenge of Islam to Christianity, but noted that there is a challenge to Islam as well: could Muslims adopt a historical-critical attitude to their own holy Book? This is what Christians have been trying to learn during the last centuries with regard to *their* book. To be sure, the churches have been reluctant and selective in their acceptance of the critical approach. Yet individual Christians and groups who have adopted it feel that they have profited even religiously.

The history of the interpretation of the Qur'an in many ways resembles the earlier history of biblical exegesis. Both in Judaism and Christianity and in Islam different schools and communities have found their own doctrines in their scriptures.[1] But no Qur'anic research comparable to the critical study of the Bible has emerged in Islam.[2] In classical as well as modern commentaries efforts are made 'to fit the text of scripture to the conditions of the era contemporary with the interpreter'.[3]

Hans Küng formulates the 'awkward but unavoidable' question:

Does revelation supposedly fall directly from heaven, to be inspired unmistakably or dictated word for word from God? . . . today it is important that the Qur'an as the word of God be regarded at the same time as the word of the human prophet.[4] . . . if we have historical criticism of the Bible (for the benefit of a contemporary biblical faith) why not then also have historical criticism of the Qur'an, and this for the benefit of a Muslim faith appropriate to modern times? . . . why not perceive the Qur'an as a great prophetic witness to the one and only powerful and merciful God . . . ?[5]

Such demands cannot of course be imposed from outside. It was thinkers within the Christian tradition who developed the historical criticism of the Bible – and fought for it, as it was (and often still is) regarded as anything but a benefit for faith by fellow believers.[6] John Hick is surely right in believing that

> the official belief-system of each tradition is capable of desirable development and modification at many points; but this can only properly be done from within those traditions and by their own thinkers . . . change has to come from within a religious tradition.[7]

Here I am looking for signs of a shift in Muslim views of the Qur'an.

The orthodox view has been that the Qur'an is God's eternal, uncreated Word.[8] Every word came directly from God. True, of old attention has also been paid to the issue of the occasions for the 'sending down' of the individual verses, though even this has often been forgotten. Daud Rahbar, then a Muslim scholar, reported a generation ago that 'Muslims of moderate education' understand the revelation 'in the sense of the Prophet's receiving the Qur'an from the physically above literally as a bound volume'. And even when very intelligent graduates heard that

> the Qur'an was a collection of intermittent revelations that were proclaimed by the Prophet orally, they became extremely surprised and even shocked. The most authentic fact that the present arrangement of the Qur'an is different from the actual order of revelation, which was one of the most primary subjects of discussion in Qur'anic learning in the classical days of Islam, is unknown to a very great majority of enlightened Muslims today.

Muslim students admitted that these discussions 'shook their faith'.[9] One hopes that the situation is better today.

Even when the historical 'occasions' of the verses have been recognized, this has not led to the assumption of anything like a causal connection between the situation of the prophet and the Qur'anic statements.[10] To say that 'revelation had a historical context' does not mean 'that the Qur'an was being composed in the life-time of the Prophet'. Even Rahbar held fast to the view that the Qur'an is 'the eternal Divine Word'. The Qur'an was there with God eternally, but the sending down of its parts awaited the events which were to occur as their occasions, and with reference to which those verses were to be understood.[11]

Also, from early on one had to wrestle with the problem that some verses had been expressly abrogated through other verses. Yet these changes were never ascribed to the prophet, but to God himself. For an outsider this view involves an obvious problem: how do such abrogations fit with the eternity of the Qur'an?[12]

'Scientific' exegesis

Since the end of the last century, a strong 'Modernist' trend has characterized Muslim thought in many circles, especially in India and Egypt.[13] One has distinguished three aspects in the modern interpretation of the Qur'an (in Egypt): 'scientific', philological and practical.[14] The philological one contains genuinely historical insights.

By contrast, a modern interpreter with a 'scientific' interest tries to combine the contents of the Qur'an with modern natural science. One has discovered the doctrines of both Darwin and Einstein in the Qur'an, and the demons called jinns have proved to be microbes.[15] Others find allusions to aeroplanes, artificial satellites, interplanetary travel and the hydrogen bomb.[16] This approach is alive and well in Maurice Bucaille's popular book *The Bible, the Qur'an and Science*.

Bucaille emphasizes e.g. that, unlike the Genesis story, the Qur'anic account of the Flood 'does not give rise to any criticisms from a historical point of view'. The Flood is not described as universal; the Qur'an 'does not date the Flood in time and gives no indication as to the duration of the cataclysm itself' (233–235).[17] True enough; but what has actually happened is that the story, like all biblical and Jewish stories in the Qur'an, has been detached from its (quasi-)historical framework. This has indeed caused some of the impossibilities in the biblical account to disappear. But Bucaille passes in silence the issue of Noah's taking a pair of every kind of animal into the ark – a not exactly historically probable feature of the biblical story which is also found in the Qur'an (11.40).

Sometimes Bucaille exploits the general difficulties in translating Arabic terms and gives his own modernizing rendering (208–210). A striking inability to understand religious language in context surfaces when he interprets 55.33 as a reference to the future 'conquest of space', another proof of the divine origin of the Qur'an (174–176). The verse reads:

> O tribe of jinn (!) and of men, if you are able to pass through the confines of heaven and earth, pass through them! You shall not pass through except with an authority.

The context is that of the last judgment and the point is clearly that man (or jinn) cannot flee anywhere from it.

A science-orientated commentator often eliminates the 'supernatural' in a quite rationalistic way. The suggestion that jinns are microbes was also an effort to explain away these 'invisible beings, either harmful or helpful, that interfere with the lives of mortals'.[18] The Qur'an tells, in accordance with a Christian legend, that Mary lived in the temple and received her food from God (3.37).[19] For rationalist interpretation this means only that visitors brought food to her.[20] The virginal conception of Jesus indicates a normal pregnancy which originated in a marriage,[21] though no husband is ever mentioned in the Qur'an, and it remains obscure why others in this case should have accused Mary of unchastity.

Surah 2 tells of a man whom God let remain dead for one hundred years, but who was then resuscitated (2.259). Rationalist interpreters have proposed that the man was under a strong suggestion and felt as if one hundred years had passed.[22] Surah 18 tells the familiar legend of the Seven who during a persecution fled to a cave; there they slept for 309 years (18.25), until God woke them up (18.19). 'Scientific' interpreters tell us that the men died; a natural phenomenon (mummification) made them look like sleepers.

Another surah reports, following a Jewish tradition, that Solomon learned the language of birds. To his army belonged

'jinns, humans and birds'; ants fled away from it. Solomon understands the speech of an ant and smiles at him. The hoopoe carries
out a spying mission (27.16ff.). A rationalist interpreter explains
away all traits which might confuse a modern person. 'Birds' and
'ants' refer to different groups of people or to different tribes;[23]
'hoopoe' is the name of a person.[24]

In all this, modern trends in Islam confirm a fact well known
from Christian theology: extreme conservatism and outright
rationalism fit well together. Scriptural conservatism is often
identified with literalism but, as James Barr has shown, this is not
always the case.[25] Precisely the conservative interpreter often gives
up literal interpretation. Remember that in the old church it was
Marcion, the radical, who read the Old Testament literally, and his
conservative critics who shunned a literal interpretation. If a literal
reading entails that the text is in error or incredible, a conservative
must avoid such a conclusion at all costs, even by way of a non-
literal explanation. This is why a modernist Muslim explains that
the talking animals are not real animals; for the same reason some
'conservative evangelical' interpreters maintain that the seven days
of creation in Genesis 1 are not normal days.[26] Many conservatives
on both sides have in fact succumbed to a scientific view of
the world in most (if not all) areas of life. One is reluctant to
believe in too great miracles and takes efforts to explain away the
miraculous (for details see below, pp. 147f.). Such an approach
precludes a genuinely historical understanding of the texts.

There is an interesting analogy between modern conservatives –
Muslim and Christian – on one side and the liberal rationalist
expositors of the Gospels of the early nineteenth century. The
latter held fast to the form of the Gospel stories: what was told had
really happened, but the eye-witnesses had misunderstood what
they saw. They believed that Jesus was walking on the sea, when
he was only walking on the shore on a foggy day; his feeding
miracle consisted in the fact that his example made people share
their food with others – compare the modernist interpretation of
the miraculous feeding of Mary in the Qur'an. The death blow to
this kind of exposition of the Gospels was given by the radical
critic D.F. Strauss who played off the supernatural and the
rationalist explanations against each other. While demonstrating

the implausibility of both, Strauss did not conceal his sympathy for the 'supernatural' explanations; though historically impossible, they at least took the content and intention of the texts as they stand seriously.

Form criticism and contextual exegesis

'Scientific' exegesis has been rejected by other Muslim interpreters, who emphasize that the Qur'an must be expounded in the light of its historical context.[27] One has to ask what the revelation could have meant to its immediate recipients. Amin al-Khuli, a leading Egyptian exegete in this century, stated that one cannot profit from the 'spiritual guidance' of the Qur'an 'before one knows the exact "literal" meaning of it as it was understood in the days of its revelation'.[28] Unlike so many Muslims, al-Khuli does not reject Western orientalism; a pupil of his even translated Theodor Nöldeke's *Geschichte des Korans* into Arabic (though the translation was never printed). Exegetical studies

> should be divided into two parts: (1) those on the background of the Koran, on the history of its genesis, on the society in which it came into being, on the language of the people to which it was primarily addressed, etc., and (2) the interpretation of the verses of the Koran in the light of these preliminary studies.

Al-Khuli considers it essential to establish first of all 'the true literal meaning' of the text, 'even if we do not look for edification through it' and 'without regard for religion'.[29] This approach is, germinally at least, comparable to the two-stage approach in biblical exegesis which emphasizes the necessity of distinguishing between 'what it meant' and 'what it means' (Krister Stendahl).[30]

Al-Khuli supervised a thesis of Muhammad Khalafallah on 'the art of story-telling in the Qur'an' in the late 1940s. Here it was suggested that the Qur'an contains legends and fables;[31] the Qur'an itself does not deny the claim of unbelievers that it includes 'histories of the old' (25.5). It does not refrain from putting a fable into the service of its message. This is what happens in the case of the ants and the hoopoe. Many stories of earlier prophets in the

Qur'an need not be historically true.[32] Yet the existence of legends does not mean that Muhammad is the author of the Qur'an. Khalafallah combines an orthodox dogmatic view[33] – God is the only 'author' of the Qur'an – with historical and literary insight. It was not God's aim to set forth 'historical' truths, but religious truths in tales which aim at influencing the will and actions of people.

God took into account the situation of Muhammad's hearers and their ability to understand. He employed ways of expression and stories familiar to them. The Qur'an is 'human with reference to expression and style'. Part of it is addressed to Muhammad to comfort him. Here the problem arises: how does this correlation with Muhammad's situation fit with the eternity of the Qur'an? Khalafallah evades the problem. Still, his view is to a degree comparable with the standard Christian notion that biblical revelation e.g. in the early stories of Genesis employs older oriental tales.

The outcome of Khalafallah's innovations was that he was dismissed from his university post. Critics concluded that he did not really believe in the divine origin of the Qur'an[34] (and indeed it can be asked whether it was consistent to hold fast to the full divinity of the book when so much was conceded in terms of human expression).[35]

The Pakistani scholar Daud Rahbar used a related approach in *God of Justice* (1960). Two features stand out: 1. the Qur'an must be interpreted by the Qur'an (rather than in the light of later theological tradition) – a principle of *sola scriptura* as it were; 2. the context must determine the interpretation of individual statements. Both principles of course belong to the basic methodology of any biblical scholar; they also correspond to al-Khuli's methodology.[36]

Rahbar claims that the Qur'anic revelation is connected with Muhammad's natural knowledge, for (contrary to a popular Muslim opinion) Muhammad had of course (!) heard a lot from Jews and Christians. In fact the way the Qur'an constantly alludes to Jewish and Christian stories assumes that they were familiar to Muhammad's hearers. But when the old stories are retold in the Qur'an, their language becomes more beautiful and their significance clearer.[37] The question of possible earlier (Jewish, Christian and pagan) 'influences' on the Qur'an is a critical issue: where their existence admitted, it is possible to speak of a really historical approach.

The hermeneutics of change

On the basis of insights which had matured in exegetical work, Rahbar tried in the 1950s to develop a critical hermeneutics of the Qur'an, starting from the needs of Islamic society. Muslims had to realize the necessity of changes, for to the essence of Islam belongs the dynamic character of the Qur'an, which always takes the situation of the recipients of the message into account. The abrogation of some precepts in new situations within the Qur'an itself shows its dynamic character.[38] Therefore the details of the Islamic law cannot be eternal.

Rahbar even took up the question of how the eternity of the Qur'an fits with its close connection with the situation of seventh-century Arabs; he solved the problem simply by appealing to God's omniscience.

Rahbar's influence on Muslim interpretation of the Qur'an was doomed to fail, for he converted to Christianity. Yet these writings of his were still conceived as Muslim contributions to the discussion within Islam.

The issue of time-bound and eternal elements

Rahbar is by no means alone in favouring Qur'anic interpretations which encourage social innovation.[39] Others too focus on the 'dynamic' aspect of the Qur'an which comes to expression in the phenomenon of 'abrogation'. Muhammad Said Al-Ashmawy, a high Egyptian official, argues that the Qur'anic principle of abrogation implies a 'law of evolution of the norms' so that Islamic legislation must be (as it was from the beginning) 'in constant movement'. Early Caliphs even cancelled Qur'anic injunctions (e.g. the harsh punishment for theft) which had not been abrogated in the Qur'an itself, without thereby becoming infidels.[40]

Abdullahi Ahmed An-Na'im was once Professor of Law in Sudan and an active fighter for human rights in the 'Republican

Brotherhood'.[41] He wants to reform the *shariah* in the spirit of human rights and modern democracy, yet on an Islamic basis. The Islamic law must be criticized in the light of the Qur'an; once more the notion of abrogation proves vital.

An-Na'im claims that it is harmful to apply the Shariah today, for it does not correspond to the principles of modern constitutionalism. Some Muslims describe the Shariah in very humane terms, but An-Na'im finds this misleading. Once more, critical study of religious history is needed as an historical conscience! The application of the Shariah today would humiliate non-Muslims and also Muslim women in a 'morally repugnant' way (59), and even undermine the freedom of belief, expression and assembly of Muslim men. In international relations the Shariah would justify the use of force; even slavery would be acceptable. So one has to go back to the Qur'an! The problem is that the Qur'an itself offers different starting-points for legislation. This is seen, for instance, as regards the proper Muslim attitude to non-Muslims. The early Meccan surahs urge peaceful persuasion only; by contrast, violence is justified in revelations from the later Medinan period. To reconcile such contradictions, Muslim lawyers resorted to the theory of abrogation: later revelation has cancelled the earlier one. The classical *shariah* is mainly based on the later Medinan revelation.

An-Na'im turns the theory of abrogation upside down: it is the later Medinan verses that are to be cancelled. A new Shariah is to be built solely on the early Meccan revelation, which he takes to have been egalitarian, humanitarian and universalist. Later revelations were adapted to the conditions of Medinan society; it was meant to be of a temporary character, to be replaced in due time by the older Meccan verses.

An-Na'im thinks that according to the Meccan revelation, which was later postponed for a while, women are entitled to the same rights as men, and non-Muslims to the same rights as Muslims. Apostasy is not a legal crime. From the viewpoint of the historical conscience one may doubt An-Na'im's exegesis; the Meccan revelation was hardly all that egalitarian either.[42]

However, An-Na'im's theory does seem to work with regard to the issue of force in Muslim relations to non-believers. The revelations from the Meccan time presuppose peaceful persuasion;[43] only in the Medinan period does violence enter the picture.[44] For the historian the reason is obvious: in his Meccan time Muhammad was in no position to use force; the situation changed in Medina.

An-Na'im holds uncompromisingly fast to the divinity of the Qur'an: 'to doubt the direct and totally divine nature of any part of the text of the Qur'an is to cease to be a Muslim' (196 n. 29). Nevertheless, his view raises far-reaching theological problems: why did God give in Medina a revelation which was inferior to that which he had already given in Mecca? An-Na'im answers (53) that the Qur'an had to contain 'all that God wanted to intimate to posterity', both that which was intended for immediate application (the Medinan revelation) and that which was to be applied under appropriate future circumstances (the Meccan revelation).

This view reminds one of the so-called accommodation theory which was prominent in 'advanced' biblical interpretation in the eighteenth century: revelation had to be adapted to the humans' capacity of reception.[45] In the eyes of an outsider it fits awkwardly with the belief that the Qur'an is pre-existent, or even uncreated. In addition, a strong tension remains between the finality of the revelation and its actual contents. If God had revealed the very same message through thousands of messengers before Muhammad, why did he bring the revelations to an end precisely in seventh-century Medina? Why did he give the *final* revelation in an environment that was not at all ripe to assimilate it?

One of An-Na'im's authorities is the late Fazlur Rahman of Chicago (died 1988).[46] He too suggested that the Shariah should be reassessed in the light of the Qur'an, read in chronological order. It is the oldest revelations that give a clear picture of the 'basic impulse' of Islam which differs from later institutions. One would also have to distinguish between the legal statements of the Qur'an and their intention. In searching for the intention one would have to pay close attention to the social context of the revelation.

Rahman set out the principles but did not derive a concrete reform programme from them; An-Na'im tries to put his principles into practice. Rahman stated frankly that Muslims were not yet ready to accept his 'honest' and 'practical' method.

As a parallel from Christendom one is reminded of Hermann Samuel Reimarus, praised by subsequent exegetes from Albert Schweitzer on, who in the eighteenth century wrote an apology for the rational worshippers of God. He completed it in 1767, but 'prudently showed it only to a few trusted friends', considering 'his society not yet ready for the truth about the Bible and revealed religion'.[47]

An-Na'im expressly abstains from any criticisms of the Qur'an. Rahman's stance seems more radical. He stated that 'the Qur'an is entirely the Word of God and, in an ordinary sense, *also entirely the word of Muhammad*'.[48] The Qur'an is 'purely divine', for there were moments when Muhammad,

> as it were, 'transcends himself' and his moral cognitive perception becomes so acute and keen that his consciousness becomes identical with the moral law itself . . . When Muhammad's moral intuitive perception rose to the highest point and became identified with the moral law itself . . . , the Word was given with the inspiration itself.

> A voice is crying from the very depths of life and impinging forcefully on the Prophet's mind in order to make itself explicit at the level of consciousness.

> The Qur'an is thus pure Divine Word, but, of course (!), it is equally intimately related to the inmost personality of the Prophet Muhammad whose relationship to it cannot be mechanically conceived like that of a record. The Divine Word flowed through the Prophet's heart.[49]

The Qur'an tackles legal problems experimentally (!) as they arise (witness its different standpoints on the use of alcohol).[50] One has to distinguish between the 'spirit' of the Qur'an and its actual legislation. The legislation 'had partly to accept the then existing society as a term of reference'; therefore the Qur'an could not possibly intend its laws to be 'literally eternal'. One must go beyond the actual legislation to reach the real intention of each

law.[51] In a rather similar vein, eighteenth-century biblical interpreters thought that by use of the 'principle of accommodation' it
was possible to identify what parts of the Bible are 'merely local
and temporal in significance'.[52]

Take the cutting off of a hand, enjoined by the Qur'an as the
penalty for theft.[53] This practice was in use among some tribes
before Muhammad; it was adopted by the Qur'an. In that social
context the concept of theft was different from that found in
modern societies. Theft violated the owner's sense of honour,
whereas in advanced urban societies it is just an economic trespass.
A shift in values requires a change in punishment. But very soon
'the Muslim lawyers and dogmaticians began to confuse the issue'
and the strictly legal injunctions of Qur'an were thought to apply
to any society; yet the real status of the Qur'an is 'the religious
source of law'.[54] Its instructions are to be applied in the twentieth
century in a different way from the way they were applied in the
seventh century.[55]

Both An-Na'im and Rahman claim that they hold fast to the full
divinity of the Qur'an. Yet one wonders whether their position
does not imply a more critical attitude. Rahman actually concedes
that his 'sociological approach' raises a serious theological
question, answering that 'the eternity of the Word of God can be
substantially (!) admitted'. The letter of the Qur'anic law results
from a 'transaction' between the eternal Word and the social situation of seventh-century Arabia.[56] One may doubt whether this
explanation serves to eliminate the problem![57]

A comparable figure is Mohammed Arkoun, an Algerian teaching at the Sorbonne, who has outlined an ambitious new programme for Qur'anic study. He strategically steers a middle course
between orthodox Islam and Western 'historicism',[58] calling for a
linguistic-semiotic analysis of the religious language of the Qur'an
along synchronic-structuralist lines; in such a programme the
hottest issues can be by-passed. Arkoun's 'daring writings'[59] are
mainly methodological in character; concrete critical points are
made almost in passing, but they are there, ready to be seized on in
a time when what is now socially 'unthinkable' within Islam may
no longer be so.[60]

Thus, Arkoun accepts crucial findings of Western orientalists.

The question of a critical history of the Qur'anic text, introduced by Nöldeke, was an 'inevitable' one, though one made tabu by Muslim orthodoxy (1982, xxii). Islamic thought 'can no longer ignore the extreme fecundity of the historical study' practised by such Western scholars as R. Blachère, J. Wansbrough and J. Burton (xxiv)! The possibility of textual corrections in the Qur'an is conceded (44.70). Arkoun also admits the existence of legends (1)[61] in the Qur'an, the language of which is mythical and symbolical (12, 64 and passim). He represents a clearly 'pluralist' stance within Islam.[62] According to Issa J. Boullata, 'a growing number of younger Arab scholars are beginning to be inspired by his writings'.[63]

The Qur'an as testimony

The Indian lawyer and diplomat Asaf A. A. Fyzee[64] went even further in the direction of an openly historical understanding of the Qur'an. In 1963, he in effect distinguished between God's word and Muhammad's testimony:

> I believe that the Koran is a message from God. It is the voice of God heard by Muhammad. Muhammad gave it to us in the words of Muhammad, in the speech of Muhammad, the Arabic language . . . God spoke to him, and he spoke to us. The Koran is a testimony of his faith in God. Muhammad was a man like us, but the word was the Word of God (109f.).

This revolutionary view comes close to the standard Christian view of the Bible. Fyzee also writes:

> We cannot go 'back' to the Koran, we have to go 'forward' with it. I wish to *understand* the Koran as it was understood by the Arabs of the time of the Prophet only (!) to *reinterpret* it and apply it to my conditions of life and to believe in it, so far as it appeals to me as a twentieth-century man . . . I must distinguish between poetic truth and factual truth . . . I must distinguish between the husk and the kernel of religion, between law and legend (94).[65]

This bold statement parallels the stance of many Christian theologians, although Fyzee has a better sense of history than many in that he frankly speaks of a *re*-interpretation. In practice the concrete legislation is not to be regarded as binding. 'Universal moral rules' (truthfulness, marital purity, honesty . . .) are to be distinguished from 'the particular moral rules', such as the prohibition of ham and wine (99). 'The former are enjoined by all religions; the latter are not. A difference of emphasis is clearly indicated in such cases.' The famous verse 'Men are in charge of women, because God has made one of them to excel the other' (4.34) should be 'reinterpreted as purely local and applicable only for the time being' (103f.).

Fyzee also notes that the Qur'an 'is to be interpreted in its historical setting and on chronological principles'. This includes the fact that 'the better we get acquainted with the contribution of Judaism and Christianity, the fuller insight we gain into the message and doctrines of the Prophet'.[66] Fyzee speaks in an appreciative way of the contribution of Western orientalists.[67] Modernist 'scientific' interpretation is rejected by him out of hand.

Fyzee speaks of his vision as 'Liberal Islam' (104); we might also call it 'Pluralist Islam'. An English article in which Fyzee originally set forth his ideas 'was repeatedly reprinted and translated into Arabic and Urdu'.[68] These thoughts have, then, elicited response from fellow Muslims.[69]

There are, then, some signs of 'liberal' trends within Islam. Their significance is perhaps not to be overestimated; on the other hand, it is difficult for an outsider to estimate what is really happening below the surface. Most Arab thinkers agree that there is an 'intellectual crisis' in the Islamic world; change is wanted, but a struggle is going on 'about the direction of this change'.[70] A critical issue is the position of the *ulama*, the established custodians of the legal tradition who have so far shown little or no interest in fresh approaches to the Qur'an.[71]

The challenge of new experiences

There are features in the classical Muslim tradition which would support the liberal trends: the discussions concerning the 'occasions of the sending down'[72] of the individual passages as well as the issue of abrogation. But in the main, new trends have been generated by the same kind of impulses which led biblical scholar-ship to new paths: on the one hand the challenge of 'modern' thought which includes rational and moral criticism of tradition, and on the other hand the accumulation of inductive observations on one's Scripture.

For Christians, the challenge of modernity consisted in the voyages of discovery[73] and the development of science and philosophy. It also included, in the aftermath of the Reformation, the shocking experience that radically different interpretations, with different practical results, were given to the same Scripture. For Islam, the main challenge consists in the encounter with Western culture and technology, the former including, along with bitter experiences of crude colonial power, the experience of democracy and human rights as understood in the West. It also includes the development of Christianity. Rahbar's attitude to the Qur'an is affected by his acquaintance with Christian study of the Bible.[74] Fyzee refers to the example both of 'Progressive Jewry' and of Luther, who 'broke down the barriers of dogma in Christianity and asserted the right of individual interpretation'.[75] Arkoun refers to questions raised about revelation and history by Jewish and Christian thinkers, deploring the absence of 'Islamic testimony' in the debate.[76] This immediately leads into the critical issue of 'influences' upon the Qur'an as well.

The process of interpreting one's tradition in the light of one's new situation is, of course, age-old. An-Na'im's vision for one could be assessed as an impressive example of the dialectic of tradition, experience and interpretation.[77] The experience of modern constitutional states has forced the Sudanese scholar to reinterpret his tradition in an innovative way. He legitimizes his interpretation by stressing that it, and even it alone, agrees with the original intentions of Islam.

There is an analogy between the situation and intentions of An-Na'im and, say, those of Paul. Paul, too, reinterpreted his Jewish tradition radically in the light of his Christ experience and in the light of his social experience of mixing with Gentiles. Because of these new experiences the sacred tradition had to be reinterpreted; one had to give up strict observance of the rules concerning circumcision and food. Paul, too, tried to justify his theology by underlining that it was he who was really affirming the true intentions of the tradition, and not his conservative critics. 'Do we overthrow the law by faith? By no means! On the contrary, we uphold the law' (Rom. 3.31).[78]

More conservative Jewish Christians were not convinced by Paul's argument. Nor is it difficult to anticipate that fellow Muslims will decline An-Naim's programme. No doubt they will be able to point out that he accepts the modern ideal of human rights as an aprioristic starting point, simply putting the 'realities of modern life' above the *shariah*.[79] Social experience is as vital to his vision as it was to Paul's.

Barriers in the way of historical criticism

For biblical scholarship, inductive study of inner-biblical parallels has been an important impulse. For a newcomer in the guild a comparison, say, of parallel passages in the Gospels was often of greatest pedagogical significance. An attentive reader of the Bible cannot but see problems arise when comparing different passages. And naturally the differences between the Old and the New Testament force even the most conservative expositor to apply some kind of historical differentiation.

For Muslims, intrinsic inconsistencies in the Qur'an have been more difficult to detect,[80] as the Qur'an consists of the proclamation of one prophet from a period of a couple of decades. The possibility of critical comparison of Qur'anic texts exists, as the distinction between Meccan and Medinan revelation shows, but only to a limited degree.[81] Still, the issue of abrogation is of great potential importance,[82] comparable to the discovery by biblical scholars of the problem of 'unity and diversity' in the New Testament. Biblical scholars have been encouraged by the discovery of the original diversity to speak for greater openness toward pluralism in the present as well; something similar might ensue from wrestling with the issue of 'abrogation' within the Qur'an. If God constantly – in hundreds of cases[83] – cancels what he has just revealed (or even what he is just revealing[84]), this seems a bit odd. It could be compared to the problem that God seems to go back on his eternal covenant in the Bible – a feature which has caused problems for biblical interpreters, as we have seen. One may wonder what benefit there is in having the eternal revelation, if the fallible attempts of humans are needed anyway to make sense of it (to tell whether verse A is cancelled by verse B or vice versa).[85]

An important step on the road towards historical criticism of the Bible based on inductive observations was the development of textual criticism. It started with the collection of existing variants by a few bold individuals; it took several centuries, however, to produce a critical edition which was able to overthrow the *textus receptus* that had been produced by Erasmus in a rather haphazard way. The attempts of textual critics to collect and assess the evidence were much resisted, as it was feared that they would endanger the faith.

One might have thought that similar processes would have begun within Islam. The issue of the 'collection' of the Qur'an ought to cause some problems for the orthodox view! If the revelation mediated through Muhammad – and that alone – is God's eternal revelation, word by word, then how can the establishment of the inerrant text be dependent on the human enterprise of Caliph Uthman and the 'commission' under him? After all, this work included the annihilation of all previously existing copies of the Qur'an some twenty years after the death of the Prophet.[86] This raises the question, 'Who was, in the final analysis, inspired by God – Muhammad, Uthman or both?'[87] Or was it the men who worked for Uthman, especially one Zayd ibn-Thabit?[88]

So far, Islamic theology has managed to evade the problem.[89] No one has tried to produce a critical edition of the Qur'an which would take account of the variants in a textual apparatus.[90] Yet all pre-Uthmanic readings were not forgotten. Classical commentaries do refer to them from time to time; the amount of known variants[91] runs to thousands.[92] One early codex[93] omitted the last two surahs altogether (113, 114) and possibly even the later all-important 'Fatiha' (Surah 1).[94]

Even Western scholars generally[95] rely very much on Uthman's work,[96] the high quality of which is recognized. But the question remains: how could this brave human effort have preserved such divine inerrancy as the orthodox view ascribes to the Qur'an?

Indeed, it is this orthodox view which is the most difficult barrier to the rise of historical criticism of the Qur'an. It is a pertinent observation that the position of the Qur'an in Islam is *not* identical with the position of the Bible in mainstream Christianity. The position of the Qur'an corresponds better to that of Jesus Christ in Christianity.[97] A closer counterpart to the Bible in Islam is the traditions about Muhammad (*hadith*).[98]

Thus it can be maintained that historical criticism of the Qur'an involves much more for a Muslim, in emotional terms, than historical criticism of the Bible does for a Christian. As an emotional analogy on the Christian side one might, with Cantwell Smith, think of a psychoanalysis of Jesus – or perhaps a thorough demythologization of christology. Yet the difference should not be exaggerated, for the Bible did not always have a secondary position in Christianity. Just think of its place in the 'biblical culture' of post-Reformation Protestantism with all the social and political consequences that followed![99] The gradual breaking down of this seventeenth-century view was a painful process which is not yet over. After all, fundamentalism, or near-fundamentalist 'evangelicalism', is a mighty force in the Protestant world, especially in the USA.[100] As for the analogies suggested by Smith, neither a psychoanalysis of Jesus nor a thorough demythologization of christology are unheard-of enterprises among Christians.[101] We saw in Chapter 6 that if a historical approach to the Bible is pursued consistently, the doctrine of Christ will be affected as well.

In the final analysis, the connection of national feelings with religion is bound to make the break-through of a historical approach to the Qur'an within Islam difficult, especially in the current situation.

But the Islamologist Frederick Denny for one looks forward to changes in Qur'anic exegesis in the 'New World', where increasing numbers of Muslims are pursuing advanced studies in the atmosphere of the freedom of expression.[102]

The anticipated changes

will be implemented, in part at least, by means of new kinds of
theological and cultural thought by Muslims and by interested
non-Muslims, such as dialogue partners and even estranged
former Muslims who nevertheless respect their heritage and
delve into its more absorbing intellectual dimensions for their
own purposes.[103]

If we still have to wait for this prediction to come true, it is good
to remember that it took Christians some seventeen centuries to
start historical-critical study of the Bible. To keep this pace, Islam
has plenty of time.

9

The Bible and the Traditions of the Nations: Isaac La Peyrère as a Precursor of Biblical Criticism

Few people today have heard of Isaac (de) La Peyrère (1596–1676). In the seventeeth century he was a celebrity. He tried to harmonize the early chapters of the Bible with recent historical and anthropological knowledge through his theory of 'pre-Adamites': there had been human beings even before Adam was created;[1] what Genesis tells us is the pritimive history of the Jews, not of humankind as a whole. The book appeared in 1655; it was burnt publicly in Paris the next year. More than one hundred works were written to refute La Peyrère's theory, the last ones in the early nineteenth century.[2]

John Bowden comments that, along with Galileo, La Peyrère is still worth dwelling on as a representative figure of his time,[3] 'because what happened in the seventeenth century is still comparatively unknown to Christians', even though it is 'far more important in the long run than the Reformation, over which so much ink has been spilt'. La Peyrère made 'a final, last-ditch attempt . . . to reconcile the new discoveries (in astronomy, geography and history) with what was said in the Bible'.[4]

> His whole argument is a mere curiosity to us now; but the discovery of what de la Peyrère thought to be a solution enabled him to look the real problems straight in the face, and to take many of the historical statements of ancient authorities more seriously than had been done before.[5]

The relation of the biblical accounts to extra-biblical traditions had become problematic because of the recent voyages of discovery and the wealth of new information about the geography of the world they had brought. Until the seventeenth century the view of the world had remained essentially that of the Bible, Jerusalem lying in the centre of the earth, which was divided in three continents (Asia, Africa and Europe), inhabited by the three sons of Noah. But it now turned out that the newly discovered areas had inhabitants of which the Bible was quite ignorant. These seemed to have no connection with the history recounted in the Bible and no religion which could be related to its God.[6]

Experience – in this case, the experience of becoming familiar with new peoples and their traditions! – affected and affects the interpretation of tradition (including the Bible), at times deeply and disturbingly. To some extent the problem which faced La Peyrère is similar to the problem which faces modern Christians as they have become aware of foreign religions and cultures in quite new ways in recent times.

Another experience which was at least as important to La Peyrère as the one just mentioned was his consciousness of the problems involved in the co-existence of Christians and Jews; in fact his theory of the origins of mankind belongs to a larger vision of salvation history in which God's dealings with the Jews are absolutely central. In writing about Jews La Peyrère demonstrated an ecumenical mind of a quality which is quite surprising in a person of his time.

La Peyrère was not an exegete. He did not know the work of biblical scholars, except of those whom he had met personally.[7] He knew no Hebrew nor, it seems, much Greek.[8] He was a maverick thinker, an alert lay reader who made acute observations and developed original theories to explain them. Part of the fascination in studying him is due to the fact that (like the classics of the field in general) he writes in a situation which is in many ways similar to that of those modern readers who approach the Bible 'on their own', being innocent of the work of critics – as so many people still are. 'Where did Cain get a wife from?' is a question that still intrigues Bible readers.

La Peyrère's life and thought[9]

Isaac La Peyrère was born in Bordeaux, the son of a well-to-do Calvinist family, probably in 1596.[10] Scholars debate his possible

Jewish background. Some think that he was a *marrano* (the descendant of Jews forced to convert to Christianity),[11] which might account for his exceptionally positive attitude to Judaism.

From 1640 on he worked in Paris in the service of the Prince of Condé. He travelled widely and became acquainted with leading intellectuals, e.g. Hugo Grotius, probably also Thomas Hobbes.

La Peyrère's great work was in essence ready in the early 1640s. Several people came to know the manuscript, among them Grotius. He considered the theory of pre-Adamites a serious threat to religion[12] and tried to refute it in a book which appeared in 1643. La Peyrère then removed the section about the origins of mankind from his manuscript; his own book of 1643, *Du Rappel des Juifs*, concentrated on imminent end-time events.[13] This work deserves to be considered in its own right (below, 150–2). The book on pre-Adamites was postponed for twelve years. In the meantime, La Peyrère collected more material to support his pre-Adamite theory. Diplomatic tasks brought him to Scandinavia, where he became acquainted with young Christina, Queen of Sweden. When La Peyrère later met Christina, who had now abdicated her throne, in Belgium, she encouraged him to publish his manuscript. She probably even funded the project.[14]

Preadamitae, written in Latin, appeared anonymously in Holland in 1655.

> Strictly speaking there were two separate writings. *Praeadamitae* or *Exercitatio* is a 50-page exegetical treatise on Romans 5.12–14. *Systema theologicum* on the other hand comprises almost 300 pages.[15] When later authors speak of *Praeadamitae*, they often mean both writings collectively.[16] Since the pagination numbers differ in different Latin editions, I refer to these writings by book and chapter only.

The work(s) appeared right away in several editions. They were widely distributed, until the book was banned. Nevertheless it soon appeared also in English and Dutch translations. Condemnations and refutations too appeared at a rapid pace.[17]

Although the book came out anonymously, it was not difficult to trace the author; too many people were familiar with La Peyrère's ideas. La Peyrère was caught in prison, and only the intervention of the Prince of Condé saved him from the stake. The condition was that La Peyrère had to apologize to the Pope and convert to Catholicism.

La Peyrère formulated his recantation carefully, even ironically. Calvinist upbringing, he said, had misled him to interpret the Bible in the light of reason and conscience; thus he had come to harbour the theory of pre-Adamites. His opponents presented neither biblical nor rational arguments against the theory, but they maintained that it militated against the views of all rabbis, church fathers and theologians. Since the Pope said that they were right, he, La Peyrère had no choice but to recant. He never admitted that anybody had managed to put forward any real evidence against his theory.[18]

Although hardly anybody can have taken his recantation seriously, the Pope accepted the apology and La Peyrère was allowed to live in peace. Soon enough he withdrew to a remote abbey. On his deathbed he is said to have refused to recant his heretical thoughts.

The theory of pre-Adamites[19]

La Peyrère opens his work with a discussion of Romans 5.12–14. In this passage Paul states that sin and death came into the world through one man, Adam (v.12). 'Sin was in the world before the law, but sin is not reckoned (or 'imputed', *peccatum non imputabatur*) when there is no law' (v.13).

According to the usual and no doubt correct explanation Paul has in mind the law given to Moses. The 'imputation' of sin to the sinner began from the time of Moses. However, La Peyrère maintains emphatically that the text must refer to an earlier law, one given to Adam. The reckoning of sin started with Adam's transgression (*Exerc.*, ch. 1), yet sin – and thus humans – existed in the world already before him (ch. 8). Until Adam sin was something natural (*peccatum naturale*), the normal defect of human nature – men, though created to be good, were made from poor material which was prone to be damaged. But from Adam on sin is transgression of the law, *peccatum legale* (*Syst.*I, ch. 2), which is imputed to humans because of Adam.

Similarly death is a natural thing, independent of Adam; it existed before Adam (*Exerc.*, ch. 10). Because of Adam, however, even 'spiritual death' invaded the world.[20] In a corresponding manner other punishments incumbent on the Fall simply added a new dimension to the existing situation (instead of creating a quite new condition). Work was cumbersome and giving birth painful by nature, before Adam; because of Adam's deed God added spiritual and mystical birth pangs to the woman. The serpent too had crawled on its belly before the Fall, due to its nature – after all, God had created the reptiles on the fifth day. After the Fall, however, the serpent had to crawl because of a divine command.

Those humans whose sins, according to Paul, were 'not like the transgression of Adam' (Rom. 5.14) were pre-Adamites (*Exerc.*, ch. 17). Adam's sin was in retrospect reckoned to them as well; for all men must become guilty, so that all can participate in the salvation in Christ (ch. 19).

No doubt La Peyrère's overall interpretation is a *tour de force* which does not correspond to the intentions of the apostle. Nevertheless it is based on shrewd observations on the Pauline text. What La Peyrère aims at is not so much a new interpretation of Romans as a reading of the book of Genesis which frees it from self-contradictions and reconciles it with extra-biblical information.[21] He tells how already as a child he had doubted certain statements in Genesis: where 'out to the field' did Cain take his brother, whom did he fear, where did he get a wife from, how did he build a city . . . ? But La Peyrère would not have dared to set forth his doubts, had he not later found confirmation of the idea of pre-Adamites in Romans (*Syst.*, *Prooemium*).

La Peyrère lists a number of observations about the story of Cain and Abel which are inexplicable, unless there were already other people in the world than the brothers and their parents. In addition, he presents 'a truly amazing compilation of the ancient pagan material'.[22] In the light of their own sources not only the history of the Chaldaeans and the Egyptians but also that of newly discovered people like the Mexicans is very long; this does not match the biblical chronology that starts with Adam and can be calculated on the basis of Genesis (*Syst*. III, chs. 5–6). Also the development of pagan astronomy, astrology, theology and magic must have taken much longer than a few thousand years.

The story of the deluge brings the chronological problem to a head. According to Eusebius, the sixteenth dynasty reigned in Egypt when Abraham was born – only three hundred years after the flood according to the biblical chronology. If the biblical flood destroyed the whole earth, all subsequent nations would have to descend from the sons of Noah, including the rulers of the first dynasty in Egypt. But then the dynasties would have changed in Egypt at an enormous speed (*Syst*. IV, ch. 9)! The opponents of La Peyrère did not delve into the problems of the non-biblical chronologies (apart from asserting that such chronologies as deviated from the Bible had to be rejected).[23]

La Peyrère concludes that Genesis does not tell everything. It does not describe the primal history of all humankind, but only the history of the Jews. Thus even the deluge in Noah's time only covered the Holy Land – Jews and those Gentiles who had mixed with them (*Syst*. IV, ch. 7)[24] – but not the whole world. The fresh leaf of the olive tree which the dove brought to the ark shows indeed that there were areas which had remained outside the flood; for in the deluge area any leaves ought to have decayed (ch. 8). To this it must be added that pagan sources only know of local floods, not of universal ones.

La Peyrère finally refutes claims that those peoples which have become recently known, especially the Indians and the Eskimos, descend from the sons of Noah.[25]

La Peyrère argues humorously and at length that the events depicted in Genesis from the formation of Adam to the making of Eve (Gen. 2) could not possibly take place in one single day, i.e. during the sixth day of Genesis 1 (*Syst*. III, ch. 2). It would not have been possible to gather all the animals of the world together in one single day for the name-giving event; after all, the elephants had to arrive from India and Africa, and many other animals from America. Neither would Adam have been able to muster the whole lot in one day and give names to all. For undoubtedly Adam also had to make a dictionary of the names, otherwise the results of his work would have been forgotten . . . (III, ch. 3).

La Peyrère concludes that the creation stories of the first two chapters of Genesis do not speak of the same thing. Chapter 1 tells of the creation of Gentiles, chapter 2 of the formation of Adam, the Jew. Thus there were pagans in existence long before Adam.

La Peyrère finally constructs a doctrine of sin and redemption which does not require Adam to be the first man.[26] He thus wants to refute the claim of Grotius that his theory is a danger for religion. La Peyrère maintains on the contrary that precisely his theory, and it alone, is able to overcome the obstacles that stand in the way of the dissemination of Christianity in his day. His theory reconciles 'Genesis and the gospel' with the astronomy, history and philosophy of pagan nations. Let therefore Chaldaean astronomers or Egyptian chronologers come, let Aristotle himself or the Chinese chronologers and philosophers or any peoples from South or North, known or still unknown, come: on the basis of La Peyrère's view they will all be able to 'accept the history of Genesis and be more willing to become Christians' (*Exerc.*, ch. 26).

The nature of the Pentateuch

La Peyrère demonstrates that if one assumes that Adam and Eve were the first human beings, and Cain and Abel their only children at the time of the fratricide, then the account as told in Genesis is incoherent. He puts forward a number of 'Socinian'[27] questions. How would Cain have been able to cultivate the land alone? Who made the tools, who baked bread from the corn? Why did Abel guard his sheep, if there were no thieves? Cain said 'let us go out' and killed Abel in the field (*in agro*): consequently the brothers were first inside the walls of a city (*Syst.* III, ch. 4). Who had built it?

Whom did Cain fear after the fratricide? God would have set the 'mark of Cain' upon him in vain, if there were no other people in the world. Where did Cain get a wife from, if not from the daughters of the pagans? Where did he later get builders for the city he founded? For whom did he build it? Who lived in the city, if there were none but descendants of Adam in the world?

The contemporary critic Maresius[28] tried to refute the critical questions of La Peyrère with a conventional answer which draws on Jewish traditions and had been put forward already by Augustine:[29] during the first 130 years many other children were born to Adam and Eve than those mentioned in the Bible. Abel and Cain married their sisters. In the year 30 'after the foundation of the world' there were already perhaps ten families in existence; one hundred years later there were 'myriads of people'.[30] Maresius thus shares with La Peyrère the view that Genesis is incomplete; it does not tell everything.[31]

However, La Peyrère is not content with proving that Genesis indirectly assumes the existence of other people. He claims in addition that Genesis in its present form is not trustworthy at all. He distinguishes sharply between the original 'autographs' and later versions, the 'apographs'.

Many books of the Bible cannot be 'original', since they refer to sources; e.g. Josh. 10.13 refers to the 'Book of Jashar'.[32] Similarly, the Pentateuch does not go directly back to Moses either; its books have been copied and compiled by others. Moses already wrote very briefly about the origin of the universe. The later versions are abbreviations of his story; that is why the account of the creation is so brief in the first chapter of Genesis (IV, ch. 2).

The problem is that such a theory of truncation contradicts the effort at harmonization which La Peyrère has just undertaken.[33] He has just taken pains to reconcile the data of Genesis both with each other and with other information, and praised his own pre-Adamite theory as the only way to resolve the apparent tensions, the underlying idea being that Genesis is reliable but incomplete. The notion that the books of Moses are *not* reliable is a rival explanation which undermines the said effort at reconciliation.[34] One wonders whether the more radical idea of the secondary nature of the present text occurred to La Peyrère at a late point so that he was not able to combine it smoothly with his own overall picture.

Largely due to this (generally overlooked) tension, scholars are in disagreement as to what La Peyrère 'really' believed. Some underline his positive attempt at harmonization,[35] others his sceptical criticism.[36] His eloquent exaltation of Judaism speaks in favour of a sincere religious conviction.[37]

La Peyrère proceeds to put forward arguments against the

notion that the Pentateuch as a whole goes back to Moses. They include the following (*Syst*. IV, ch. 1):

– The Pentateuch speaks of the death of Moses.

– According to Deut. 1.1 Moses spoke in the desert 'beyond the Jordan' (*trans Iordanem*). Moses himself would have written 'on this side of Jordan' (*cis Iordanem*), as he was himself never allowed to cross the river.

– The phrase 'to this day' (e.g. Deut. 3.14) refers to a time after Moses.

– The reference to 'The Book of the Wars of the Lord' (Num. 21.14 shows that the fourth book 'of Moses' is much later than Moses. First the Book of the Wars had to be written (La Peyrère assumes that it was based on notes taken by Moses). Then some time must have elapsed before the writing of Numbers, so that what we have now is only the copy of a copy (*apographum apographi*).

La Peyrère rises to polemics: the books of Moses cannot possibly be Mosaic 'archetypes', for they contain so much obscure, confused, misplaced and mutilated stuff. The twentieth chapter of Genesis, for example, is misplaced, for how could Abimelech have coveted Sarah, an old woman according to Genesis 18? (Maresius replied: perhaps Sara got back her former beauty when she gave birth to Isaac!)[38] In the 'muddle of the apographs' passages are found which are opposed to each other as bluntly as cold is opposed to hot or dry to wet. No wonder critics regarded this passage as particularly blasphemous.[39] The contradictions within Genesis can only be accounted for if its authors have used multifarious sources.

La Peyrère connects the difficulty in interpreting Scripture with a surprising view of revelation which bluntly contradicts the Protestant principle of 'perspicuity': God has not wanted to reveal much of himself, but has spoken in a perplexing and obscure manner. God lives in the dark (I Kings 8.12). No wonder, then, if it is his will that there are problems in the transmission of the scriptures. Only what is essential to man's salvation has been revealed clearly. Therefore God allowed the autographs to disappear, letting only the obscure and confused apographs be preserved to us. La Peyrère believes that the autographs were dictated by the Holy Spirit, but the apographs are only a weak reflection of them. It is a difficult task to discern the text of the autograph from an apograph (*Syst.* IV, chs. 1–2).

La Peyrère's 'positive' theory about the pre-Adamites is today of historical interest only. By contrast, his 'negative' observations on the immanent problems in the books of Moses are of lasting significance. It was his second, more radical explanation which pointed to the direction where a lasting solution can be found: the Pentateuch consists of various sources of different nature and age. Of their character La Peyrère could not yet have a realistic view. But when his observations were taken up by Spinoza and Richard Simon, the study of the Pentateuch began to make dramatic progress. La Peyrère was not the first to raise questions about the Mosaic origin of the Pentateuch, but he certainly developed the beginning doubts to unheard-of lengths. Popkin notes that Thomas Hobbes is generally given the credit of being the first to deny the Mosaic authorship of the Pentateuch, and yet 'Hobbes's contention is certainly more modest and less sweeping than La Peyrère's'.[40]

The miracles of the Bible

To corroborate the thesis that Adam was only the ancestor of the Jews, La Peyrère included a discussion of analogous phenomena in the Bible which are likewise to be understood 'more specifically' than they are usually explained (*Syst.* IV, ch. 3). The section widens to a statement on biblical miracles as a whole. In this matter, too, many of La Peyrère's fresh observations continue to be of interest even when his constructive theory is rejected.

Thus, the star seen by the Magi could not be an ordinary luminary (however conspicuous) in the sky. For in that case others too would have seen it, including Herod who, however, had to make inquiries about it. Therefore the 'star' was a luminous phenomenon seen by the magi only, similar to the pillar of fire once seen just by the Israelites. If it had been a star in the sky, how could it have stood upon one single house? And had it been visible to all, historians would remember it.

La Peyrère's interpretation does not explain the 'miracle' away.

A miraculous phenomenon in the service of providence remains, but it is a local, not a universal, matter.[41] It is incorrect to claim that La Peyrère denies miracles.[42]

King Hezekiah was given a miraculous sign (II Kings 20: the shadow on the dial 'went back ten steps'). La Peyrère states that the sun did not really move back. It was only the shadow that moved – a miracle too no doubt, but a more 'reasonable' one (*Syst.* IV, ch. 4.). For the whole of nature would have gone into disorder if the sun had really changed its direction of movement. Would it be thinkable that no other source has ever mentioned anything about this? Moreover, would it not be out of all proportion if Hezekiah (who was to recover) had been given a more marvellous sign that the one given to Christ when he was dying?

The situation presupposed in Joshua 10 is explained by La Peyrère: the sun 'stood still' only in the area of Gibeon, not else-where (*Syst.* IV, ch. 5). This time La Peyrère comes close to a 'natural' explanation: the sun did set, but its radiation remained in the sky. Even this is considered a miracle by La Peyrère, although he mentions having seen a similar phenomenon himself.[43]

La Peyrère refuses to believe in miracles which are *wholly* against reason. He does believe in the miracles of Joshua and the dial of Ahaz, provided that the miracles are 'kept in limits' (*Syst.* IV, ch. 5). Where all reason disappears, faith collapses too (*Syst.* III, ch. 1). La Peyrère regards it as a merit of his theory of pre-Adamites that it reconciles faith with reason (*Exerc.*, ch. 8).

It is fascinating to note that it is commonplace among many modern fundamentalists to 'mitigate' such biblical miracles as the flood, the dial of Ahaz and the sun in Gibeon in ways very similar to those suggested by the arch-heretic La Peyrère! If God had really stopped the movement of the sun, 'the disturbances on the earth and the solar system would have been enormous', and evidence of this enormous disturbance of the solar system would be available through astronomical investigations, yet there is no such evidence. Even though the omnipotent God would have been able to do such a thing, the record 'does not call for a miracle of such gigantic proportions',[44] writes a leading fundamentalist expositor 'with his engaging frankness'.[45] Another spokesman for biblical inerrancy actually repeats La Peyrère's explanation of

Joshua 10 in attributing the standing still of the sun to a mistranslation: 'Possibly cease *shining* rather than cease *moving* should be understood!'[46] And of course it even 'seems probable' to a prominent ultra-conservative commentator that 'the Biblical Deluge was a comparatively local affair'.[47]

La Peyrère and the Epistle to the Romans

While the merits of La Peyrère in the history of Old Testament study are generally acknowledged, scholars have not appreciated his exegesis of the New Testament; this has been considered abstruse[48] and arbitrary.[49] True, his contention that Paul presupposes the existence of pre-Adamites in Rom. 5.12–14 cannot correspond to Paul's intentions. Yet La Peyrère's interpretation of Romans is understandable and clever[50] on the assumption that the apostle is consistent in his reasoning and does not contradict the Old Testament.

La Peyrère correctly perceives that Romans 5 is governed by a juxtaposition of Adam and Christ which logically leaves no room for Moses. Paul's idea that sin was not 'reckoned' until the law of Moses is curious; it is quite understandable that La Peyrère tries to move such an oddity from the thought of the apostle. La Peyrère points out that if Paul had the law of Moses in mind here, he would contradict the whole book of Genesis (and no doubt this is what actually happens!). For what is the meaning of the 'non-reckoning' of sin, La Peyrère asks, if Adam and Eve were nevertheless expelled from Paradise and if death entered the world because of this very sin? How could death 'reign' in the world, if sin was not reckoned (*Exerc.*, ch. 5)? If it was not reckoned, why was the earth cursed? Why was Cain's punishment greater than he could bear? Why did God punish the Pharaoh with plagues because of Sarah? Why did he tell the Sodomites that their sin was grave? 'What was this aggravation of sin, if not an imputation of sin?' Why were sacrifices ordered to expiate for sins? And why the flood?

This problem was already seen by many of the church fathers, but they were unable to solve it. Oecumenius and Photius for instance maintained that sin was 'reckoned' even before the time of

Moses (it was a transgression of the 'law of nature'), but it was not reckoned quite as severely as afterwards.[51] Ursinus, an early opponent of La Peyrère, appeals to Origen: due to God's righteousness, sin could never be left unpunished; what could not be 'reckoned' until Moses' time was sin as 'transgression'. On such a reading the only accomplishment of the Mosaic law seems to be that the sin to be punished is, as it were, registered in a different column, or under a different heading ('transgression' rather than 'sin') in the heavenly book of accounts. In the subject-matter itself nothing changes.[52]

Even those modern exegetes who assume that Paul is fully consistent in his reasoning are bound to propose artificial explanations in the vein of the fathers for the 'reckoning' of sin from Moses on (but not before); these explanations do not meet La Peyrère's challenge.[53] Consider the attempt of Stephen Westerholm, one of the more perceptive interpreters of the tangle of Paul's conception of the law, to show that Rom. 5.13 makes sense after all:

> That sin is 'not counted' in the absence of the law does not mean that it goes unpunished – the immediate context affirms the opposite – but simply that God cannot judge 'according to the book'. Ample power to punish sin is at his disposal – forty days of uninterrupted rain are more than adequate for the task – but God's grievance against humanity is not one which a court of law would recognize: no statute has been transgressed. For the due registration of wrongs committed, and the consequent demonstration of human culpability and divine justice in punishing, the institution of the law proves necessary.[54]

Westerholm goes on to ask the obvious question: 'Does its coming make a difference?' Answer:

> Not, perhaps, one which the objects of divine wrath have the inclination or the leisure to appreciate; but it cannot be said that a display of human guilt and a vindication of God's justice are matters of 'no consequence' to Paul . . .[55]

While trying to do the opposite, Westerholm's answer confirms my point: on this reading, the coming of the law makes no real difference whatsoever.

Rudolf Bultmann saw correctly that 'verse 13 is completely unintelligible' (at least if we try to understand it as part of a Pauline system of thought). 'What sort of sin was it if it did not originate as contradiction of the Law? And how can it have brought death after it if it was not 'counted'? These questions cannot be answered.'[56]

It must be recognized that La Peyrère made astute observations on this passage, even if the theory of pre-Adamites is a forced solution to the problems he noticed. In the seventeenth century it would have been impossible to solve the problems simply by referring to Paul's inconsistency,[57] a solution that causes offence even today.

A pioneer of inter-religious dialogue

La Peyrère's view of the common future of Jews and Christians seems amazingly modern. 'Given the intolerance that prevailed in the early seventeenth century, it is wonderful to see a theologian, albeit an odd one, advancing such a completely universalistic theory.'[58] His key text is Romans 11, the chapter which plays a central role in modern dialogue too, as we have seen (Chapters 1 and 2 above).

The systematic-theological part of *Preadamitae* opens with a long praise of the Jews and continues with an even longer treatment of the election of Jews and Gentiles. This indicates what the final aim of the whole work is. Actually the book is dedicated to all synagogues of the world. At bottom, La Peyrère's theory about pre-Adamites is indeed a theory about the relationship of Gentiles and Jews, and it serves his messianic vision, presented in detail in his 1643 book called *Du Rappel des Juifs*.[59]

God elected the Jews to be his people when he formed their ancestor Adam from the dust of the earth. To the Jews also belongs the Holy Land (from the Nile to the Euphrates).[60] Later on God rejected the Jews for a time and elected the Gentiles (Romans 11) 'to belong to Jews through a mystical election'; Gentiles were adopted as Jews, as it were (one is reminded here of Krister Stendahl's phrase that a Gentile Christian might be called 'an honorary Jew'[61]).

Nevertheless, the Jews still have a specific place in salvation history. They have the right to wait for the Messiah promised to them. In this La Peyrère comes close to Marcion's ideas, although his overall vision of Jewish-Christian relations is very different from that of Marcion.[62]

La Peyrère thought that God will soon recall the Jews he had rejected for the time being. The Jews will accept the call – in France. The king of France will lead them to Palestine, which will be rebuilt.[63] Jerusalem will become the centre of the world. Jews and Christians will unite; the Christian denominations will forget their quarrels. In the end of the day, all humans will be saved and the whole creation renewed.

More interesting than the role of the French king in this grandiose eschatological vision is the idea that Jesus will return to the world as a political Messiah who will liberate the Jews. Obviously La Peyrère tried to combine the Christian doctrine of the second coming with the Jewish conviction that Jesus of Nazareth could not be the Messiah (since he had not freed the Jews from their affliction which, of course, was an essential part of the role designed for the Messiah). In a way he thus admits that Jesus can really be acknowledged as the Messiah only after he has acted in a properly messianic way. In fact he expressly suggests that there are two kinds of Messianism (apparently both legitimate): Jewish Messianism as set forth in the book of Isaiah, and Christian Messianism as proclaimed by Paul. While he was on earth in the past, Jesus acted according the role preserved for him in the Christian version; in his second coming he will fulfil the work by acting out the role of the Messiah in the Jewish scenario. Thus La Peyrère actually presents a kind of two-covenant soteriology (presented in linear-chronological terms). It actually does more justice to Judaism than the ruminations of those modern followers of Paul who expect Jews to adopt the Christian view of Jesus as the Messiah at the parousia.[64]

La Peyrère also suggested that one should preach to Jews in the manner of the primitive church – on the basis of the Acts of the

Apostles rather than according to later creeds. This would amount
to a great simplification of Christian dogmatics.

The anti-Judaism of Christendom forms a dire chapter in the
effective history of the Bible. La Peyrère's vision, which is quite
different, say, from that of (the old) Luther, is a rare spark of
light in the darkness. In his own time his vision was rejected. It is
only in the Jewish-Christian dialogue of recent years that voices
reminiscent of his have been heard.

La Peyrère's significance

La Peyrère's book on pre-Adamites is not just an elaboration of a
curious idea.[65] As Don Cameron Allen puts it, 'In announcing his
thesis and arguing it so well, Isaac de la Peyrère gave Christian
Europe a tremendous jolt.'[66] To be sure, at times the reader might
have hoped for a more compact manner of presentation. But the
work contains, at least in an embryonic form, a number of new
critical questions[67] which before long came to revolutionize
people's attitude to the Bible. New empirical knowledge could no
longer be integrated into the historical and chronological framework of the Bible without further ado. 'Whether La Peyrère
realized it or not, when he developed his critique of Scripture in
order to buttress his case for the pre-Adamite theory, he also began
a chain of analyses that would end up transforming the evaluation
of Scripture from a holy to a profane work.'[68]

La Peyrère exerted a direct influence on the thought of Baruch
Spinoza and of his friend Richard Simon.[69] He has gained an
acknowledged position in the history of Old Testament study,[70]
but his influence reached much wider, to deists and to Enlightenment thinkers from Tindal to Voltaire.[71]

Contemporary critics perceived La Peyrère's enterprise as a
frontal attack on the Bible. All Christian denominations alike
were unable to discern the genuine questions behind La Peyrère's
theories.[72] His was, however, a valiant effort to meet the challenges
posed by new experiences.

10

A Bible-Believer Improves the Bible:
Joseph Smith's Contribution to Exegesis

Mormonism is an intriguing chapter in the effective history of the
Bible. The movement started with Joseph Smith's publication in
1830 of the Book of Mormon, a work reminiscent of the Bible in
form and content. Smith, an illiterate but gifted son of a poor and
pious family in Palmyra, New York, told that he had been directed
by an angel to a hill where he had found golden plates (never seen
by anyone else) written in 'reformed Egyptian'. With them there
was a miraculous stone 'Urim and Thummim', with the help of
which Smith was able to translate the texts. They told the history
of the earlier inhabitants of the American continent; they also told
how Jesus had visited America after his resurrection and founded
his church there.

Without the Bible, the Book of Mormon would have been
incomprehensible. It was printed in biblical fashion as a collection
of books, originally divided into chapters and later into verses.[1]

> For its earliest adherents, the Book of Mormon was important,
> almost independent of its specific contents, because it existed; it
> was proof that God had spoken again, just as in biblical times.
> The sine qua non of the Mormon message . . . in 1830 was its
> distinctive biblical nature: not the Bible as a final authority but,
> rather, the restoration of the authority, teachings, and prophetic
> methods reflected in the Bible. Convert after convert reported
> embracing Mormonism because it satisfied their yearnings for a
> truly biblical Christianity.[2]

Indeed, Mormonism was born in a Bible-impregnated
atmosphere. The Bible 'played a role in shaping American culture
for which there was no European equivalent'.[3] 'Joseph Smith grew

up in a Bible-drenched society, and he showed it. Like those
around him, his religious conceptions and his everyday speech
were biblically informed.[4] He shared his era's assumptions about
the literality, historicity and inspiration of the Bible.' But 'he
differed from his evangelical contemporaries in that he found the
unaided Bible an inadequate religious compass'. Instead of turning
to scholarly or ecclesiastical authority to address this lack, he 'produced more scripture – scripture that at once challenged yet
reinforced biblical authority, and that echoed biblical themes,
interpreted biblical passages, shared biblical content, corrected
biblical errors, filled biblical gaps . . .' Joseph Smith 'was a Bible-
believing Christian with a difference'.[5]

Mormons thoroughly identified themselves with the biblical
Israel.[6] They were recapitulating, living through the stories of
Israel and early Christianity.[7] 'It likely never occurred to Joseph
Smith that he was anything but a Christian, just as Paul of Tarsus
may not have considered himself an apostate from the religion of
Israel.'[8]

One might have thought that such a man and such a church
would have caught the attention of biblical scholars and posed a
hermeneutical challenge to the theologians of other churches. For
its rise and development remind one in an astonishing way of the
birth of Christianity within Judaism and its gradual separation
from the latter.

Actually Smith's work has seldom been taken seriously in
Europe.[9] It has been easy to show that the Book of Mormon is a
nineteenth-century product; after that, people have been content
to glean a selection of 'oddities' from the Mormon doctrines to
bring the discussion to a close. Yet precisely a historical-critical
scrutiny of Smith's production reveals features which might raise
wider interest in the rise of the Mormon church, or at least provide
mainstream theology with new stimuli to reflect on its own nature.

Things are different in America.[10] There Mormonism is taken
seriously as a discussion partner, as will be readily seen in some
statements by top theologians at a conference held at Brigham
Young University, Salt Lake City in 1978. The papers of the
conference are collected in a volume called *Reflections on
Mormonism*. In it, W.D. Davies calls Mormonism 'the Jewish-

Christian tradition in an American key'.[11] John Dillenberger compares 'grace and works in Martin Luther and Joseph Smith', trying to diminish the gap perceived to exist between the two.[12] Ernest Benz considers Smith's later idea of man's deification and finds early Christian analogies in patristic thought, summarized in Athanasius' words 'God became man so that we might become God'.[13]

The Sermon on the Mount in the Book of Mormon

Exegetically, the most fascinating contribution to the volume is Krister Stendahl's article, which compares Matthew's Sermon on the Mount with the corresponding sermon in the Book of Mormon.[14] In the 'Third Book of Nephi', the risen Jesus instructs the American 'Nephites' roughly with the words of the Sermon on the Mount. Stendahl examines this speech redaction-critically. He compares it with the Sermon on the Mount in the King James Version, and points out the new emphases which Smith has put on the material.

Typically, the 3 Nephi sermon opens with 'extra' beatitudes not found in Matthew. In them, the significance of faith is stressed.[15] '. . . blessed are ye if ye shall believe in me and be baptized . . . more blessed are they who shall believe in your words . . .' (3 Nephi 12.1–2).[16] In Matthew's Sermon there is no talk about faith in Jesus and in his words.

Another typical enlargement is the addition to Matt. 5.6 (3 Nephi 12.6). The Gospel of Matthew in KJV reads here: 'Blessed are they which do hunger and thirst after righteousness: for they shall be filled.' 3 Nephi adds: they shall be filled 'with the Holy Ghost'.

Additions of this kind are formally similar to the changes made to the original biblical texts in the Targums, the Aramaic translations of the Hebrew Bible. They are also comparable to 'the pseudepigraphic recasting of biblical material'.

The targumic tendencies are those of clarifying and actualizing translations, usually by expansion and more specific application to the need and situation of the community. The pseudepigraphic . . . tend to fill out the gaps in our knowledge . . . the Book of Mormon stands within both of these traditions if considered as a phenomenon of religious texts.[17]

In terms of content, Smith's additions to the Sermon on the Mount could be labelled Christianizing or spiritualizing. To be more precise, the Nephi sermon with its tendency to centre upon faith in Jesus gives Matthew's sermon a more Johannine stamp.[18] Even elsewhere in 3 Nephi the image of Jesus 'is that of a revealer, stressing faith "in me" rather than what is right according to God's will'.[19]

A redaction-critical analysis of the Book of Mormon thus reveals, paradoxically perhaps, that 3 Nephi is at central points 'more Christian' than the Sermon in Matthew – if conventional Christian theology is taken as a criterion of what is 'Christian'. Both in standard Christian proclamation and in the 3 Nephi sermon the person of Jesus acquires a soteriological significance which it lacks in Matthew's sermon.

There is nothing peculiar in the fact that Joseph Smith views the Sermon on the Mount through 'Johannine' spectacles; on the contrary, he is quite conventional here. It has been typical of Christian thought at large to interpret the Synoptic Gospels from a Johannine (or Pauline) point of view. But whereas others have been content to explain the Sermon on the Mount from a viewpoint extraneous to the sermon itself, Smith includes the explanations within the Sermon.

Here Smith actually follows the example, not just of the Targums and the Pseudepigrapha, but of the biblical writers themselves. For of course the alteration of earlier texts for theological reasons is a common phenomenon even in the processes which led to the birth of biblical books. Stendahl refers in passing to the retelling of the accounts of the books of Samuel and Kings in Chronicles as 'a kind of parallel to what is going on in the Book of Mormon'.[20] Moving beyond narrative texts, one can point as a striking parallel to the freedom with which Paul, time and again, drastically interferes with the wording of the Bible when he quotes it.[21]

Smith's spiritualizing of Matt. 5.6 continues a trajectory which started within the New Testament. For undoubtedly Luke has preserved an older wording and thought (from Q) when he writes: 'Blessed are ye that hunger now: for ye shall be filled' (Luke 6.21 KJV). A word which speaks of actual hunger is given a religious-ethical content by Matthew when he speaks of hunger (and thirst) 'after righteousness' (a term which in Matthew's Gospel refers to man's doing of God's will). The Book of Mormon continues this development, moving further in a 'spiritual' direction. Stendahl comments that 'there is nothing wrong in that; it is our common Christian tradition and experience to widen and deepen the meaning of holy words'.[22]

Conventional theology blames Joseph Smith for falsifying Jesus' words to fit his own theology.[23] I find it hard to join this criticism, for biblical writers proceed in just the same way when using each other's works. The Book of Mormon can only be criticized fairly with content-critical arguments; this is what Stendahl gently does when he finally states that 'there is sometimes too much glitter in the Christmas tree'.[24]

On the background of the Book of Mormon

Thomas F. O'Dea noted in his classic analysis of Mormonism that the Book of Mormon is 'in a fundamental sense a work of the Christian imagination that may show a lack of discipline but nevertheless arranges its materials within the general framework of tradition'.[25] By contrast, Smith's later revelations (in the 1840s) go in a novel polytheistic direction. To the Mormon church, these later revelations, included in the work called *Doctrines and Covenants*, have become much more important than the Book of Mormon itself. Here I am less concerned with present-day Mormonism than with the treatment of the Bible in Smith's earlier ministry: in the Book of Mormon and in the 'translation' of the Bible accomplished by Smith soon after (see below). Had Mormonism stayed closer to the thought-world of these documents, it would today be closer to traditional Christianity than it now is.

In a study devoted to the question 'why Joseph Smith wrote the Book of Mormon', Robert N. Hullinger suggests that one reason was Smith's desire to protect Christian faith from the attacks of Deist critics, notably Tom Paine's *The Age of Reason*.[26] Smith stood up to defend the biblical message and the biblical God. Simultaneously, the conflicts between Christian denominations would be settled. Yet at many points young Joseph could not but admit the justification of Deist criticisms. The God of the Bible often repents of his earlier decisions and makes new ones; thus his nature is mutable. We are reminded of Marcion's problems. Again, many biblical passages contradict each other. The predictions of the prophets are ambiguous. The idea of a closed canon means that God has ceased to speak to people in the same immediate way he once did. Such a change in God's ways was intolerable to the Deists. If God really had revealed himself to people of old, he must use a similar method even today; otherwise there was no trusting the old stories either.

Joseph Smith adopted such critical thoughts, but they did not make him a Deist. Instead, he became the mediator of a new revelation. God was speaking again to humankind just as in the good old days! One of Deism's accusations against Christianity had thus been annulled.

The 'Inspired Version'

Still confronted with other Deist accusations, Smith began, like a new Marcion, to purify the Bible from features unworthy of the true God. However, he did not throw the Old Testament overboard. On the contrary, in a good Protestant fashion he regarded the whole Bible as the inerrant word of God – in principle. Since, however, there are undoubtedly mistakes and shortcomings in our Bible, Smith inferred – just as Muhammad, and even Isaac La Peyrère had done – that at some point the book must have been corrupted in the hands of its transmitters. In its original form the Bible must have been blameless.

Interestingly, this idea still surfaces in evangelical fundamentalism, when no other way to eliminate a problem exists: admittedly, the extant copies do contain an error, but then the original manuscript must have been different.[27] Smith made the necessary textual changes openly. What the Bible ought to look like, according to Joseph Smith, is shown by the Book of Mormon, which repeats more or less freely large parts of the Bible, as well as Smith's subsequent 'translation' of the Bible, called 'The Inspired Version' (IV).

The Inspired Version is a most interesting document from an exegetical point of view. It is much less known than the Book of Mormon. This is very understandable, for the main branch of the Mormon church has never acknowledged it as authoritative (!); on the contrary, it still uses the King James Version as the best translation. (It is given as a reason that Smith never finished his own translation, although it was, at least essentially, ready as early as 1833.) No doubt acknowledging the Inspired Version would bring a number of revelation-theological difficulties with it (how to explain the differences of the Inspired Version from both the Book of Mormon and the authoritative KJV?). But a smaller branch, called the 'Reorganized Church of Jesus Christ of Latter Day Saints', has published the work, and Mormon scholars do pay attention to it in their work.[28] Although the Inspired Version has not functioned as scripture in the Mormon community, it is an important and interesting source for someone who wants to get a picture of Joseph Smith as a 'biblical critic'. We move here in a little worked area of scholarship, that of the 'wild' reception of the Bible which belongs to 'the intellectual history of the common man'.[29]

Smith's changes show how much there was in the Bible that caused difficulties for a believer. His point of departure is the inerrancy of God's word; when he notes contradictions, he eliminates them. Many of his actual devices are familiar from the arsenal of today's evangelicalism. The difference is that where evangelical commentators resort to harmonizing exegesis, Smith's Inspired Version alters the text itself.[30]

Examples

How did Judas Iscariot die? The statement 'he hanged himself' of the KJV (Matt. 27.5; IV 27.6) is expanded: 'on a tree. And straightway he fell down, and his bowels gushed out, and he died.' Thus the account is brought into harmony with Acts 1.18. The same explanation is found in evangelical works even today.[31] The number of angels at Jesus' tomb is now the same in all Gospels: a second angel (as in Luke and John) is introduced into the narratives of Mark and Matthew as well. However, Smith has more devices at his disposal than an evangelical expositor. The latter must show that no extant version is wrong; when numbers differ, he must choose the highest one. When Matthew mentions two demoniacs and Mark just one, Mark too must be thinking of two, though he does not care to mention both.[32] By contrast, Smith has removed the second demoniac from Matthew's story (Matt. 8.28ff.); likewise he has removed the colt from Matt. 21 so that there, as in Mark, the ass alone serves as Jesus' riding animal. In the crucifixion scene, Smith introduces the second thief, the penitent one, from Luke into Matthew's and Mark's accounts as well.[33] Problems of this sort were well known already to the church fathers, who were bothered by them.[34] To remove the slightest chance of contradiction, Origen even suggested (as a possibility) that perhaps there were four robbers crucified with Jesus!

Smith brings the differing statements on Christian sin in the First Epistle of John into internal harmony. In 2.1 the author states: 'these things write I unto you, that ye sin not. And if any man sin, we have an advocate . . .' (KJV). However, in 3.9 it is claimed that 'whosoever is born of God doth not commit sin; for his seed remaineth in him and he cannot sin . . .' In Smith's version 2.1 reads: 'if any man sin *and repent* . . .'. Again, 3.9 states that 'whosoever is born of God doth not *continue in* sin; for the *Spirit of God* remaineth in him . . .' The picture is now coherent, and it conforms to the traditional picture of Christian life.

Matthew 23.2 'All . . . whatsoever they bid you observe, that observe and do' (KJV), seems to contradict a number of other Gospel passages: why should Pharisaic ordinances be obeyed? Consequently Smith changes the wording: 'All . . . whatsoever they bid you observe, *they will make you* observe and do' (IV).

There is an important difference between Exodus and the Gospel of John. John (1.19) claims that 'no man hath seen God at any time'. The Inspired Version takes the Exodus accounts of Moses seeing God seriously and adds to John's Gospel: '*except he hath borne record of the Son . . .*' (Smith's ability to write in the style of the King James John when handling the Fourth Gospel is noteworthy!).

The classical problem of the divine names – the name Yahweh is only revealed in Ex. 6.3, and yet humans use it in Genesis narratives already – is cleverly solved through a slight change in wording. Smith turns the end of the verse into a rhetorical question: I appeared to the fathers as God Almighty, 'the Lord JEHOVAH. And was not my name known unto them?'

The imminent expectation of the end has always been a problem for conservative exegesis. Here too Smith presents an interpretation which, in its intentions, agrees with evangelical exegesis. Once again the difference is that he is not content with expository acrobatics, but frankly changes the difficult texts themselves. Paul does not claim that 'we' are still alive when the Lord comes, but that *they who* are alive shall not 'prevent' those who are asleep (I Thess. 4.15). I Cor. 7.29 does not announce that 'the time is short'; it says that 'the time that remaineth is but short, *that ye shall be sent forth unto the ministry*'. Hebrews 9.26 does not claim that Jesus has appeared 'in the end of the world' but in the *meridian* of time. The statement 'this generation shall not pass, till all these things be fulfilled' (Matt. 24.34) is expanded as follows: 'This generation, *in which these things shall be shown forth*, shall not pass away, until all I have told you shall be fulfilled.' Correspondingly, in the previous verses it is not 'ye' who shall 'see all these things', but '*mine elect*'.

A Mormon commentator innocently remarks:

From the account in the King James Version it could be inferred that Jesus expected his second coming to be soon after his death . . . Changes made by the Prophet Joseph Smith transfer the time of Jesus' second coming to a date later than during the natural life of those to whom he spoke, and in truth this has been the case.[35]

Alterations are also made where the implied notion of God seems offensive. As the Deists had made clear, God does not repent. Therefore, in the opening of the Flood story in the Inspired Version (Gen. 6.7; IV 8.13) it is Noah who repented that the Lord had created man. The statement 'it repenteth me that I have set up Saul to be king' is replaced with 'I have set up Saul to be a king and *he repenteth not* . . .' (I Sam. 15.11). In the Inspired Version God never hardens the Pharaoh; he always hardens his own heart (e.g. Ex. 10.20). In Acts 13.48 the order of the verbs is changed: 'as many as believed were ordained unto eternal life'. The petition 'lead us not into temptation' in the Lord's Prayer is changed into '*suffer us not to be led* into temptation' (Matt. 6.13).

Perhaps the most striking innovation in Smith's interpretation of the Bible is this: according to him humans are from the very beginning fully aware of Messiah Jesus' future coming and mission. They even have in advance the chance to enjoy the salvation offered by him. The Inspired Version clearly teaches that 'the ancient prophets, from Adam to Abraham . . . taught and practised the gospel; they knew Christ and worshipped the Father in his name'.[36] A number of additions and expansions make this clear.

God decreed to his descendants that they had to repent, and promised: 'And as many as believed in the Son, and repented of their sins, should be saved' (Gen. 5.1–2 IV). So the gospel was preached right in the beginning (Gen. 5.44–45), even before the Flood. In one of the Inspired Version's numerous additions to Genesis, Enoch summarizes what God had told Adam:

> If thou wilt, turn unto me and hearken unto my voice, and believe, and repent of all thy transgressions, and be baptized, even in water, in the name of mine Only Begotten Son, who is full of grace and truth, which is Jesus Christ, the only name which shall be given under heaven, whereby salvation shall come unto the children of men; and ye shall receive the gift of the Holy Ghost . . . (Gen. 6.63 IV).

The long speech of the patriarch is summarized in the following words: 'This is the plan of salvation unto all men, through the blood of mine Only Begotten, who shall come in the meridian of time' (Gen. 6.60 IV). Adam was actually baptized (Gen. 6.67 IV).

A Mormon scholar commenting on the Inspired Version notes: 'Since these early patriarchs had the gospel and obeyed its ordinances, it is evident that the plan of salvation is constant and has been the same throughout the history of the world. This is not so obvious in the King James Version.'[37] Indeed it isn't!

For all the naiveté of Joseph Smith's solution, he has touched a sensitive point in biblical salvation history, as we have seen in connection with Marcion and his critics. The New Testament too speaks of God's eternal plan of salvation. But what is one to think of this plan, if Christ actually opened a *new* way of salvation which was unknown to the ancients? Or was the way to salvation open to ancient generations, too, if they repented of their sins or gladly accepted God's law? If not, did not God himself lead them astray by giving them a law which promised them life (e.g. Lev. 18.5) and in no way suggested that it was just a provisional arrangement? On the other hand, if the people of old *could* reach salvation, what was Christ really needed for? Had God's first plan failed so that he now came up with a better idea (as e.g. Oscar Cullmann seems to think)?[38] This would make Christ an emergency measure on God's part.

Either way, we are caught in a dilemma. One has to sacrifice either the immutability of God's plan or else the crucial significance of Christ. The problem surfaces in I Clement. Clement confirms in New Testament terminology that God has from eternity always justified everyone in the same way: through faith (I Clem. 32.4). God 'gave those who wanted to turn to him, from generation to generation, opportunity for repentance' (I Clem. 7.5). The 'difference between Christians and the pious men of the Old Testament disappears'.[39] Clement preserves the immutability of God's plan, but the price paid for this is that the role of Christ is quite vague. In fact, Paul already faced the same problem (though he seems to be unaware of it) when he introduced the figure of Abraham as the first Christian (as it were). If Abraham was justified by faith, and faith without works was thus a possibility open to humankind a millennium or two before Christ, why was it necessary for God at all to send Christ?

Like Clement of Rome, Joseph Smith definitely holds that 'God had always related to man on the basis of his faith, and any other terms would, indeed, make God mutable'.[40] (Ironically, Joseph Smith himself set forth in his later revelations that actually God himself made progress in his own development.[41]) But unlike

Clement, Smith does not let Christ's role remain vague. Without inhibitions, he projects the Christian soteriology in its totality on to Paradise. Obviously he has sensed the artificiality of the standard christological reading of the Old Testament as it stands. If the Old Testament really is a testimony to Christ (as Christians of all times have asserted), then it should actually speak of Jesus. Even the New Testament notion of Christ's pre-existence and the idea of God's eternal plan, which has now been revealed in Christ, leaves the problem of the time between the creation and the incarnation unsolved.

For all its lack of sense of history, in purely logical terms Smith's solution is admirable. Nor is he quite alone in the full-blown christocentrism of his exposition of the primeval stories. A Christian addition to the Jewish pseudepigraphon, the Testament of Adam, lets Adam teach his sons as follows:

> I have heard, my son Seth, that the Messiah[42] is coming from heaven and will be born of a virgin, working miracles and performing signs and great deeds, walking on the waves of the seas upon boards of wood, rebuking the winds and they are silenced, beckoning to the waves and they are stilled; also opening the eyes of the blind and cleansing the lepers and causing the deaf to hear. And the mute speak. And he shall cast out evil spirits, and raise the buried from the midst of their graves. Concerning this the Messiah spoke to me in paradise . . . (Testament of Adam 3.1–3).[43]

Actually it can happen today as well that the biblical text is improved in a similar vein. *The Children's Bible* by Anne de Vries, a Christian bestseller (originally Dutch), sold in millions of copies, appends without scruples several mentions of Jesus to Old Testament stories. The story of the Fall ends like this: 'Who would this child be? The Lord Jesus. When Jesus would come, God would no longer be angry . . . When they [Adam and Eve] thought of that they became again a bit glad.'[44] To Abraham the promise is given: 'Your children will live in the land, and later Lord Jesus too will be born there.'[45]

In its notorious stress on the baptism for the dead, later

Mormon thought has hit on a somewhat analogous salvation-historical problem. For this baptism, Mormon authors refer to such biblical passages as I Cor. 15.29 (if the dead are not raised, why are some people receiving baptism on their behalf?); I Peter 3.18f.; 4.6 (Christ's descent to Hades); Mal. 4.5f. – and John 3.5 ('no one can see the kingdom of God without being born of water and Spirit'). No doubt baptism for the dead was, historically speaking, a marginal phenomenon in early Christianity; we only hear that it was practised by some Corinthians in Paul's time (but Paul does not condemn it) and, later on, by some Gnostic circles. Yet even here a genuine problem lurks, which is mostly overlooked in the New Testament apart from I Peter: can those who have died before Christ participate in salvation, and how?

Mormon authors reckon, in accordance with John 3.5, with the absolute necessity of water baptism. This they cleverly combine with the New Testament mention of the baptism for the dead in I Cor. 15.29. Interestingly, Hermas already arrived at a rather similar idea, with express reference to John 3.5 (*Sim.* IX, 16): even the pious people of the Old Testament can only partake of salvation after they have been baptized; therefore apostles and teachers had preached to them and baptized them – in Hades, after their death. The difference from Mormon theology is that this idea is not modelled on I Cor. 15, but on the example of Jesus in I Peter.

To return to the Inspired Version, the law does not become a problem there in the way it does in standard Christian theology, for Adam already learned that animal sacrifices are 'a similitude of the sacrifice of the Only Begotten of the Father' (Gen. 4.7 IV). The typological theology of the law of Hebrews is projected into the beginnings of salvation history.[46] Christ has brought the law to an end, for it was fulfilled in him (3 Nephi 9.17; 29.4) who, being identical with the God of Israel (!), was also the giver of the law (3 Nephi 29.5). He *is* actually the law and the light (3 Nephi 29.9). Apart from the identification of Father and Son, Smith agrees in these assertions with classical patristic solutions.[47]

One further problem connected with the continuity of salvation history is Paul's talk of the law as the cause of sin, or of its function of increasing sin. Smith is forced to weaken such statements. Once more he finds himself in good company; the church fathers too, in opposing Marcion, took efforts to render the apostle harmless on such points.[48] Paul speaks in Rom. 7.5 of the sinful desires in our members that were 'by the law' (KJV). In the Inspired Version this becomes 'sinful desires . . . *not* according to the law'. The other offensive statement that the commandment 'ordained to life' actually was 'unto death' (Rom. 7.10) is avoided through the following rendering of Rom. 7.9–10: 'For once I was alive without *transgression* of the law,[49] but when the commandment *of Christ* came, sin revived, and I died. And when I *believed not* the commandment of Christ which came, which was ordained to life, I found it *condemned* me unto death.' Even the claim of verse 11 that sin took 'occasion' by the law is toned down: 'For sin, taking occasion, *denied* the commandment and deceived me.' The close connection which Paul here establishes between law and sin is flatly denied by Joseph Smith. Some modern interpreters will assess this as a dilution of Paul's profoundly dialectical view of the law. Others, however, find that Paul's view is beset with internal and external difficulties; Smith exhibits common sense in regarding only the transgression of the divine law as a negative matter, not the law itself.[50] Chrysostom (who watered down Paul's assertion in Rom. 7.8 and 7.11) observed that logically even the New Testament precepts would have had the same effect of engendering sin; 'this particular charge could never be directed against the Old Testament law without involving the New Testament also'.[51]

Smith's interpretation of Rom. 7.14–25 is amazingly modern. This passage, in which Paul speaks of the misery of an 'I', is often taken as a description of Paul's Christian life. This, however, would contradict Paul's general picture of life in the Spirit, not least in Romans 8. So the majority of modern critics think that he must really mean non-Christian existence 'under the law'.

Sensing the problem, the Inspired Version anticipates the critics and alters the text thoroughly. 'I am carnal, sold under sin' now becomes: '*when I was under the law*, I was *yet* carnal, sold under sin' (Rom. 7.14). Then a new contrast to 'I was carnal' is added: '*But now I am spiritual.*' The sequel 'For that which I do I allow not: for what I would, that I do not . . .' (Rom. 7.15 KJV) is replaced with: 'for that which *I am commanded to do, I do*; *and that which I am commanded not to allow, I allow not*' (IV). The

Inspired Version consistently transforms the apparent tension of flesh and spirit in Paul's heart into a contrast between two succeeding stages in his life; the alternative that the 'I'-form is rhetorical and that Paul is speaking of the non-Christian under the law has, understandably, not occurred to Smith.

The Inspired Version even omits the last clause 'with the flesh (I serve) the law of sin' (Rom. 7.25), which many modern scholars too have ascribed to a post-Pauline interpreter. Both these scholars and the Inspired Version let Paul close the chapter with the statement 'with the mind I myself serve the law of God' (Rom. 7.27 IV). If the modern majority interpretation is correct, then Joseph Smith's interpretation of the passage is closer to Paul's intentions than was e.g. that of Martin Luther.

There is much to learn from Smith's implicit criticism of the Bible. The parallels to mainstream conservatism of today are very intriguing; so are the parallels to the apologetics of the church fathers. In Smith's work one can, as with a magnifying glass, study the mechanisms operative in all apologetic interpretation of the Bible. Even if his answers seem fanciful at times, he asks genuine questions and perceives many of the problems quite sharply.

The story of the Book of Mormon

The greatest and best known peculiarity of Joseph Smith is, however, the fanciful story of the Book of Mormon, on which Smith staked the whole authority of the book. In itself, a revelatory book which claims to confirm and complement – often also to correct – earlier scriptures is no novelty in the world of religions. Similarities to the Qur'an and the rise of Islam are especially striking.[52] Many features in the Book of Mormon that seem odd at first glance are easily explained from the presuppositions of the age and environment, often even from Smith's and his adherents' belief in the Bible. Eduard Meyer, comparing the Book of Mormon to the Bible, observed:

> It followed without further ado from the Bible, and was not in doubt in the believer's mind, that the aborigines of America must be descended from Noah; they must have come from the

old world after the Babylonian confusion of tongues. Even the idea that they were connected with the 'lost' tribes of Israel, traces of which were sought everywhere in the world, came in naturally: for in the narrow horizon of a simple person who believed in the inspiration of the Bible, the history of Israel transmitted in the Old Testament was the history of the world.[53]

What may appear absurd to us in the Book of Mormon is no more so than many features of the Old Testament:

The journey of the Jaredites to America in miraculously closed, God-guided ships is no more absurd than the story of the Flood, understood literally; whoever is able to believe literally this or, say, the stories of Daniel or of the Apocalypse or the war stories of the Chronicles and much else, is without the slightest difficulties able to swallow in faith even the Book of Mormon.[54]

One theologian criticizes the 'miraculous atmosphere' of the Book of Mormon, claiming that 'God does not make use of such means . . . He acts in history through guidance, visitation and incarnation . . .'[55] But especially in the Old Testament God does act through quite spectacular miracles as well! One could ask whether Smith's alleged gold plates which contained the Book of Mormon are really a more conspicuous miracle than Moses' stone tablets, fashioned by God (!), written with God's (!) finger (Ex. 31.18; 32.16; Deut. 4.13; 9.10).

Mormons have officially staked everything on the historical correctness of Smith's claims of the origin of the Book of Mormon.[56] The words of one Mormon leader have often been quoted: 'This book must be either true or false . . . If false, it is one of the most cunning, wicked, bold, deep-laid impositions ever palmed upon the world, calculated to deceive and ruin millions.'[57] However, other kinds of thoughts have been entertained by some people. Already in the 1950s Thomas F. O'Dea reported about intellectual problems in the Mormon community which had caused some members to put inherited 'values' consciously over above mere 'facts'.[58]

Indeed, the Mormon church has had internal problems comparable to those of other religious communities with regard to holy scriptures and the criticism applied to them. Philip Barlow shows that the reception of biblical criticism among Mormons resembles the developments among Baptists or even Roman Catholics (prior to the encyclical of 1943).[59]

The Mormon church has had its own conservatives and liberals, and its own strife about heresy. In the beginning of our century one William Chamberlin was 'effectively forced to resign' his post in Brigham Young University (despite the support of most students) for treating the Bible 'as an incomparable record of religious experience', but also 'full of legend, myth, poetry, parable . . . and error for which God could not be accountable'.[60] In 1988 Professor David P. Wright was fired. Three of his unacceptable views were specified: 1. the Book of Mormon is best explained as an inspired nineteenth-century work; 2. the prophets of the Hebrew Bible generally spoke for their own time; 3. the historical accuracy of many Old Testament incidents is questionable.[61]

Barlow, himself a Mormon scholar, sums up:

> Among LDS religious educators, historico-critical methods are discreetly adopted by a minority, attacked by another minority, but often simply ignored, either because teachers are innocent of them, contemptuous of them, or because they believe their public use might cost them their jobs.[62]

He notes, however, that 'liberal views among Mormon leaders are less visible now than formerly'.[63] If so, the development has run parallel to the inner development of Islam. The future will show whether the Mormon church can afford some kind of demythologization on any larger scale. As shown e.g. by the book *Reflections on Mormonism*, discussed above, unprejudiced outsiders can today appreciate the theological potential inherent in Mormonism, although – or perhaps because! – they do not agree with the community's interpretation of the nature of its scriptures.

Apart from that, mainstream Christians might profit from taking the questions once asked by Joseph Smith very seriously, even if they may not accept the answers suggested by him or his followers.

11

Ideals and Problems of Universal Wisdom:
Mahatma Gandhi and the Sermon
on the Mount

Some time ago, a Finnish writer claimed that Mohandas Gandhi
(1869–1948) was 'the greatest *Christian* statesman in our century'.
Jesus' Sermon on the Mount 'became the religious kernel in his
doctrine of *satyagraha*'.

> He even wanted to make of the Preacher of the Sermon on the
> Mount the most important teacher in Indian politics . . . After
> he had become acquainted with the teaching of the Preacher on
> the Mount, he decided to try it in practice . . . Afterwards he
> found the same principles in the (Bhagavad) Gita.[1]

It was once customary to describe Gandhi's mission in Christian
terms.[2] According to Friedrich Heiler, Jesus taught Gandhi something quite novel: 'the universal validity of the ideal of non-
violence'.[3] Heiler could call Gandhi 'an unbaptized Christian'; 'it
was the gospel of Jesus that formed this heroic personality'.[4] One
may perceive in such inclusivism traces of imperialism, the
usurpation of a non-Christian 'hero'; but on the other hand such a
view is connected with Christian self-criticism: 'we do not live
according to our doctrine ourselves'.

In modern Gandhi research the convictions of the Mahatma are
no longer Christianized; they are traced back to Indian tradition.
Among Christians, however, the idea that the Sermon on the
Mount had a crucial influence on him is still popular. He is viewed
as 'a paradigm of the immense impact which Jesus and his teaching
can have upon adherents of another faith'; it is held that his whole

life, like that of Francis of Assisi, was orientated towards the Sermon on the Mount.[5]

This chapter tries to shed some light on the actual role of the Sermon on the Mount in Gandhi's life and thought and on his place in its reception history. In this connection some problems connected with Gandhi's 'non-violent resistance' surface. The treatment of Gandhi finally leads into a discussion of problems inherent in the Matthean sermon itself.

From the voluminous corpus of Gandhi's production I have used here 1. the unfinished autobiography *The Story of My Experiments With the Truth* (cited as *Autobiography*; because of the different pagination in different editions, the references are by chapter only);[6] and 2. the three-volume selection *The Moral and Political Writings of Mahatma Gandhi*, edited by R. Iyer (Oxford 1986–1987, cited as *MPW*), intended 'to rescue Gandhi's essential writings from the wealth of detail (and ephemera) in the *Collected Works*' and to be 'a comprehensive, balanced, and accessible collection' (*MPW* 1, viii).

On Gandhi's action and thought

Gandhi is often regarded as the father of the Indian nation. After a study period in London he fought for two decades for the civil and human rights of the Indian immigrants in South Africa. Here he developed his method of non-violent resistance which he later practised in India. Yet in India operations which had started without violence often ended up in outbreaks of violence, and towards the end of his life Gandhi thought that his efforts had failed.[7] His hope of unity between Hindus and Muslims came to nothing, and he himself was murdered for the sake of his Muslim sympathies by a fanatical Hindu.

Gandhi's actual significance for the political independence of India is ambiguous,[8] but he certainly became a national symbol. He has also become something of an inter-faith saint. A portrait is often drawn of him with hagiographical features,[9] but very critical assessments have also been put forward,[10] and it would be unwise to neglect them. Precisely because Gandhi's work holds some promise and hope, we cannot afford simply to glorify it.[11]

Gandhi's politics were founded on the ideal of 'non-violence'.[12] *Ahimsa* was an age-old and generally accepted principle in India. It meant both physical abstention from doing harm and spiritual non-violence in thoughts and words. Gandhi widened the concept by applying it also to politics, economic life and social institutions. *Ahimsa* now also gained a positive side; it came to mean the greatest love, that of even the enemy and the stranger.

Gandhi called his method of realizing *ahimsa* in society *satyagraha* (holding to truth). He was convinced that he worked for the eternal truth, identical with God. His ultimate aim was the Hindu goal of spiritual self-realization. Perfect *ahimsa* is *moksha*, release from body and from karmic activity.[13] In working for *satyagraha*, Gandhi was working for his own liberation as well. Nevertheless, *satyagraha* amounts to voluntary communal suffering through which the adversary is conquered. By contrast, it does *not* imply the abandonment of resistance. It is nothing for the weak; it is manly. Gandhi came emphatically to reject the term 'passive' resistance (which he had originally adopted). *Satyagraha* means resistance, but resistance without violence.

The origins of Gandhi's non-violent resistance

The Christianized picture of Gandhi is connected with the assumption that the New Testament played a great part in his development. According to a more cautious assessment, *satyagraha* is a blending of Hindu elements and elements of Jesus' teaching as interpreted by Tolstoy.

The opposite position was taken by the theologian Otto Wolff in a polemical work of 1955. Gandhi puts us before a choice, he maintains: either the Mahatma or the Christ. Wolff holds that the New Testament did not play any major role in Gandhi's development. It was certain impressions and events in his childhood that proved decisive. Jainism, too, had a great influence. Later discoveries in Tolstoy, in the Bible and in the Bhagavadgita only confirmed an already existing conviction. Wolff even asserts that the Mahatma crudely abused the Sermon on the Mount for political ends.

Wolff's charge of abuse misses the mark,[14] but he may have seen the historical relation between the Sermon on the Mount and *satyagraha* correctly.

When young Gandhi in London got a Bible, he started reading it in order. The books of Moses sent him to sleep, but the Sermon on the Mount went straight away in his heart. 'But I say unto ye, that ye resist not evil: but whosoever shall smite thee on the right cheek, turn to him the other also. And if any man take away thy coat let him have thy cloak too.' Such verses delighted Gandhi 'beyond measure'. 'That renunciation was the highest form of religion appealed to me greatly.' He states expressly that the Sermon reminded him of a native poem which had made a deep impression on him in his childhood: 'But the truly noble know all men as one, And return with gladness good for evil done' (*Autobiography*, Part 1, ch. 20).

A few years later (1893) in South Africa Gandhi, in the midst of a somewhat anguished religious quest, returned to the New Testament. His retrospective statement on that encounter is ambiguous. On the one hand he states that it was the New Testament, i.e. the Sermon on the Mount, that brought the truth and value of non-violent resistance into his consciousness. But on the other hand he notes that he was delighted beyond measure at such verses as Matt. 5.39 and 5.44f., for he now found confirmation for his view where he had least expected it. He goes on to state that that impression was deepened by the Bhagavad Gita and given final form through Tolstoy's *The Kingdom of God Is Within You*.

Obviously, the reading of the Sermon on the Mount and, later, of Tolstoy activated and helped to articulate and, still later, legitimate something that lay in Gandhi's heart from the early days of childhood. To the crucial childhood experiences belonged a 'confession of sin' before the father who, contrary to the son's expectation, was not angry but forgave his transgression with tears. This behaviour was later regarded by Gandhi as 'pure *ahimsa*' (*Autobiography*, Part 1, ch. 8).

Christianity did act as a catalyst. Gandhi was indebted to his Christian friends 'for the religious quest that they awakened in me' (*Autobiography*, Part 2, ch. 15).[15] But he delighted in his first

discovery of the Sermon on the Mount roughly in the same
way that he had somewhat earlier delighted in finally finding a
vegetarian restaurant in London (*Autobiography*, Part 1, ch. 14).
In both cases he found something familiar in the new cultural
environment.

There is one all-important point with regard to Gandhi's
relation to the Sermon on the Mount and the origin of his *satyagraha* that usually escapes attention. How did Gandhi come to
regard resistance as an integral part of *ahimsa* in the first place?
Clearly, the notion of non-retaliation was available to him both in
his own tradition and in the Sermon on the Mount or in Tolstoy,
and Christian tradition may have contributed to the positive aspect
of *ahimsa* as universal love.[16] But whence came the central idea that
this *ahimsa* should express itself actively as resistance to evil? This
activist aspect is not an obvious outcome of Indian tradition. Nor
can it be traced back simply to a reading of the Sermon on the
Mount, for there the opposite point is explicitly made: 'Do not
resist evil' (Matt. 5.39)[17].

In fact, the practice of *satyagraha* started spontaneously, as a
series of instinctive reactions to certain incidents, not as a thought-
out programme (nor as a response to the Sermon on the Mount or
to any other text).[18] One of Gandhi's first experiences in South
Africa was that the magistrate asked him, the lawyer, to take off his
native turban in the court. Gandhi left the court; to avoid contro-
versy, he thought of starting to wear an English hat. It was his
Indian Muslim employer who disapproved of the idea and moved
him from passivity to resistance. Gandhi then wrote to the press,
explaining and defending his use of the turban. Then followed the
well-known incident in a train where Gandhi was forced to leave
his compartment and other insults that were 'more than I could
bear' (*Autobiography*, Part 2, ch. 9).

The simple Indian workers in South Africa were not in a
position to claim their rights, and the merchant class pocketed
insults in order to keep the business going. Gandhi the lawyer was
in a different position; instead of giving up his right to travel first
class he started looking for loopholes in the railway regulations.
When time passed, he came to know 'that South Africa was no
country for a self-respecting Indian', and his mind was 'more and

more occupied with the question as to how this state of things might be improved' (*Autobiography*, Part 2, ch. 13). Here, in the almost instinctive reactions of a self-respecting middle-class Indian to his alarming experiences, the beginnings of non-violent resistance are to be found; neither the New Testament nor Tolstoy played a part. But after it had become clear that resistance there must be, the New Testament and Tolstoy helped Gandhi insist on the claim that this resistance had to be of a non-violent kind.[19]

The significance of the Sermon on the Mount and of Jesus

Gandhi is somewhat selective in his use of the Sermon on the Mount. He often refers to the passage about turning the other cheek. Often he also cites Matt. 6.33: 'Seek first the Kingdom of God and his righteousness, and everything else will be added to you.' At a mature age (1927) Gandhi recalled from his 'early studies of the Bible' that that verse 'seized me immediately as I read the passage' (*MPW* 1, 497). This need not mean that the verse had a direct innovative influence, for Gandhi equates the reign of God with the Hindu concept of *moksha*, 'liberation':[20]

> I am a humble seeker after truth. I am impatient to realize myself, to attain *moksha* in this very existence. My national service is part of my training for freeing my soul from the bondage of flesh. Thus considered, my service may be regarded as purely selfish. I have no desire for the perishable kingdom of earth. I am striving for the Kingdom of Heaven which is *moksha* . . .[21] For me the road to salvation lies through the incessant toil in the service of my country and therethrough of humanity (*MPW* 1, 18f.).

A third favourite sentence is Matt. 7.20: 'You will know them by their fruits.'[21]

By contrast, a verse that plays no part whatsoever is Matt. 5.34: 'Do not swear at all'. This ruling was quite central to Tolstoy. Gandhi, on the contrary, asserted that Jesus was pre-eminently a man of vows! Gandhi himself made lavish use of oaths and vows, which became part of the *satyagraha* technique. Some oaths were more or less coercively imposed on others. There were mass vows which had later to be confirmed in writing by the individuals. In Gandhi's ashram the inmates had to take a number of vows, including those of celibacy and diet.[22]

The injunctions against public fasting (Matt. 6.16–18) do not belong to Gandhi's repertoire either. The role of fasting, sometimes spectacular, as a method of political pressure (though seen by Gandhi himself merely as a penitential act) is well-known. Here again he clearly stands on Indian ground.[23]

Inevitably, Gandhi had to relate his understanding of the Sermon on the Mount to other aspects of Jesus' teaching as described in the New Testament. He speaks of Jesus' bold and wise resistance which has wrongly been regarded as weakness in Europe.

> . . . you have to pay a very heavy price when your resistance is passive, in the sense of the weakness of the resister. Europe mistook the bold and brave resistance full of wisdom by Jesus of Nazareth for passive resistance, as if it was of the weak. As I read the New Testament for the first time, I detected no passivity, no weakness about Jesus as depicted in the four gospels and the meaning became clearer to me when I read Tolstoy's *Harmony of the Gospels* and his other kindred writings. Has not the West paid heavily in regarding Jesus as a Passive Resister? Christendom has been responsible for wars which put to shame even those described in the Old Testament and other records . . . (*MPW* 3, 25–6).

Gandhi reminds his readers of how Jesus 'drove out the money-changers from the temple' and 'drew down curses from Heaven on the hypocrites and the Pharisees', comparing Jesus to Buddha who 'brought down on its knees an arrogant priesthood' (*MPW* 1, 44). He interprets the debate over the tribute to Caesar in the sense that Jesus refused to pay taxes (*MPW* 1, 511).

Gandhi thus interprets the Sermon on the Mount in the light of such more 'activist' passages, which are indeed found in the Gospels. As anything but a fundamentalist reader of the Gospels, he would have been free to take a different tack and to state that

some acts or sayings of Jesus were not in accord with his basic
ahimsa.[24] Had he wished to do so, Gandhi could have criticized
Jesus' activity in the temple (which can only with difficulty be
deemed wholly non-violent!) from this viewpoint, as a Hindu
philosopher among his admirers was subsequently to do.[25] With
even better reasons he could have criticized Jesus' curses on
Pharisees and Sadducees. But in general he does not even contemplate this order of priorities. He does not choose the apparent non-
resistance of Matt. 5.38ff. as a vantage point from which to criticize
(or to reinterpret) the other, more 'combative' or 'activist' Gospel
passages; quite the contrary.

Still more important to Gandhi is another emphasis which does
not literally go back to the Sermon on the Mount, but to the gospel
message in general: the emphasis on the cross as a symbol of
personal suffering which is such a central aspect in Gandhi's concept of *satyagraha*. It is probably here that biblical influence on
Gandhi is the clearest, although the cross, too, is given a Hindu
turn in that Jesus' destiny comes to stand for an eternal 'law' or
principle of the cross.

Indeed, Gandhi always tends to move from the particular to the
general. He states that even 'if the man called Jesus never lived',
the Sermon on the Mount 'would still be true for me'.[26] The
Sermon is an expression of general principles. In it, 'Jesus has
given a definition of perfect *dharma*'.[27] For Gandhi, all the great
religious teachers proclaimed one and the same message. We may
regard him as a Hindu representative of an 'inclusivist' approach
to inter-religious dialogue.

Apparently Gandhi wished to underline the significance of his
satyagraha and to legitimize his struggle before Christians by
referring to the Sermon on the Mount and to the history of Jesus.
He successfully appealed to Western consciences by appealing to
Christ: ' . . . today's Christianity is a denial of his central teaching –
"Love your enemy" ' (*MPW* 2, 333). The Sermon on the Mount
thus gave resonance to Gandhi's message in Christian hearts.[28]
That is not to say that he omitted to speak of Jesus to Hindus. He
did mention Jesus to them too, but not as if he were coming
forward with something new.[29]

Gandhi had warm feelings towards Jesus, but he pointed out

that Christianity deviated from Jesus' own teaching. Jesus did not preach a new religion but a new life. Gandhi could say, not just of the conduct, but also of the beliefs of Western Christians: '. . . much of what passes as Christianity is a negation of the Sermon on the Mount' (*MPW* 1, 498). He could accept Jesus 'as a martyr, an embodiment of sacrifice, and a divine teacher',[30] but not as the redeemer, not even as the most perfect man – for he missed in Jesus such love towards all living creatures, not just human beings, as he found in the Buddha (*Autobiography*, Part 2, ch. 22).

Apart from the last point, Gandhi's thoughts on Jesus do not differ much from the liberal Christian theology of the time. Hans Windisch, for one, pointed out: 'If seen from the viewpoint of Paul, Luther, or Calvin, the soteriology of the Sermon on the Mount is incurably heretical.'[31] A difference is that Gandhi puts all religions and their founders on the same level, whereas the liberal Christians reserved a special place for Jesus the man. More recent exegetical research has confirmed that the idea of redemptive death is lacking precisely in the thought-world of those circles (the 'Q' group) which preserved (or even created?[32]) the bulk of the Jesus material that went into the Sermon on the Mount.[33]

Inherent problems in Gandhi's interpretation of non-violence

There are inherent problems both in Gandhi's theory and in his practice.[34] His 'attitude remains a *complexio oppositorum*, even if we try to understand his environment with the greatest possible empathy'; 'extraordinary admiration and constant perplexity incessantly counterbalance each other'.[35] Gandhi suggests that he is rejecting all violence in accordance with the eternal Truth. Non-violence is an absolute principle,[36] equated with Truth itself. In actual fact Gandhi does not reject violence, however; he only wants to reduce it to a minimum, and not even that consistently.[37]

According to Gandhi there are different degrees of violence. It is best to act non-violently. But if this is impossible, the second best alternative is – violent defence. Worst of all is non-violent resignation before violence; it is of equal value with aggressive violence! 'Anything is better than cowardice' (*MPW* 3, 582).

Gandhi once told the story of 'a Negro clergyman with a

Herculean frame in South Africa saying "pardon me brother", when insulted by a white man, and sneaking into a coloured man's compartment'. Gandhi commented: 'That is not non-violence. It is a travesty of Jesus' teaching. It would have been more manly to retaliate' (*MPW* 3, 582.). More manly, no doubt – but would retaliation really have amounted to 'turning the other cheek' or to enacting the eternal principle of *ahimsa*?

Gandhi claims that he declines all mental *himsa* (violence) as well. He does not admit (or realize) how much violence is actually involved in several of his methods (fasts, imposed vows and oaths, methods of upbringing).[38] Gandhi's treatment of his own family was hardly void of coercion and mental violence; one critic speaks of 'the cruelty of Gandhi's relations to those nearest to him: the harsh treatment of his children, who could not live up to his inhuman rectitude, his callous destruction of marriages and families . . . those terrible distractions along the way of *brahmacharya*'.[39]

Most bewildering, however, was Gandhi's way of legitimating his participation in and his propaganda for the Boer War, the defeat of the Zulu 'rebellion' and the First World War. Without seriously raising the issue of justice, let alone of *ahimsa* in this connection, he put himself quite opportunistically[40] on the side of the British empire for the simple reason that Indians might profit.[41] In 1918, Gandhi made the almost incredible point that for the Indian people the war was a golden opportunity to learn to use weapons and to demonstrate, by joining the army, that they were no cowards.[42]

Reinhold Niebuhr concluded that Gandhi was really saying that 'even violence is justified if it proceeds from perfect moral good-will', adding that Gandhi was probably right on this.[43] But this is *not* what Gandhi himself claimed he was up to. He used to say that he did not 'accept the limitations that are sought to be put upon the teaching of The Sermon on the Mount' and that he could 'discover no justification in the New Testament for wars'.[44] Gandhi's actual practice leaves the door wide open for the use of double standards.[45]

Gandhi in the reception history of the Sermon on the Mount[46]

I am using the term 'Sermon on the Mount' here loosely (as it was used both by Gandhi and by those who debated with him) to denote the main points in Jesus' ethical message in so far as they find expression in Matt. 5–7 – and other equally radical demands in the Synoptic tradition as well.

The designation 'Sermon on the Mount' was first used by Augustine. It only became common in the sixteenth century. Exegetically speaking, the Sermon is a creation of Matthew, based on the much shorter 'Sermon on the Plain' found in his source, Q (Luke 6.20–49). It is of some significance that Matt. 5.39a ('do not resist evil') is almost certainly an addition of the evangelist rather than a saying of Jesus himself. But neither Gandhi nor his Christian dispute partners made any such distinctions; they (understandably) took the Sermon on the Mount at face value as a speech of Jesus.

1. Until Christianity became the religion of the Roman state, the sayings ascribed to Jesus were taken literally and regarded as rules of perfection. Later on, the Sermon on the Mount was applied literally by mediaeval sects and mendicant orders and, still later, by the 'left wing' of the Reformation. The Anabaptists demanded the separation of church and state and abstained from oaths and violence. A Christian could not participate in state administration. The Anabaptists did not think that society could be governed by the Sermon on the Mount; they wanted to be a small flock of saints who followed Christ. They met with ridicule and persecution.

Primitive Christianity, the Anabaptists and the 'peace churches' which originated with the latter represent a literal interpretation of the Sermon on the Mount. The Sermon is regarded as valid for a small group with no important role in society at large.

2. With the emergence of the state church, the radical precepts had to be reinterpreted. This led to a distinction between two groups of recipients. The Catholic Church continued to understand the Sermon on the Mount literally, but it was no longer thought to be an absolute rule for all Christians. It was valid – as 'counsels' – for those who (in monasteries) strove for perfection.

3. The Reformers rejected both the Catholic and the Anabaptist interpretation. Luther distinguished between the spiritual and the worldly 'reign'. He came to lay the foundations for an individualistic interpretation of the Sermon on the Mount. One had to distinguish between one's actions as an individual and one's duties in relation to other people as master, husband or official. In carrying out the duties of his office a man has to do things he is not allowed to do as a private person. Luther agreed with the Anabaptists that the Sermon on the Mount is meant for all Christians. But he tried to interpret it in such a way as to not part company with state and culture. When a Christian goes to war or sits on a tribunal to punish his fellow men, or hands in an official complaint, he does not do that as a Christian but as a soldier, judge or lawyer. At the same time he preserves the heart of a Christian.[47]

In later Protestant theology the Sermon on the Mount has often been regarded as a 'mirror'. It is meant for all Christians, but not as a norm to be actually followed. It is designed to expose man's moral misery and to drive him to seek the mercy of Christ.[48] A liberal version has it that the commands are meant to found a new consciousness, not to lead to real action.

4. In these interpretations,[49] either the literalness of the Sermon on the Mount is abandoned or its scope is narrowed down. By contrast, Leo Tolstoy combined a literal interpretation with the conviction that the Sermon was meant for all and sundry. He believed that its demands could be fulfilled and identified the kernel of Christianity with non-violence: 'Do not resist evil'. War was rejected by him in all its forms.[50]

To reject violence was to reject the state, the right of ownership, the administration of justice, the upholding of order. The outcome seemed to be pure anarchy. But Tolstoy believed that when the source of violence had been removed, no one would behave violently any more.

Obviously, Gandhi largely agrees with this line of interpretation, even though his *satyagraha* had been formed before his acquaintance with Tolstoy. *Satyagraha* is meant for all those who have enough courage. The Sermon on the Mount 'has no meaning if it is not of vital use in everyday life to everyone' (*MPW* 1, 517).

It is largely acknowledged by scholars today that the commands collected in Matthew's Sermon on the Mount were addressed to all recipients. It was not generally doubted in early Christianity that they could be put into practice.[51] Whether they could function as the ethics of a society, or even as rules in normal relations between individuals, is another matter.[52]

Actually there was a greater difference between Gandhi and Tolstoy than either of them realized. Tolstoy wished to abstain from all resistance to evil. But precisely this attitude was strictly rejected by Gandhi; for him it was mere weakness.[53] According to Tolstoy, an individual is not allowed to defend himself or his family, even against the most brutal kind of violence. Here Gandhi was, as we have seen, of a quite different opinion (and often had to oppose his own followers who had drawn different conclusions from his teaching of *ahimsa*). Gandhi differs from Tolstoy in that he actually rejects a literal interpretation of the command of turning the other cheek.[54]

It is not difficult to regard Gandhi as the more realistic of the two. But for better or for worse, it is Tolstoy who seems to be closer to the wording of the Sermon on the Mount – and closer to the non-resistant strand in Indian traditions for that matter. In his actual statements on war, or on the different degrees of violence, Gandhi tacitly moved quite some way in the direction of a conformist 'state church' interpretation (like that of Luther).[55]

The Sermon on the Mount envisages *non*-resistance, not just 'non-violent resistance'. Matthew 5.39 ('do not resist evil', 'turn the other cheek') is quite clear on this,[56] and so is Matt. 5.41, which recommends one who is forced (by soldiers) to walk a mile not to sit down and refuse co-operation, but to walk an extra mile.[57] The Anabaptists and Tolstoy were no doubt right in their exegesis.[58] There is then a difference between the Sermon on the Mount and Gandhi.

Gandhi's reception of the Sermon on the Mount thus amounts to a reinterpretation in an activist, in part even *realpolitisch* direction. In this regard he resembles other interpreters who have refused to regard the Sermon just as the 'law' for some small group. Gandhi himself does not admit that a reinterpretation has taken place; for him it is all the time a question of the eternal Truth.

Gandhi's 'activist' reinterpretation which replaces the passive turning of the cheek with non-violent resistance seems in itself a meaningful application. But it would clarify things a great deal if one could admit that a *re*interpretation has actually taken place: 'what it means' is not identical with 'what it meant'. It would be even more important to admit that a relativization of Gandhi's own ideal of *ahimsa* has taken place as well; a 'relative truth' can, and should, be made the subject of rational discussion and debate (which Gandhi was not disposed to do[59]). Here the immanent critique of the problems inherent in Gandhi's philosophy and the assessment of his interpretation of the New Testament converge.

The context of the commands

The difficulties of the interpreters of the Sermon on the Mount are partly due to the lack of a clear interpretative context for its commands in the New Testament itself. The command of love for enemies is singular (!) in the Gospel tradition,[60] and its motivation is not disclosed.[61] It does not become clear what kinds of insults or enemies are in view; there are no stories about Jesus himself to exemplify the expected behaviour in practice.

In Acts it is said that Stephen died praying for the forgiveness of his executioners (Acts 7.60). In the received text of Luke's Gospel a similar prayer is put into the mouth of Jesus: 'Father, forgive them; for they do not know what they are doing' (Luke 23.34); but on a textual basis this is probably a later addition to the Gospel.[62]

The sources do not suggest that preaching non-violence or love for one's enemies amounted to anything like a concrete 'programme' of Jesus (as it was, for all his problems, a central part in the programme of Gandhi, or in that of Martin Luther King – or as contemporary Cynics strove to give 'credibility to their more extreme ascetic maxims by consistently following them themselves'[63]). If the Gospels are any guide, 'Jesus did not apparently offer an explanation by personal example'.[64]

Moreover, there is a palpable tension between the command to love and the actual harshness of much of the Gospel tradition, a tension which reminds one of the ambiguities in Gandhi's career.

Jesus' relationship to his own actual adversaries, Pharisees and scribes, does not look compassionate or mild. Far from blessing his adversaries, Jesus curses them. In the very Gospel of Matthew which programmatically underlines the importance of loving one's enemies, Jesus himself puts forward harsh polemic against his ideological critics, branding them as 'children of hell', 'snakes' and 'brood of vipers' (Matt. 23.15, 33).[65] Long ago the Jewish scholar C.G. Montefiore commented: 'One cannot help wishing that Jesus had practised what he taught. With the exception of the spurious verse in Luke,[66] we have no account of any prayer offered up by Jesus for his enemies, or of any love shown by him to them.'[67] Instead, Jesus bitterly exclaims that 'this generation will be charged with the blood of all the prophets shed since the foundation of the world' (Luke 11.50; Matt. 23.35–36).

The common picture of Jesus as a gentle philanthropist who accepts people as they are, without conditions, is essentially based on stories about his relations with those who accepted his message about the kingdom and his own central role in it.[68] On those who did not, Jesus seems to have pronounced a judgment of rejection in God's name: 'whoever denies me before others will be denied before the angels of God' (Luke 12.8–9; Matt. 10.32–33). As often happens, love seems to be converted to threats, if the message is not accepted. Ulrich Luz suggests that Matthew's anti-Judaism, palpable in his terrible claim that the blood of Jesus is to come upon the children of the Jewish crowd (Matt. 27.25), is rooted in Jesus' own exclusive claims over against his generation.[69]

Distinctive or traditional?

Thus, there are grounds for doubting the actual centrality of the love for enemies in the real 'programme' of Jesus, the proclamation of the eschatological kingdom of God.[70] There are even better grounds for doubting the Christian myth that the teaching on non-violence and non-retaliation by the Matthean Jesus is unique, something qualitatively different from other teachings. This myth is one of the reasons for the assumption that someone like Gandhi *must* have learnt his ethics from Jesus.

Despite the antitheses which the evangelist prefaces to central injunctions in the Sermon on the Mount, these injunctions are not 'distinctively Christian'. Non-retaliation and doing good to one's enemy is an ideal often found outside early Christianity. The thoughtful study of Gordon Zerbe, while carefully differentiating between the various literary and social contexts, concludes: certain differences notwithstanding, 'the non-retaliatory ethics of the New Testament stand solidly in the tradition of the non-retaliatory ethics in early Judaism'.[71]

Nor should similarities with popular Graeco-Roman philosophy be ignored.[72] Origen mentions non-Christians (Lycurgus, Zeno) who did good to their enemies (*Contra Celsum* 8.35). Even Celsus accepts the command to turn the other cheek, but states that 'this is nothing new, and it has been better said by others, especially by Plato' (*Crito* 49B–E). According to Seneca, 'we shall never cease to work for the common good, to help all, to aid even our enemies' (*De otio* 1.4). Seneca differs from New Testament authors mainly with regard to the social context. He speaks of giving up hatred and bearing slander as a virtue of rulers or masters – people who (like Gandhi in South Africa) have the possibility to choose whether or not they will pocket insults.[73]

Epictetus the slave philosopher is socially closer to early Christians. He says that the true Cynic must 'let himself be flogged like an ass and, when beaten, love those who beat him as if he were their father and brother' (*Diss.*, 3.22.54). Epictetus' description of the Cynic reminds one of many legends about philosophers such as Socrates who are beaten because they are troubling teachers and who abstain from retaliating.[74] Basil the Great actually quotes such a story and finds that it corresponds exactly to Jesus' demand to turn the other cheek.[75] William Klassen summarizes: 'Both first-century Jews and Christians shared with their pagan counterparts a commitment to benevolence rather than violence as the best expression of the human.'[76]

It is often claimed that such correspondences are superficial; behind apparently similar teachings in philosophy and in early Christianity there are different motivations.[77] But it seems more correct to say that both share a moral tradition which is applied in different ways (there are diverse emphases even within the New Testament in these matters). Unlike the Stoics, New Testament authors are not concerned with training the unshakable character of the sage; on the other hand, the Stoics do not dwell on divine vengeance, as many parts of the New Testament do. The philosophers do display a sense of superiority over others, but then the Christians also possess an 'elitist group ethos'[78] which distinguishes them from 'Gentiles', 'tax collectors' or 'sinners' (Matt. 5.46–47; Luke 6.32–34).[79]

The second-century sermon attributed to Clement of Rome puts forward sincere self-criticism which demonstrates both the values common to Christians and others and the gap between ideals and reality (II Clem. 13.3–4): when pagans hear Christians talk about loving enemies, 'they admire this abundant goodness. But when they then see that we do not love even those who love us, not to speak of those who hate us, they laugh at us and the name of the Lord is mocked'.

Universal wisdom

It can be said that the wisdom stream of the Jesus tradition took up some of the best Jewish and Graeco-Roman moral traditions in adopting the ideals of non-retaliation and non-violence. In the Sermon on the Mount something is underlined and crystallized which was already there. There is common ground with Indian tradition as well; Gandhi did not need Jesus to become aware of the way of non-violence. The positive commands of love for enemies and praying for persecutors enhance the ideals,[80] even if the New Testament writings – the Book of Revelation in particular – also contain materials which allow to exclude one's religious and ideological adversaries outside the sphere of this command.

If exclusive eschatological and christological claims separate early Christianity from many other traditions, the wisdom material unites it with them. It is not by chance that precisely the Sermon on the Mount found its way to Gandhi's heart, or that the Golden Rule, a maxim of popular wisdom, forms the core in Hans Küng's effort to create a global ethic on the basis of what is common to different religions.[81] Eschatology may have been the more central strand in the Jesus tradition originally; but the wisdom layers (whether authentically Jesuanic or not) may turn out more helpful today.

This ties in with a point made by Sugirtharajah in the book discussed in the first chapter: 'Probably one way to initiate multi-faith hermeneutics is to retrieve the Wisdom tradition.' Its strength is that it is universal.

> The undue concentration on the distinctive features of Jesus' teaching . . . encouraged a dim view of other cultures. The bracketing of Jesus' message with that of other sages is not to minimize his importance, but to point to the creative possibilities of the commonly held universal elements in his message. These common elements should provide starting points to engage in multi-faith hermeneutics in a way that the traditional missionary view that Christians have the superior truth, does not.[82]

It goes without saying that the wisdom tradition is no magic key to global harmony. In what ways counsels of non-retaliation can be applied always depends on the particular social and political situation. Even Gandhi's vision and practice must be subjected to critical analysis; it is in some revised form that it may have a future. The same, of course, can be said of Matthew's vision.

The movement set in motion by Gandhi seemed for decades to be of no major significance in India.[83] Since then, the times have changed somewhat; one can even speak of 'the rapid spread of the politics of non-violence' in many parts of the world.[84]

Of Gandhi's foreign disciples, Martin Luther King has undoubtedly been the most important. He assimilated Gandhism with what he had learnt from the Social Gospel, from liberal Protestantism and Reinhold Niebuhr.[85] For King the Sermon on the Mount became, along with Christian *agape*, the motivating force for working for civil rights; his strategy and tactics he learnt from Gandhi. Actually King's statement that non-violent resistance 'is not a method for cowards; it does resist'[86] parallels Gandhi closer than it does the Christ of Matthew 5. In King's case, too, the appeal to the Sermon on the Mount helped to call forth a response, albeit a painfully slow one, from white Christians.[87]

One may regard the resistance practised by King as a form of *satyagraha* from which Gandhi's most striking idiosyncracies have been removed.[88] In some such revised form Gandhi's and Matthew's combined version of the universal wisdom might be able to contribute positively to the future of humankind.[89]

12

Conclusion: The Pluralist Imperative

My starting point was the new global situation and the new demands it presents for Christian thought in relation to other traditions. Our historical consciousness has changed, partly due to a new awareness of other cultural and religious traditions. In the words of Paul Knitter,

> there has been a genuinely new evolution in the 'texture' of human experience, very different from the 'context' of the New Testament and past dogmatic statements about Jesus. This texture includes a new 'historical consciousness' of the relativity of all cultures and historical achievements, a new awareness of pluralism . . . Not to understand Jesus anew in this new context . . . is to run the risk of confining the past in an idolatrous 'deposit of faith'.[1]

In this book I have approached the subject from a much more limited angle, from an exegetical point of view; but for what they are worth, my findings clearly converge with those of Knitter. It is part of our changed historical consciousness that our view of Scripture has inevitably changed – or ought to have changed.

If biblical studies are taken really seriously – which happens rarely – traditional ways of using the Bible in theology become unviable. Biblical scholarship has recognized the wide diversity of beliefs within the New Testament itself on one hand and the inherently problematic nature of many New Testament beliefs on the other. For this state of affairs alone a new approach to inter-religious dialogue is inevitable.

Inherent problems in exclusivism

Maurice Wiles frankly notes that an open inter-religious dialogue is something new in our history: it seems to be 'closer to a U-turn than to a minor deviation' within Christian tradition.[2] The 'historical conscience' of the biblical scholar which I have tried to voice in this book must support him. Historically, exclusivism has a point. If the exclusivism of the tradition, already powerfully present in the Bible, is tacitly suppressed, it cannot be dealt with adequately.

Still, Wiles suggests certain 'ways of assessing our Christian past, which may serve to moderate any sense of its monolithic opposition to an open dialogue with other religions'. He notes in particular that the old tradition itself does not stand up to the test of consistency: the God of universal love is understood to be denying to the majority of humankind any possibility of salvation. Therefore 'a radically revised understanding of other religions' cannot be 'ruled out *a priori* as liable to disrupt an otherwise fully coherent system of belief'.[3] The old system was never that coherent.

I have not dealt in this book with the particular problem of universal love as opposed to the damnation of the majority. But in several connections I have touched a no less formidable theological problem: the salvation-historical dilemma of the discontinuity of God's actions. The problem of a salvation-historical break is inherent in the basics of Christianity. The logical conclusion seems to be that God had, contrary to his own solemn declarations, changed his mind when he sent Jesus and apparently made salvation exclusively dependent on faith in him. This implies that the previous 'eternal' covenant he had established is no longer fully valid.

The New Testament speaks of God's eternal plan of salvation. But what is one to think of this plan, if Christ actually opened a *new* way of salvation which was not available to the ancients? Alternatively, if salvation *was* available before Christ, why is his significance so crucial?

Either way, we are caught in a dilemma. One has to sacrifice either the immutability of God's plan or the absolute necessity of Christ's work. Both Marcion and his critics, both the Deists and Joseph Smith, took offence at this problem and tried in different ways to overcome it. Marcion postulated two gods and thus cut the roots of salvation history. The 'orthodox' church fathers, who opposed him, resorted to an artificial usurpation of the Old Testament. At many points, Joseph Smith had to admit that Deist criticisms were justified; he ended up by projecting the full Christian salvation back into Paradise. In much, he in effect agreed with patristic solutions.

Outsiders can often help us see what we do not notice ourselves. A sympathetic assessment of the cases of Marcion and Joseph Smith may help us to see problems, logical and moral, in what became our classic tradition. Neither of the two is able to offer answers that are viable today; but each is asking genuine questions and often perceives the problems involved quite sharply.

The issue of continuity or discontinuity is justly raised in the inter-religious dialogue today.[4]

To bring Wiles' point to a head: the problems of coherence in the classic tradition are of such magnitude that they make 'absoluteness' seem impossible and strongly tip the scales in favour of some kind of religious pluralism.

No reified conception of salvation history seems plausible. On an 'objective' level it seems impossible to join an Old Testament 'covenant theology' with an exclusive christological soteriology. The one excludes the other because there cannot be two different bases for salvation in the absolute sense (cf. Ch. 2). From the conviction that there was no salvation outside Christ it would seem to follow that the old covenant was not meant seriously except as preparation for Christ. Those early Christian authors who claimed that Christians were free from biblical law could provide only troublesome answers to the question why God had given the law in the first place.[5] The problematic nature of these answers should prevent a Christian theologian today from absolutizing his or her own christological tradition. That so few Jews in the course of history have been persuaded by these answers should not surprise us.

The diversity of the New Testament

Nor are the claims to absoluteness strengthened when we contemplate the nature of the New Testament in general in the light of two centuries of critical research.

The New Testament is a book filled with strong tensions, many of them by no means peripheral. There are different expectations of the future and different notions of salvation. For some parts of the New Testament Jesus' death, interpreted in vicarious terms, is an indispensable part of God's plan for human salvation; to others, it is the typical fate of a prophet brought about by men's iniquity, but not invested with soteriological significance.[6] There are different perceptions of the person and work of Christ. Some regard his divine sonship as based on the raising by God of the man Jesus from the dead, others on his eternal pre-existence.

Ernst Käsemann's dictum that 'the New Testament canon does not, as such, constitute the foundation of the unity of the church', but 'the basis for the multiplicity of the confessions'[7] is explicitly endorsed by a scholar no more radical than James Dunn,[8] though the latter pays lip service to unity by never using the word 'contra-diction' (only 'diversity'). Of course there are also constant features (many of which, like monotheism, are not 'distinctively Christian'), but they are not very impressive. Thus, what Dunn finds to be the unifying factor between all the different writings and strands is the conviction of the 'unity between the historical Jesus and the exalted Christ' – a thin and elusive bond and more-over hardly in harmony with Dunn's own findings. For his claim that the 'adoptionist' christology of the early Jerusalem church is 'ultimately one and the same' as John's incarnational theology stretches the reader's imagination to breaking-point: to hold that Jesus received his high status after his death is different from the belief that it was his from all eternity.[9]

Therefore, Islam with its monotheist, anti-trinitarian 'christo-logy' can justly be called a reminder of Christians' own past (cf. Ch. 6). Conservative Jewish Christianity seems to form the historical link between Christianity and Islam; and on Dunn's own showing, Jewish Christianity best retained the religious and theo-logical outlook of the earliest community in Jerusalem, its only 'fault' being that it remained too conservative and refused to change![10]

It must be said that the New Testament lacks that uniqueness on which some generations of biblical scholars used to put a lot of stress. A 'pluralist imperative' would seem to follow. Alan Race correctly notes: 'Some form of pluralism in the Christian theology of religions is inevitable . . . if historical studies are treated seriously.'[11]

In the words of Gerd Theissen, historical-critical scholarship shows

> how the religious traditions of mankind are all connected together historically. Christianity was the development of a Jewish heresy, and Judaism was a supreme example of Near Eastern religion. In other words, whereas every historical phenomenon is indeed unique . . . none is ever to be found in complete isolation.
>
> In short, historical criticism shows that religious traditions are very earthly, very relative and very questionable.

Theissen rightly deems this 'an irreversible insight'.[12]

Theissen correctly speaks of 'traditions' in the plural. Others may help us see problems inherent in our tradition, but critical communication is a two-way traffic. Christian scholars can in turn address critical questions to other traditions. Marcion's outspoken criticism of the Hebrew Bible was not born out of nothing; there *are* problems in central strands of the Old Testament which should trouble even Jewish believers.

A moderately critical attitude to one's own scripture is, of course, just as much part of today's Judaism as it is of modern Christianity. Not so in Islam. In all fairness the question can be raised (cf. Ch. 8) whether Muslims might not, and should not, some day be able to adopt a more historical attitude to their Book and whether this might not be beneficial for them – and for the world. Biblical scholars have been encouraged by the discovery of the original diversity of Scripture to speak for greater openness towards pluralism in the present as well; something similar might ensue from wrestling with the issue of 'abrogation' within the Qur'an.[13] After all, in the eyes of a detached observer, a God who constantly (literally in hundreds of cases) cancels what he has just revealed seems no less odd than a God who goes back on his eternal covenants. A reified conception of revelation should cause problems even to Muslim believers.

Moral problems of exclusivism

That some of the darkest sides of the influence of the Bible on human relations are linked with quite central points of traditional Christian faith does set one thinking. The very notion of the absoluteness of Christ has contributed to the annihilation of those who disagreed, trusting their own traditions. 'If my faith is universal in its claim, then woe unto those who do not see the world as I do.'[14]

In antiquity, the rise of Christianity induced a rise in religious intolerance and the open coercion of religious belief. 'The assumption of Christian superiority' has had destructive effects on relations between European and North American Christians and black and brown peoples. In the eighteenth and nineteenth centuries 'the conviction of the decisive superiority of Christianity infused the imperial expansion of the West with a powerful moral impetus and an effective religious validation without which the enterprise might well not have been psychologically viable'. And of course there is a clear connection between centuries of the 'absoluteness' of Christianity, 'with its corollary of the radical inferiority and perverseness of the Judaism it "superseded", and the consequent endemic anti-Semitism of Christian civilization'.[15] Judaism itself is not quite innocent either. The late Deuteronomic attitude to neighbours is not just ancient history, as the events in the modern state of Israel have shown.

The tree is known by its fruits, we are taught. Marcion applied this principle to the Old Testament and its god. Modern scholars must apply it to the Bible and to other scriptures. The New Testament in its canonical status can be just as dangerous as the Old. The example of Marcion and Harnack reminds us of the urgency of moral criticism of Scripture (Ch. 5). Muslim scholars might be invited to take some steps in a similar direction in their home field too.

Tradition – experience – interpretation

Biblical criticism cannot prescribe what one should think or how one should behave. But it might be able to provide a sort of formal model for theology, including the dialogical enterprise. It shows that the formation of biblical (or any other) tradition can be viewed as a process of interaction between tradition, experience and reinterpretation. The biblical thought world developed in a process in which traditions were time and again interpreted in the light of new experiences, mostly social experiences, and *vice versa*: experiences were interpreted in the light of traditions.[16]

The emphasis can be put on different sides in this process: one can stress the role of the tradition which determines every experience or, conversely, the significance of new experiences which lead to changes in the tradition. When a more peaceful stage of a religion is studied, the main emphasis may lie on the tradition which guides the life and thought of its adherents. But when a time of upheaval is in focus, such as the Exile or the rise of Christianity (or of Buddhism, or of Islam), more emphasis must necessarily be put on the experiences which lead to major reinterpretations of the tradition and to the rise of new traditions.

The process of interpreting one's tradition in the light of one's new situation and experience is, of course, universal. The portraits of Jesus and other divine messengers in the Qur'an consistently reflect Muhammad's own experience and situation (Ch. 6). The visions of modern Muslim thinkers (e.g. An-Na'im) of a reformed Shariah can likewise be assessed as impressive examples of the dialectic of tradition, experience and interpretation (Ch. 8). La Peyrère tried to cope with the new intellectual situation created by the voyages of discovery (Ch. 9). Gandhi drew on both familiar (Hindu) and alien (Christian) tradition in trying to cope with his apartheid experiences in South Africa; this led to a powerful vision and an effective programme (Ch. 11).

Stress on the new situation

The process in question has always been going on: before, in and after the Bible. Of course people have not always been conscious of it; they have pretended simply to interpret the Bible when they have in fact been presenting a strong reinterpretation. For Christianity has always been 'adapting itself to something that can be believed' (T.S. Eliot). Knitter notes that 'to propose a *new* understanding of the gospel and Christian tradition is not a novelty . . . Christianity has always been profoundly dependent on the ever changing contexts of history.'[17]

A striking example is the perception of Christianity as a religion of love, which today is almost self-evident to so many people. Langdon Gilkey reminds us that not so long ago, 'defending the faith' for the greater glory of God was regarded 'as an unquestionable Christian demand, one that clearly outranked the obligation to love the other'; John Calvin's attitude to Miguel Servetus is a case in point. 'In the modern period . . . this dominance of faith over love shifted . . .'[18]

It would not be difficult to list biblical examples of the transforming impact of new experiences on the tradition. As a graphic illustration the story of Peter in the house of Cornelius (Acts 10.1– 11.18) can be cited. There a series of new experiences (in this case, ecstatic experiences: a vision, an experience of glossolalia) leads to a new interpretation of God's will concerning the relation of Jews to Gentiles. This experience, along with the interpretation given to it, then leads to a new practice: the abandonment of circumcision as a rite of entrance into the community of the righteous. This may not be a long step in the direction of true pluralism or universalism – it is concerned with the group's relation to those 'others' who show sympathy towards it anyway. But it is a step all right, and a radical one in the circumstances. Indeed this step initiated a series of events which finally led to the emergence of a new religion.

It is a logical continuation of the process thus initiated if Christians – and others – engage in conscious reinterpretation of their traditions in the light of their present experience.

The word 'conscious' is crucial. Surely Marcion is not to be followed in his attempt to purge the New Testament by way of a fictitious reconstruction of its original message. Nor can we adopt without modifications the analogous attempts to restore an unblemished past by, say, Muhammad (Ch. 6), Joseph Smith (Ch. 10), or Abdullahi Ahmad An-Na'im (who calls for a return to the older parts of the Qur'an, Ch. 8), or by the nineteenth-century spokesmen of the quest of the historical Jesus. We have to go the more difficult way of coming to terms with our canon as it is, with all the fruits it has borne. We have to be critical and consciously selective. For our enterprise takes place in a situation in which our historical consciousness has changed: we must be conscious of taking *new* steps, resorting to *new* interpretations. We know that we are not just restoring something that existed in the tradition all along.

Theology could be understood as an attempt to make sense of our experience of reality with the aid of our tradition (which includes a strong religious, partly biblical element) as the starting-point, and as making sense of our tradition in the light of our interpreted experience of reality. This kind of theology does not presuppose any predetermined results.[19]

Reading selectively: Matthew 25

What a selective reinterpretation of biblical texts might involve may be clarified in a discussion with Francis Watson's fresh attempt to 'liberate the reader' to an exegetical practice with an open 'orientation towards the political-theological task'. We are coming full circle here, for we started in the first chapter with a discussion of the demand that biblical scholars adopt a practice which aims at transforming the world. Discussing the parable of the sheep and the goats (Matt. 25.31–46), Watson records a striking difference between the treatment of this text in liberation theology and in historical exegesis. Liberation theology finds in the text the demand of universal love of one's neighbour; the 'least brothers' of Jesus denote any poor and oppressed people in the world. By contrast, historical exegesis tends to identify these least brothers with Christian missionaries (as in Matt. 10.42 – whoever gives a cup of water 'to one of these little ones', which in this context clearly means the messengers sent by Jesus). But read in this way the text of Matt. 25 becomes, in Watson's words, 'theo-logically worthless'.[20]

Watson writes, with explicit reference to my choice of phrase:

In its self-appointed role as historical conscience exegesis informs theology that the real meaning of the parable . . . is more or less the opposite of what it [theology] had supposed: the allegedly universal criterion turns out to be thoroughly particularist.[21]

Actually, the particularist reading is not at all an invention of historical critics. Down to our time, it has *always* predominated in the history of interpretation; it is only in the twentieth century that the universal interpretation of the least brothers has become common.[22]

More to the point, however, it is not my view that 'original' meaning necessarily equals 'real' meaning. I do not think that exegetes should act as new popes who determine which application or *use* of a text is right or wrong. Watson is quite correct in stating that in so far as the historical (particularist) reading attempts to exclude the theological (universalist) one 'by representing itself as what the text "really" means, it oversteps the limits of its own competence'.[23] Historical critics have tried to make sense of the parable in the framework of Matthew's Gospel; in that overall context, a tension between universalist and particularist-confessional elements is unavoidable.

Watson tries, according to his own description, to 'practise the theological and the exegetical tasks simultaneously'.[24] He makes 'eclectic use of a number of the hermeneutical and exegetical strategies currently available';[25] for instance, he stresses the freedom 'to actualize certain potential connections and not others, the freedom to emphasize and de-emphasize in accordance with one's own criteria of relevance',[26] i.e. with ethical criteria.[27] But Watson properly characterizes this task as 'a theological appropriation of a text'.[28] I have no quarrel with this, as long as the meaning so discovered is not called 'the real' meaning of the text (and from this Watson refrains). While it is very hard to tell exactly when an application becomes artificial, I would certainly not regard a 'universalist' interpretation of the 'least brothers' in Matthew 25 as 'overly strained'.

Watson, however, is *using* the text, appropriating it for a purpose (a very worth-while purpose for that matter), not trying to understand it (historically). These are, I insist, two different tasks, both legitimate. And I still wonder whether it is wise to fuse them together consciously.

Reading against the grain

A comparable tension can be detected in Luke's work. David Seeley has argued that there is a sense in which Jesus seems unnecessary in Lukan soteriology, in which salvation is 'by generosity'.[29] 'Sell your possessions and give alms' and you will have a treasure in heaven (Luke 12.33); invite to dinner the poor and sick who cannot repay you, and 'you will be repaid at the resurrection of the just' (14.12–14). The story of Zacchaeus is 'perhaps the clearest example of Luke making salvation dependent on generosity'[30] – Zacchaeus promises to give half of his goods to the poor and to restore fourfold if he has 'defrauded any one of anything'; Jesus replies: 'Today salvation has come to this house . . .' (Luke 19.8–9). And of course there is the parable of the Good Samaritan where 'the obvious implication' is that if one wants to reach eternal life (Luke 10.25), 'one should love God and act like the Samaritan, i.e., with unbounded generosity'.[31]

It would seem that Jesus is not necessary; 'presumably, anyone could have preached about generosity'.[32]

The story of the rich man and Lazarus in Luke 16 reveals that 'Moses and the prophets contain everything people need to know'. The messages of Moses and the prophets and of Jesus are 'essentially the same. Rejection of the first is tantamount to rejecting the second . . .'[33]

Seeley asks, 'Why would Luke come so close to admitting that there was no effective need for what Jesus said?' Answer: because of 'his eagerness to affirm . . . the fundamental unity of Judaism and Christianity . . . Unfortunately for Luke, he overdid things, and left the impression that this unity was so complete as to render Jesus expendable.'[34]

In Chapter 1, I noted a similar contradiction between christological exclusivism and a tendency toward openness to others (in that case, towards Gentiles) in the Areopagus speech (Acts 17). I concluded that this prevents us from regarding Luke as a truly 'inclusivist' theologian. But from another angle we might see Luke as seriously wrestling with the problem of pluralism and exclusivism. Somehow he seems to sense the problematic nature of his own exclusivist standpoint. He is – fortunately – not able simply to brush aside the considerations dictated by universal morality. A kind of incipient universalism does get the opportunity to enter through the back door. I think that this is a case of genuine ambiguity (rather than conscious inclusivism).

The tension exists in Luke's tradition already. Some of the tension can be found even in Paul who, for all his christocentrism, can occasionally argue that salvation is by deeds (Romans 2).[35] We may exploit this kind of tension creatively in our struggle for dialogue. Indeed, if I am on the right track in my reading of Romans 9–11, it is Paul's struggle, his wrestling with his tradition in the light of his new experiences, that might be seen as a model for us, as his weightiest contribution to contemporary struggles (Ch. 2). But we should not forget that in seizing on the tensions we are not reproducing *the* 'New Testament message'. We are selecting, re-emphasizing, deciding anew which elements are important and which are not, often reading texts against the grain.

The relevance of wisdom

Such an enterprise of a selective reading could, for example, mean a new positive emphasis on the wisdom tradition. In the Old Testament, this tradition represents a universalist current markedly different from the exclusive stand of the Deuteronomic history. As John Eaton puts it,

> it is a striking fact that the fundamental tradition of Old Testament wisdom did not speak of the peculiar national forms of religion but of universal values. It was discourse in which the sages of other lands could readily join.[36]

According to Eaton,

> the universality of the old wisdom tradition retains its value, and the ecumenical task appropriate to our time can be encouraged

by the figure of primal Wisdom. Her delight is with the whole race. Her address is to all peoples . . .[37]

Here is no 'thus says the Lord' or even 'thus said Moses'. The characteristic appeal of Wisdom is to experience: taste and see! Go and watch the ant! Look upon the rainbow![38]

We saw in the last chapter that while exclusive eschatological and christological claims separate early Christianity from many other traditions, the wisdom material unites it with them. We also noted that the wisdom strand of the Jesus tradition took up some of the best Jewish and Graeco-Roman moral traditions. In the Sermon on the Mount, with its stress on non-violence and non-retaliation, something is beautifully crystallized which was already in existence.

An impressive early example of keeping the different tasks of historical understanding and contemporizing application apart was provided a century ago by Johannes Weiss. He realized that the kingdom of God as proclaimed by Jesus (a supernatural, though earthly future reality) was quite different from the 'kingdom' as interpreted by Albrecht Ritschl and his followers. The Ritschlians regarded the kingdom as a community of morally acting people. This did not correspond to Jesus' thoughts; still, Weiss found the Ritschlian notion theologically helpful. One might say that Weiss opted for a personal theology which came much closer to a wisdom than an eschatological interpretation of Jesus' teaching.[39] The point is that he knew what he was doing in using the concept of the kingdom in a different sense from that in which it had been used in the beginning. Although he clearly perceived the centrality of eschatology both in the message of Jesus and in the life of early Christianity in general, he himself took only the *non*-eschatological part of the message to be of lasting religious value. This is what I mean by 'historical conscience': we are free to reinterpret, but we should know and acknowledge what we are doing.

I am reminded of the nice apocryphal story about Jesus when he saw a man working in the field on a Sabbath. Jesus said to him: 'Man, if you know what you are doing, you are blessed. But if you do not know, you are cursed and a transgressor of the Law' (Luke 6.5 D).

There should be no pressure necessarily to agree with this or that biblical strand; one should in fact feel free to decide against all biblical options, if need be. A modern attitude to the New Testament might perhaps resemble the attitude taken by someone like Paul towards the Old Testament – with the significant difference that the radical re-application of scripture should be done consciously, not in a hidden or pre-critical manner. We might then take the New Testament in a radically typological sense: we use its words and symbols, but we use them as fore-shadowings of something new which is demanded by our very different situation.

In the process of selective and conscious reinterpretation biblical ideas and concepts may well turn into 'symbols' (which is a more elusive notion). 'Kingdom of God', 'resurrection', 'redemption', 'Christ', even 'God' may be thoroughly problematic as concepts or ideas, but they may still serve as evocative and challenging symbols. Symbols, values and stories can be freely moulded and used by people in the light of their experience and their sense of reality and responsibility. Reflecting on the history of the doctrine of incarnation, Maurice Wiles comments:

> If what held Christians together were seen as the use of the same myths rather than the holding of the same beliefs, it might be easier for Christians to accept the measure of variety that there both should and will be between them.[40]

'Love language'

The experience-reinterpretation-model allows everybody to start where he or she stands, working with her or his own tradition. Exclusive statements may 'have no meaning outside the community of faith', but they 'continue to be valid [or should we simply say 'meaningful'?] for those of us who belong to that tradition or confession'.[41] In Krister Stendahl's famous phrase, the language of a religious confession such as Acts 4.12 ('there is no other name . . .') should really be taken (by us) 'as love language, as caressing language'; as a confession, not as a proposition.[42]

John Hick, consistently questioning the absoluteness of
Christianity as a consequence of his non-literal christology,[43] asks
the question that is bound to arise in the mind of many Christians.
Why then should one be a Christian, rather than a Muslim or a
Jew, or indeed a Buddhist or a Hindu? He answers that

> for one who has been born into Christianity, or into a culture in
> which Christianity was the only religious option effectively
> presented to one, and who has been spiritually formed largely
> by the influences of the Christian tradition, Christianity will
> normally provide the best framework for one's relationship to
> God.[44]

Analogous questions could be raised – and analogous answers
given – from the viewpoint of other traditions.

This, then, is the challenge: can we admit pluralism on the
one hand and commit ourselves to wrestling with one particular
tradition on the other? The task would then be to make sense of
the tradition of our love, trying to reform it in the light of other
traditions and of our experience, and in the light of the fruit it has
borne so far. Could it not be the ultimate goal of the dialogue that
Christians should become better – more humane – Christians,
Muslims better Muslims, Hindus better Hindus, humanists better
humanists, and so on? And should not each try to help the other to
reach this goal?

Bibliography

(For the abbreviations see S. Schwertner, *International Glossary of Abbreviations for Theology and Related Subjects*, Berlin and New York 1974.)

Adams, C.J., 1987: 'Qur'an', in Eliade (ed.) 12, 156–76

Åkerman, S., 1988: 'Queen Christina of Sweden and Messianic Thought', in D.S. Katz and J.I. Israel (ed.), *Sceptics, Millenarians and Jews. In Honour of R.H. Popkin*, Brill's Studies in Intellectual History 17, Leiden, 142–60

Aland, B., 1973: 'Marcion. Versuch einer neuen Interpretation', *ZThK* 70, 420–47

—, 1992: 'Marcion (ca. 85–160)/ Marcioniten', *TRE* 22, 89–101

Al-Ashmawy, M.S., 1989: *L'islamisme contre l'islam*, Paris

Al-Husayni, I.M., 1960: 'Christ in the Qur'an and in Modern Arabic Literature', *MW* 50, 297–302

Allen, D.C., 1963: *The Legend of Noah*, Urbana (reprint)

An-Na'im, A.A., 1990: *Toward an Islamic Reformation. Civil Liberties, Human Rights, and International Law*, Syracuse, NY

Antes, P., 1981: 'Schriftverständnis im Islam', *ThQ* 161, 179–91

Arberry, A.J., 1986: *The Koran Interpreted*, Oxford (reprint)

Ariarajah, W., 1985: *The Bible and People of Other Faiths*, Geneva

Arkoun, M., 1982: *Lectures du Coran*, Islam d'hier et d'aujourd'hui 17, Paris

Armstrong, K., 1994: *A History of God. From Abraham to the Present: The 4000-year Quest for God*, London

Ateek, N.S., 1991: 'A Palestinian Perspective: Biblical Perspectives on the Land', in Sugirtharajah (ed.) 1991, 267–76

Aula, O., 1967: *Gandhi ja väkivallattoman vastarinnan peruskuviot*, Porvoo and Helsinki 1967

Ayoub, M.M., 1980: 'Towards an Islamic Christology, II: The Death of Jesus, Reality or Delusion. A Study of the Death of Jesus in

Tafsir Literature', *MW* 70, 91–121

—, 1989: 'Roots of Muslim-Christian Conflict', *MW* 79, 25–45

Baird, W.B., 1992: *History of New Testament Research 1. From Deism to Tübingen*, Minneapolis

Balic, S., 1987: 'Jesus Christus 3. Islamisch', in A.T. Khoury (ed.), *Lexikon religiöser Grundbegriffe: Judentum, Christentum, Islam*, Graz, Vienna and Cologne

Baljon, J.M.S., 1968: *Modern Muslim Koran Interpretation (1880–1960)*, Leiden

Barlow, P.L., 1991: *Mormons and the Bible. The Place of Latter-day Saints in American Religion*, New York and Oxford

Barr, J., 1971: 'The Old Testament and the New Crisis of Biblical Authority', *Interpretation* 25, 24–40

—, 1977: *Fundamentalism*, London

Barrett, C.K., 1973 (1957): *A Commentary on the Epistle to the Romans*, BNTC, London

—, 1982: *Essays on Paul*, London

Barth, G., 1980: 'Bergpredigt I: Im Neuen Testament', *TRE* V, 611–15

Bauckham, R., 1993: *The Climax of Prophecy. Studies on the Book of Revelation*, Edinburgh

Bauer, W., 1967: *Aufsätze und kleine Schriften*, Tübingen

Baum, G., 1979: 'Catholic Dogma After Auschwitz', in A.T. Davies (ed.), 137–50

Beck, N., 1985: *Mature Christianity. The Recognition and Repudiation of the Anti-Jewish Polemic of the New Testament*, Selingsgrove, PA

Beker, J.C., 1980: *Paul the Apostle. The Triumph of God in Life and Thought*, Philadelphia

Bell, R., 1960: *The Qur'an translated, with a critical rearrangement of the Surahs*, Edinburgh

Benz, E., 1978: '*Imago Dei*: Man in the Image of God', in Madsen (ed.), 201–21

Berner, U., 1985: *Die Bergpredigt: Rezeption und Auslegung im 20. Jahrhundert*, Göttingen, third edition

Blackman, E.C., 1948: *Marcion and his Influence*, London

Blumenkranz, B., 1968: 'Patristik und Frühmittelalter', in Rengstorf and von Kortzfleisch (ed.), 84–135

Bondurant, J.V., 1965: *Conquest of Violence: The Gandhian Philosophy of Conflict*, Berkeley (revised edition)

Boone, K.C., 1990: *The Bible Tells Them So. The Discourse of Protestant Fundamentalism*, Albany, NY and London

Borman, W., 1986: *Gandhi and Non-Violence*, Albany, NY

Borowsky, I.J., 1995: 'An Historic Bible Translation', *Explorations* 9:3, 1–2

Boullata, I.J., 1990: *Trends and Issues in Contemporary Arab Thought*, Albany, NY

Bouman, J., 1980: *Das Wort vom Kreuz und das Bekenntnis zu Allah. Die Grundlehren des Korans als nachbiblische Religion*, Frankfurt am Main

Bovon, F., 1983: 'Israel, die Kirche und die Völker im lukanischen Doppelwerk', *ThLZ* 108, 403–14

Bowden, J., 1988: *Jesus: The Unanswered Questions*, London and Nashville

Brandon, S.G.F., 1962: *Man and His Destiny in the Great Religions. An historical and comparative study containing the Wilde lectures 1954–1957*, Manchester

Braun, R., 1990–91: *Tertullien. Contra Marcionem 1–2*, SChr 365, 368, Paris

Bright, J., 1967: *The Authority of the Old Testament*, Nashville and London

Broer, I., 1993: 'Zur Wirkungsgeschichte des Talio-Verbots in der Alten Kirche', *Biblische Notizen* 66, 23–31

Brown, J.M., 1972: *Gandhi's Rise to Power. Indian Politics 1915–1922*, Cambridge

—, 1977: *Gandhi and Civil Disobedience. The Mahatma in Indian Politics 1928–34*, Cambridge

—, 1990: *Gandhi. Prisoner of Hope*, Delhi

Brown, P., 1967: *Augustine of Hippo. A Biography*, Berkeley, Los Angeles and London

Brown, R.E., 1977: *The Birth of the Messiah: A Commentary on the Infancy Narratives in Matthew and Luke*, New York and London

—, 1983: 'Rome', in R.E. Brown and J.P. Meier, *Antioch and Rome: New Testament Cradles of Catholic Christianity*, London, 87–216

Brox, N., 1979: *Der erste Petrusbrief*, EKK 21, Zürich, etc.

Brunt, J.C., 1985: 'Rejected, Ignored, or Misunderstood? The Fate of

Paul's Approach to the Problem of Food Offered to Idols in Early Christianity', *NTS* 31, 113–24

Bucaille, M., n.d. (first French ed. 1976): *The Bible, the Qur'an and Science. The Holy Scriptures Examined in the Light of Modern Knowledge*, Paris

Bultmann, R., 1951–1955: *Theology of the New Testament 1–2*, New York and London

von Campenhausen, H., 1984: *The Formation of the Christian Bible*, Philadelphia and London (second edition)

Carroll, J.T., 1988: *Response to the End of History. Eschatology and Situation in Luke-Acts*, SBLDS 92, Atlanta

Carroll, R.P., 1991: *Wolf in the Sheepfold. The Bible as a Problem for Christianity*, London and Philadelphia

Casey, P.M., 1991: *From Jewish Prophet to Gentile God. The Origins and Development of New Testament Christology*, Cambridge

Chadwick, H., 1967: *The Early Church*, Harmondsworth

Charlesworth, J.H., 1978: 'Messianism in the Pseudepigrapha and the Book of Mormon', in Madsen (ed.), 99–137

Chatterjee, M., 1983: *Gandhi's Religious Thought*, London

Collins, A.Y., 1986: 'Vilification and Self-Definition in the Book of Revelation', *HThR* 79, 308–20

—, 1989: 'Persecution and Vengeance in the Book of Revelation', in D.Hellholm (ed.), *Apocalypticism in the Mediterranean World and the Near East*, Tübingen, 729–49 (second edition)

Colpe, C., 1987: 'Jesus und die Besiegelung der Prophetie', *Berliner Theologische Zeitschrift* 4, 2–18

Conybeare, F.C., 1958 (1909): *The Origins of Christianity*, Evanston and New York

Conzelmann, H., 1960: *The Theology of St Luke*, London

Cook, M.J., 1988: 'The Mission to the Jews in Acts: Unraveling Luke's "Myth of the Myriads"', in Tyson (ed.), 102–23

Cope, L., 1990: 'First Corinthians 8–10: Continuity or Contradiction?', in A.J. Hultgren and B. Hall (ed.), *Christ and His Communities. In Honour of R.H. Fuller*, AThR Suppl. Series 11, Evanston, 114–23

Cracknell, K., 1986: *Towards a New Relationship. Christians and People of Other Faith*, London

Cragg, K., 1956: *The Call of the Minaret*, London and New York

Cranfield, C.E.B., 1975: *A Critical and Exegetical Commentary on the Epistle to the Romans 1*, Edinburgh

Cullmann, O., 1967: *Salvation in History*, London and New York

Davies, A.T., 1979 (ed.): *Antisemitism and the Foundations of Christianity*, New York

Davies, W.D., 1978: 'Israel, the Mormons and the Land', in Madsen (ed.), 79–97

Denny, F.M., 1989: 'Fazlur Rahman: Muslim Intellectual', *MW* 79, 91–101

—, 1994: 'Islamic Theology in the New World. Some Issues and Prospects', *JAAR* 62, 1069–84

Devaraja, N.K., 1969: *Hinduism and Christianity*, London

Dibelius, M., 1956: *Studies in the Acts of Apostles*, London

Dillenberger, J., 1978: 'Grace and Works in Martin Luther and Joseph Smith', in Madsen (ed.), 175–86

Dodd, C.H., 1947 (1932): *The Epistle of Paul to the Romans*, MNTC, London

Douglas, R.C., 1995: '"Love Your Enemies." Rhetoric, Tradents, and Ethos', in J.S. Kloppenborg (ed.), *Conflict and Invention. Literary, Rhetorical, and Social Studies on the Sayings Gospel Q*, Valley Forge, Pa., 116–31

Drane, J.W., 1975: *Paul, Libertine or Legalist? A Study in the Theology of the Major Pauline Epistles*, London

Driver, T.F., 1988: 'The Case for Pluralism', in Hick and Knitter (ed.), 203–18

Dunn, J.D.G., 1988: *Romans 9–16*, Word Biblical Commentary 38B, Dallas

—, 1990: *Unity and Diversity in the New Testament*, London (second edition)

—, 1991: *The Partings of the Ways Between Christianity and Judaism and their Significance for the Character of Christianity*, London

Eaton, J., 1989: *The Contemplative Face of Old Testament Wisdom in the Context of World Religions*, London

Eckert, W., 1968: 'Hoch- und Spätmittelalter. Katholischer Humanismus', in Rengstorf and von Kortzfleisch (ed.), 210–306

Edwardes, M., 1986: *The Myth of the Mahatma. Gandhi, the British and the Raj*, London

Efroymson, D.P., 1979: 'The Patristic Connection', in A.T. Davies (ed.), 98–117

Ehrhardt, A., 1964: *The Framework of the New Testament Stories*, Manchester

Eickelman, D.F., 1993: 'Islamic Liberalism Strikes Back', *The Middle East Studies Association Bulletin* 27, 163–8

Eliade, M. (ed.), 1987: *Encyclopedia of Religion*, New York and London

Eltester, W., 1972: 'Israel im lukanischen Werk und die Nazareth-perikope', in E.Grässer et al., *Jesus in Nazareth*, BZNW 40, Berlin, 76–147

Esler, P.F., 1987: *Community and Gospel in Luke-Acts. The Social and Political Motivations of Lucan Theology*, MSSNTS 57, Cambridge

Evans, C.F., 1990: *Saint Luke*, TPI New Testament Commentaries, London and Philadelphia

Evans, E., 1972 (ed.) : *Tertullian, Adversus Marcionem*, OECT, Oxford

Fiedler, P., 1990: '"Das Israel Gottes" im Neuen Testament – die Kirche oder das jüdische Volk?', in: H.Frohnhofen (ed.), *Christlicher Antijudaismus und jüdischer Antipaganismus. Ihre Motive und Hintergründe in den ersten drei Jahrhunderten*, Hamburger Theologische Studien 3, Hamburg, 64–87

Fiorenza, E.Schüssler, 1993: *Revelation. Vision of a Just World*, Edinburgh

Fischer, K.M., 1985: *Das Urchristentum*, Berlin

Fitzmyer, J.A., 1981, 1985: *The Gospel According to Luke*, AncB 28 A, New York

Fornberg, T., 1995: 'The Bible and the Many Faiths: Harmony or Conflict?', in id. (ed.), *Bible, Hermeneutics, Mission. A Contribution to the Contextual Study of Holy Scripture*, Uppsala, 131–48

—, and Hellholm, D. (ed.), 1995: *Texts and Contexts. Biblical Texts in Their Textual and Situational Contexts. In Honour of L. Hartman*, Oslo etc.

Frank, G., 1865: *Geschichte der protestantischen Theologie* 2, Leipzig

Fredouille, J.-C., 1981: 'Götzendienst', *RAC* 11, 828–95

Fredriksen, P., 1988: *From Jesus to Christ. The Origins of the New Testament Images of Jesus*, New Haven

Friedrich, M., 1988: *Zwischen Abwehr und Bekehrung. Die Stellung der deutschen evangelischen Theologie zum Judentum im 17.Jahrhundert*, BHTh 72, Tübingen

Fyzee, A.A.A., 1963: *A Modern Approach to Islam*, Bombay

Gager, J.G., 1983: *The Origins of Anti-Semitism. Attitudes Toward Judaism in Pagan and Christian Antiquity*, New York and Oxford

Gandhi, M.K., 1982: *An Autobiography or The Story of My Experiments With the Truth*, Harmondsworth (reprint)

—, 1986–87: *The Moral and Political Writings of Mahatma Gandhi*, ed. R. Iyer, Oxford

Gaston, L., 1986: 'Anti-Judaism and the Passion Narrative in Luke and Acts', in P. Richardson and D. Granskou (ed.), *Anti-Judaism in Early Christianity 1: Paul and the Gospels*, Studies in Christianity and Judaism 2, Waterloo, 127–53

—, 1987: *Paul and the Torah*, Vancouver

Gätje, H., 1976: *The Qur'an and its Exegesis: Selected Texts with Classical and Modern Muslim Interpretation*, London

George, A., 1968: 'Israël dans l'oeuvre de Luc', *RB* 75, 481–525

Gilkey, L., 1988: 'Plurality and Its Theological Implications', in Hick and Knitter (ed.), 37–50

Glassé, C., 1989: *The Concise Encyclopaedia of Islam*, London

Gnilka, J., 1986: *Das Matthäusevangelium* I, Freiburg, Basel and Vienna

Goldziher, I., 1963 (1925), *Vorlesungen über den Islam*, Heidelberg (second edition)

Gould, J.W., 1989: 'Gandhi's Relevance Today', in Hick and Hempel (ed.), 7–17

Grimme, H., 1895: *Mohammed II. Einleitung in den Koran; System der koranischen Theologie*, Münster

Guthrie, D., 1981: *New Testament Theology*, Leicester

Haenchen, E., 1974: *The Acts of the Apostles*, Oxford and Philadelphia

Hall, S.G., III, 1993: *Christian Anti-Semitism and Paul's Theology*, Minneapolis

Hanson, R.P.C., 1985: *Studies in Christian Antiquity*, Edinburgh

Harnack, A. von, 1985 (1921): *Marcion: Das Evangelium vom fremden Gott. Eine Monographie zur Grundlegung der katholischen Kirche. Neue Studien zu Marcion*, Darmstadt

Harrison, R.K., 1970: *Introduction to the Old Testament*, London

Harvey, A.E., 1990: *Strenuous Commands. The Ethic of Jesus*, London

Hayes, J.H., and Prussner, F.C., 1985: *Old Testament Theology. Its History and Development*, Philadelphia and London

Hecht, R.H., 1987: 'Philo and Messiah', in J. Neusner et al. (ed.), *Judaisms and Their Messiahs at the Turn of the Christian Era*, Cambridge, 139–68

Heiler, F., 1926: *Christlicher Glaube und indisches Geistesleben*, Munich

—, 1961: *Erscheinungsform und Wesen der Religion*, RM 1, Stuttgart

Hendriksen, W., 1982: *New Testament Commentary. Exposition of the Gospel according to Matthew*, Grand Rapids

Henninger, J., 1945: 'Spuren christlicher Glaubenswahrheiten im Koran', *NZMW* 1, 135–40, 304–14

Hick, J., 1977: 'Jesus and the World Religions', in id., (ed.), *The Myth of God Incarnate*, London and Philadephia, 167–85

—, 1983: Foreword to M.Chatterjee, *Gandhi's Religious Thought*, London, ix–xii

—, 1988: 'The Non-Absoluteness of Christianity', in Hick and Knitter (ed.), 16–36

—, 1989: 'Trinity, Incarnation and Religious Pluralism', in id. and E.S. Meltzer (ed.), *Three Faiths – One God: A Jewish, Christian, Muslim Encounter*, London, 197–210

—, 1995: *The Rainbow of Faiths. Critical Dialogues on Religious Pluralism*, London and Louisville

—, and Hempel, L.C. (ed.), 1989: *Gandhi's Significance Today*, London

—, and Knitter, P.F. (ed.), 1988: *The Myth of Christian Uniqueness*, Maryknoll, NY and London

Hill, C., 1994: *The English Bible and the Seventeenth-Century Revolution*, London

Hoffmann, R. J., 1984: *Marcion: On the Restitution of Christianity. An Essay on the Development of Radical Paulinist Theology in the Second Century*, AAR Academy Series 46, Chico

Holmquist, H., 1907: *Gamla kyrkans historia till sjunde århundradets början*, Stockholm

Höpfl, H., 1985: *The Christian Polity of John Calvin*, Cambridge (reprint)

Horsley, R.A., 1987: *Jesus and the Spiral of Violence. Popular Jewish Resistance in Roman Palestine*, San Francisco

Hübner, H., 1984: *Gottes Ich und Israel. Zum Schriftgebrauch des*

Paulus in Römer 9–11, Göttingen

Hullinger, R.N., 1980: *Mormon Answer to Scepticism. Why Joseph Smith Wrote the Book of Mormon*, St Louis

Hurtado, L.W., 1988: *One God, One Lord. Early Christian Devotion and Ancient Jewish Monotheism*, Philadelphia and London

Hutten, K., 1953: *Seher, Grübler, Enthusiasten*, Stuttgart 1953 (third edition)

Jansen, J.J.G., 1980: *The Interpretation of the Koran in Modern Egypt*, Leiden (second edition)

Jeffery, A., 1937: *Materials for the History of the Text of the Qur'an. The Old Codices*, Leiden

Jervell, J., 1972: *Luke and the People of God: A New Look at Luke-Acts*, Minneapolis

Jewett, R., 1984: *The Captain America Complex. The Dilemma of Zealous Nationalism*, Santa Fe

Johnson, E.E., 1989: *The Function of Apocalyptic and Wisdom Traditions in Romans 9–11*, SBL Diss. 109, Atlanta

Jomier, J., 1954: 'Quelques positions actuelles de l'exegese coranique en Egypte révélées par un polémique récente (1947–1951)', *MIDEO* 1, 39–72

Juergensmeyer, M., 1989: 'Shoring Up The Saint: Some Suggestions for Improving Satyagraha', in Hick and Hempel (ed.), 36–50

Källstad, T., 1974: *John Wesley and the Bible. A Psychological Study*, Uppsala

Kantzenbach, F.W., 1982: *Die Bergpredigt. Annäherung – Wirkungsgeschichte*, Stuttgart

Käsemann, E., 1964: *Essays on New Testament Themes*, London

Kasher, A., and Biderman, S., 1988: 'Why Was Baruch de Spinoza Excommunicated?', in D.S. Katz and J.I. Israel (ed.), *Sceptics, Millenarians and Jews. In honour of R.H. Popkin*, Brill's Studies in Intellectual History 17, Leiden, 98–141

Kiddle, M., 1941: *The Revelation of St. John*, MNTC, London

Kissinger, W., 1975: *The Sermon on the Mount: A History of Interpretation and Bibliography*, Metuchen, NJ

Klassen, W., 1984: *Love of Enemies*, Philadelphia

Klauck, H-J., 1982: *Herrenmahl und hellenistischer Kult. Eine religionsgeschichtliche Untersuchung zum ersten Korintherbrief*, NTA 15,

Münster (second edition)

—, 1992: 'Das Sendschreiben nach Pergamon und der Kaiserkult in der Johannesoffenbarung', *Bib* 73, 153–82

Klempt, A., 1960: *Die Säkularisierung der universalhistorischen Auffassung. Zum Wandel des Geschichtsdenkens im 16. und 17. Jahrhundert*, Göttinger Bausteine zur Geschichtswissenschaft 31, Göttingen

Kloppenborg, J., 1991: 'Literary Convention, Self-Evidence, and the Social History of the Q People', *Semeia* 55, 77–102

Knight, D.F., 1993: 'Idols, Idolatry', in Metzger and Coogan (ed.), 297–8

Knitter, P.F., 1985: *No Other Name? A Critical Survey of Christian Attitudes Toward World Religions*, Maryknoll and London

Koch, D.-A., 1986: *Die Schrift als Zeuge des Evangeliums. Untersuchungen zur Verwendung und zum Verständnis der Schrift bei Paulus*, BHTh 69, Tübingen

Koschorke, K., 1978: *Die Polemik der Gnostiker gegen das kirchliche Christentum unter besonderer Berücksichtigung der Nag Hammadi-Traktate "Apokalypse des Petrus" (NHC VII,3) und "Testimonium Veritatis" (NHC IX,3)*, Nag Hammadi Studies 12, Leiden

Kotila, M., 1988: *Umstrittener Zeuge. Studien zur Stellung des Gesetzes in der johanneischen Theologiegeschichte*, AASF Diss.hum.litt. 48, Helsinki

Kötting, B., 1968: 'Die Entwicklung im Osten bis Justinian', in Rengstorf and von Kortzfleisch (ed.), 136–74

Kraemer, H., 1938: *The Christian Message in a Non-Christian World*, London

—, 1956: *Religion and the Christian Faith*, London

Kraus, H-J., 1982: *Geschichte der historisch-kritischen Erforschung des Alten Testaments*, Neukirchen-Vluyn (third edition)

Küng, H., 1987a: 'Christianity and World Religions: The Dialogue with Islam as one Model', *MW* 77, 1987, 80–95

—, 1987b: *Christianity and the World Religions. Paths of Dialogue with Islam, Hinduism, and Buddhism*, New York and London

— and Kuschel, K.-J. (ed.), 1993: *A Global Ethic. The Declaration of the World Parliament of Religions*, London and New York

Lampe, P., 1989: *Die stadtrömischen Christen in den ersten beiden Jahrhunderten. Untersuchungen zur Sozialgeschichte*, WUNT 2. Reihe

18, Tübingen (second edition)

Lane Fox, R., 1986: *Pagans and Christians*, London and New York

Lang, B., 1993: 'Segregation and Intolerance', in M. Smith and R.J. Hoffmann (ed.), *What the Bible Really Says*, New York, 115–35

La Peyrère, I., 1643: *Du Rappel des Juives*, n.p.

—, 1655: *Praeadamitae sive Exercitatio super Versibus duodecimo, decimotertio, & decimoquarto, capitis quinti Epistolae D. Pauli ad Romanos. Quibus inducuntur Primi Homines ante Adamum conditi*

—, 1655: *Systema Theologicum ex Prae-adamitarum Hypothesi. Pars prima*

Laurila, K.S., 1946: *Leo Tolstoi und Martin Luther als Ausleger der Bergpredigt*, AASF B 55.1, Helsinki

Leaney, A.R.C., 1966: *A Commentary on the Gospel according to Luke*, BNTC, London (second edition)

Levenson, J., 1985a: 'Is There a Counterpart in the Hebrew Bible to New Testament Antisemitism?', *JES* 22, 242–60

—, 1985b: *Sinai and Zion. An Entry into the Jewish Bible*, Minneapolis

Lietzmann, H., 1949: *The Beginnings of the Christian Church*, London

Lindars, B., 1972: *The Gospel of John*, NCeB, London

Lindemann, A., 1995: 'Die Christuspredigt des Paulus in Athen (Act 17,16–33)', in Fornberg and Hellholm (ed.), 245–55

Lohfink, G., 1975: *Die Sammlung Israels: Eine Untersuchung zur lukanischen Ekklesiologie*, StANT 39, Munich

Lohse, E., 1971: *Die Offenbarung des Johannes*, NTD 11, Göttingen

Lüdemann, G. 1996: *Heretics. The Other Side of Early Christianity*, London and Louisville

Lüling, G. 1981: *Die Wiederentdeckung des Propheten Muhammad. Eine Kritik am 'christlichen' Abendland*, Erlangen

Luz, U. 1967: 'Der alte und neue Bund bei Paulus und im Hebräerbrief', *EvTh* 27, 318–36

—, 1968: *Das Geschichtsverständnis des Paulus*, BEvTh 49, Munich

—, 1989: *Matthew 1–7: A Commentary*, Minneapolis

—, 1993: 'Der Antijudaismus im Matthäusevangelium als historisches und theologisches Problem. Eine Skizze', *EvTh* 53, 310–27

—, 1994: *Matthew in History. Interpretation, Influence, and Effects*, Minneapolis

—, and Lampe, P., 1987: 'Nachpaulinisches Christentum und pagane Gesellschaft', in J.Becker et al., *Die Anfänge des Christentums. Alte Welt und neue Hoffnung*, Stuttgart, 185–216

Maddox, R., 1982: *The Purpose of Luke-Acts*, FRLANT 126, Göttingen

Madsen, T.G. (ed.), 1978: *Reflections on Mormonism. Judaeo-Christian Parallels*, Provo

Maier, G., 1979–1980: *Matthäus-Evangelium 1–2*, Neuhausen and Stuttgart

Manson, T.W., 1949: *The Sayings of Jesus as Recorded in the Gospels According to St. Matthew and St. Luke*, London

Maqsood, R.W., 1991: *The Separated Ones. Jesus, the Pharisees and Islam*, London

Maresius (Desmarets), S., 1656: *Refutatio Fabulae Praeadamicae*, Groningae, Editio altera

Margoliouth, D.S., 1939: *Mohammed*, London and Glasgow

Martyn, J.L., 1991: 'Events in Galatia. Modified Covenantal Nomism versus God's Invasion of the Cosmos in the Singular Gospel', in J.M. Bassler (ed.), *Pauline Theology I*, Minneapolis, 160–79

Masson, D., 1958: *Le Coran et la révélation Judéo-Chrétienne 1*, Paris

Matthews, R.J., 1980: *'A Plainer Translation'. Joseph Smith's Translation of the Bible. A History and Commentary*, Provo (third edition)

May, G., 1987–88: 'Marcion in Contemporary Views: Results and Open Questions', *The Second Century* 6, 129–51

Mayes, A.D.H., 1990: 'Joshua', in R.J. Coggins and J.L. Houlden (ed.), *A Dictionary of Biblical Interpretation*, London, 368–9

McCurley, F., and Reumann, J., 1980: *Word and Witness*, Understanding the Bible 2, Philadelphia

McGrath, A.E., 1990: *A Life of John Calvin. A Study in the Shaping of Western Culture*, Oxford

McKee, D.R., 1944: 'Isaac de la Peyrère, a Precursor of Eighteenth-Century Critical Deists', *PMLA* 59, 456–85

McSorley, H.J., 1967: *Luthers Lehre vom unfreien Willen*, BÖT 1, Munich

Meeks, W.A., 1993: *The Origins of Christian Morality. The First Two Centuries*, New Haven

Mehta, V., 1977: *Mahatma Gandhi and His Apostles*, London

Meijering, E.P., 1977: *Tertullian contra Marcion. Gotteslehre in der Polemik. Adversus Marcionem I–II*, PhP 3, Leiden

Meinhold, P., 1962: *Ökumenische Kirchenkunde*, Stuttgart

Merkel, H., 1971: *Widersprüche zwischen den Evangelien. Ihre polemische und apologetische Behandlung in der Alten Kirche bis zu*

Augustin, Tübingen

Metzger, B.M. and Coogan, M.D. (ed.), 1993: *The Oxford Companion to the Bible*, Oxford

Meyer, E., 1912: *Ursprung und Geschichte der Mormonen*, Halle

—, 1923: *Ursprung und Anfänge des Christentums 2, Die Apostelgeschichte und die Anfänge des Christentums*, Stuttgart

Michaud, H. 1960: *Jésus selon le Coran*, Neuchâtel

Moessner, D.P., 1988: 'The Ironic Fulfillment of Israel's Glory', in Tyson (ed.), 35–50

Montefiore, C.G., 1909: *The Synoptic Gospels 1–2*, London

Morgan, R., 1990: 'Reimarus, H.S', in R.J. Coggins and J.L. Houlden (ed.), *A Dictionary of Biblical Interpretation*, London, 585–6

Mühlmann, W., 1950: *Mahatma Gandhi. Der Mann, sein Werk und seine Wirkung*, Tübingen

Muslim-Christian Research Group, 1989: *The Challenge of the Scriptures. The Bible and the Qur'an*, Maryknoll

Mussner, F., 1984: *Tractate on the Jews. The Significance of Judaism for Christian Faith*, Philadelphia

—, 1995: 'Kommende Schwerpunkte Biblischer Theologie', in C.Dohmen and T.Söding (ed.), *Eine Bibel – zwei Testamente*, UTB 1893, Paderborn, etc., 237–51

Nasr, S.H., 1987: 'Response to Hans Küng's Paper on Christian-Muslim Dialogue', *MW* 77, 96–105

Niditch, S., 1995: *War in the Hebrew Bible. A Study in the Ethics of Violence*, New York and Oxford

Niebuhr, R., 1963: *Moral Man and Immoral Society*, London (reprint)

—, 1984: 'Reply to Interpretation and Criticism', in C.W. Kegley (ed.), *Reinhold Niebuhr: His Religious, Social and Political Thought*, New York, 507–27

Nöldeke, T., and Schwally, F. 1909, 1919: *Geschichte des Korans I–II*, Leipzig (second edition)

Nygren, G. 1956: *Das Prädestinationsproblem in der Theologie Augustins. Eine systematisch-theologische Studie*, FKDG 5, Göttingen

O'Dea, T.F., 1958: *The Mormons*, Chicago

Olsson, B., 1982: *Första Petrusbrevet*, Kommentar till Nya Testamentet 17, Stockholm

Otto, R., 1959: *The Idea of the Holy*, London

Paret, R., 1966: *Der Koran*, Stuttgart
—, 1980: *Mohammed und der Koran. Geschichte und Verkündigung des arabischen Propheten*, UB 32, Stuttgart (fifth edition)
Parkes, J., 1979: 'Preface', in A.T. Davies (ed.), v–xi
Parrinder, G., 1965: *Jesus in the Qur'an*, London
Pelikan, J., 1985: *Jesus Through the Centuries. His Place in the History of Culture*, London
Piper, J., 1979: *'Love Your Enemies.' Jesus' Love Command in the Synoptic Gospels and the Early Christian Paraenesis*, MSSNTS 38, Cambridge
—, 1983: *The Justification of God. An Exegetical and Theological Study of Romans 9,1–23*, Grand Rapids
Piper, R.A., 1995: 'The Language of Violence and the Aphoristic Sayings in Q. A Study of Q 6:27–36', in J.S. Kloppenborg (ed.), *Conflict and Invention. Literary, Rhetorical, and Social Studies on the Sayings Gospel Q*, Valley Forge, 53–72
Popkin, R.H., 1979: *The History of Scepticism from Erasmus to Spinoza*, Berkeley
—, 1987: *Isaac La Peyrère (1596–1676). His Life, Work and Influence*, Brill's Studies in Intellectual History 1, Leiden
Powers, D.S., 1988: 'The Exegetical Genre *nasikh al-Qur'an wa mansukhuhu*', in A. Rippin (ed.), *Approaches to the History of the Interpretation of the Qur'an*, Oxford, 117–38
Pregeant, R., 1978: *Christology Beyond Dogma. Matthew's Christ in Process Hermeneutic*, Philadelphia
Prickett, S., 1995: 'The Bible as a Holy Book', in P. Byrne and J.L. Houlden (ed.), *Companion Encyclopedia of Theology*, London, 142–59
Propp, W.H., 1993: 'Graven Image', in Metzger and Coogan (ed.), 261–2

Race, A., 1983: *Christians and Religious Pluralism. Patterns in the Christian Theology of Religions*, London and Maryknoll
Rad, G. von, 1962–1965: *Old Testament Theology 1–2*, Edinburgh
Rafiq, B.A. 1980: 'The Impact of the International Conference on the Deliverance of Jesus from the Cross', *RR(R)* 75, 50–5
Rahbar, D. 1958a: 'The Call of the Minaret', *MW* 48, 40–51

—, 1958b: 'The Challenge of Modern Ideas and Social Values to Muslim Society', *MW* 48, 274–85

—, 1960: *God of Justice. A Study of the Ethical Doctrine of the Qur'an*, Leiden

Rahman, F. 1968: *Islam*, New York

—, 1970: 'Islamic Modernism: Its Scope, Methods and Alternatives', *IJMES* 1, 317–33

—, 1980: *Major Themes of the Qur'an*, Minneapolis and Chicago

Räisänen, H., 1971: *Das koranische Jesusbild. Ein Beitrag zur Theologie des Korans*, Schriften der Finnischen Gesellschaft für Missiologie und Ökumenik 20, Helsinki

—, 1976: *The Idea of Divine Hardening. A Comparative Study of the Notion of Divine Hardening, Leading Astray and Inciting to Evil in the Bible and the Qur'an*, Publications of the Finnish Exegetical Society 25, Helsinki (second edition)

—, 1980: 'The Portrait of Jesus in the Qur'an: Reflections of a Biblical Scholar', *MW* 70, 122–33

—, 1987a: *Paul and the Law*, WUNT 29, Tübingen (second edition)

—, 1987b: 'Römer 9–11. Analyse eines geistigen Ringens', *ANRW* II.25.4, 2891–939

—, 1988: 'Paul, God and History. Romans 9–11 in Recent Research', in J.Neusner et al. (ed.), *The Social World of Formative Christianity and Judaism. In Honor of H.C. Kee*, Philadelphia, 178–206

—, 1990: *Beyond New Testament Theology. A Story and a Programme*, London

—, 1992: *Jesus, Paul and Torah. Collected Essays*, JSNTS 43, Sheffield

—, 1995a: 'Romans 9–11 and the "History of Early Christian Religion"', in Fornberg and Hellholm (ed.), 743–65

—, 1995b: 'The Nicolaitans: Apoc. 2; Acta 6', *ANRW* II.26.2, 1602–44

—, 1996: 'Liberating Exegesis?', *BJRL* 78, 193–204

Rauf, M.A., 1970: 'The Qur'an and Free Will', *MW* 60, 205–17, 289–99

Rengstorf, K.H. and von Kortzfleisch, S. (ed.), 1968: *Kirche und Synagoge* 1, Handbuch zur Geschichte von Christen und Juden, Stuttgart

Reventlow, H. Graf, 1995: 'The Role of the Old Testament in the German Liberal Protestant Theology of the Nineteenth Century', in H. Graf Reventlow and W. Farmer (ed.), *Biblical Studies and the*

Shifting of Paradigms, 1850–1914, JSOTS 192, Sheffield, 132–48

Richards, G., 1991: *The Philosophy of Gandhi,* Calcutta

Riches, J.K., 1993: 'Biblical Theology and the Pressing Concerns of the Church', in R.Barbour (ed.), *The Kingdom of God and Human Society,* Edinburgh, 256–79

Riddle, D.W., 1943: 'The Jewishness of Paul', *JR* 23, 240–4

Ries, J., 1987: 'Idolatry', in Eliade (ed.) 7, 72–8

Ringgren, H., 1955: *Studies in Arabian Fatalism,* UUÅ 1955:2, Uppsala

Rippin, A., 1987: 'Tafsir', in Eliade (ed.) 14, 236–44

Risse, G. 1989: *'Gott ist Christus, der Sohn der Maria.' Eine Studie zum Christusbild im Koran,* Begegnung 2, Bonn

Robinson, N., 1991: *Christ in Islam and Christianity. The Representation of Jesus in the Qur'an and the Classical Muslim Commentaries,* London

—, 1996: *Discovering the Qur'an. A Contemporary Approach to a Veiled Text,* London

Rogerson, J., 1995: 'The Old Testament: Historical Study and New Roles', in P. Byrne and J.L. Houlden (ed.), *Companion Encyclopedia of Theology,* London, 64–84

Rudolph, K., 1975: 'Jesus nach dem Koran', in W. Trilling and I. Berndt (ed.), *Was haltet ihr von Jesus? Beiträge zum Gespräch über Jesus von Nazaret,* Leipzig, 260–87

—, 1980: 'Neue Wege der Qoranforschung?', *ThLZ* 105, 1–19

—, 1983: *Gnosis. The Nature and History of an Ancient Religion,* Edinburgh

Ruether, R.R. 1974: *Faith and Fratricide. The Theological Roots of Anti-Semitism,* New York

—, 1979: 'The Faith and Fratricide Discussion: Old Problems and New Dimensions', in A.T. Davies (ed.), 230–55

—, and Ruether, H.J., 1989: *The Wrath of Jonah. The Crisis of Religious Nationalism in the Israeli-Palestinian Conflict,* San Francisco

Sandelin, K.-G., 1991: 'The Danger of Idolatry According to Philo of Alexandria', *Tem.* 27, 109–50

—, 1995: '"Do Not Be Idolaters!" (1 Cor 10:7)', in Fornberg and Hellholm (ed.), 257–73

Sanders, E.P., 1977: *Paul and Palestinian Judaism. A Comparison of*

Patterns of Religion, London and Philadelphia

—, 1983: *Paul, the Law, and the Jewish People*, Philadelphia and London

Sanders, J.T., 1987: *The Jews in Luke-Acts*, London

—, 1988: 'The Jewish People in Luke-Acts', in Tyson (ed.), 51–75

Sänger, D., 1994: *Die Verkündigung des Gekreuzigten und Israel. Studien zum Verhältnis von Kirche und Israel bei Paulus und im frühen Christentum*, WUNT 75, Tübingen

Sauer, J., 1985: 'Traditionsgeschichtliche Erwägungen zu den synoptischen und paulinischen Aussagen über Feindesliebe und Wiedervergeltungsverzicht', *ZNW* 76, 1–28

Schedl, C., 1978: *Muhammad und Jesus. Die christologisch relevanten Texte des Koran neu übersetzt und erklärt*, Vienna, Freiburg and Basel

Schelkle, K.H., 1959: *Paulus, Lehrer der Väter. Die altkirchliche Auslegung von Römer 1–11*, Düsseldorf (second edition)

Schlunk, M., 1953: *Die Weltreligionen und das Christentum. Eine Auseinandersetzung vom Christentum aus*, Frankfurt am Main

Schoeps, H.J., 1952: *Philosemitismus im Barock. Religions- und geistesgeschichtliche Untersuchungen*, Tübingen

Scholder, K., 1990: *The Birth of Modern Critical Theology*, London

Schottroff, L., 1975: 'Gewaltverzicht und Feindesliebe in der urchristlichen Jesustradition', in G. Strecker (ed.), *Jesus Christus in Historie und Theologie. FS H. Conzelmann*, Tübingen, 197–221

Schutter, W.L., 1989: *Hermeneutic and Composition in 1 Peter*, WUNT, 2. Reihe 30, Tübingen

Seale, M.S., 1964: *Muslim Theology. A Study of Origins with Reference to the Church Fathers*, London

Seeley, D., 1994: *Deconstructing the New Testament*, Leiden, New York and Cologne

Segal, A., 1990: *Paul the Convert. The Apostolate and Apostasy of Saul the Pharisee*, New Haven and London

Simon, M., 1986: *Verus Israel. A Study of the Relations between Christians and Jews in the Roman Empire (135–425)*, Oxford

Smart, N., 1989: *The World's Religions. Old Traditions and Modern Transformations*, Cambridge

Smith, J., 1974: *The Holy Scriptures, Inspired Version containing the Old and New Testaments: An Inspired Version of the Authorized Version by Joseph Smith, Jr*, Independence

Smith, K.L., and Zepp, I.G., 1975: *Search for the Beloved Community: The Thinking of Martin Luther King, Jr*, Valley Forge (second edition)

Smith, W.C., 1957: *Islam in Modern History*, New York and Toronto

—, 1988: 'Idolatry in Comparative Perspective', in Hick and Knitter (ed.), 53–68

Sonn, T., 1991: 'Fazlur Rahman's Islamic Methodology', *MW* 81, 212–30

Stendahl, K., 1978: 'The Sermon on the Mount and Third Nephi', in Madsen (ed.), 139–54 (= Stendahl 1984, 99–113)

—, 1984: *Meanings. The Bible as Document and as Guide*, Philadelphia

—, 1995: *Final Account. Paul's Letter to the Romans*, Minneapolis

Stieglecker, H., 1962: *Die Glaubenslehren des Islam*, Paderborn

Strauss, L., 1930: *Die Religionskritik Spinozas als Grundlage seiner Bibelwissenschaft. Untersuchungen zu Spinozas theologisch-politischem Traktat*, Veröffentlichungen der Akademie für die Wissenschaft des Judentums, Philosophische Sektion 2, Berlin

Strecker, G., 1979: *Eschaton und Historie. Aufsätze*, Göttingen

Ström, Å., 1994: 'Mormonen', *TRE* 23, 311–18

Strong, J.S., 1987: 'Images', in Eliade (ed.) 7, 97–104

Sugirtharajah, R., 1991: 'Postscript: Achievements and Items for a Future Agenda', in id. (ed.) 1991, 434–44

—, 1993: 'The Bible and its Asian Readers', *Biblical Interpretation* 1, 54–66

—, 1995: 'Inter-faith Hermeneutics: An Example and Some Implications', in Sugirtharajah (ed.), 1995, 306–18

—, (ed.), 1991: *Voices from the Margin. Interpreting the Bible in the Third World*, London

—, (ed.), 1995: *Voices from the Margin. Interpreting the Bible in the Third World*, London (new edition)

Syreeni, K., 1987: *The Making of the Sermon on the Mount: A Procedural Analysis of Matthew's Redactoral Activity. Part I: Methodology & Compositional Analysis*, AASF Diss.hum. 44, Helsinki

Tähtinen, U., 1964: *Non-Violence as an Ethical Principle with Special Reference to the Views of Mahatma Gandhi*, Annales Universitatis Turkuensis B 92, Turku

Tannehill, R.C., 1985: 'Israel in Luke-Acts: A Tragic Story', *JBL* 104, 69–85

—, 1986: *The Narrative Unity of Luke-Acts: A Literary Interpretation. Vol. 1: The Gospel According to Luke*, Philadelphia

—, 1988: 'Rejection by the Jews and Turning to Gentiles: the Pattern of Paul's Mission in Acts', in Tyson (ed.), 83–101

—, 1989: 'The Narrator's Strategy in the Scenes of Paul's Defense (Acts 21:27 – 26:32)', Address to the Luke-Acts Seminar of SNTS (manuscript)

Tanner, J., and Tanner, S., 1980: *The Changing World of Mormonism*, Chicago

Theissen, G., 1979a: *On Having a Critical Faith*, London

—, 1979b: *Studien zur Soziologie des Urchristentums*, WUNT 19, Tübingen

Theobald, M., 1987: 'Kirche und Israel nach Röm 9–11', *Kairos* 29, 1–22

Thompson, L.L., 1990: *The Book of Revelation. Apocalypse and Empire*, New York

Thurén, L., 1990: *The Rhetorical Strategy of 1 Peter. With Special Regard to Ambiguous Expressions*, Åbo

Tiede, D.L., 1986: 'The Exaltation of Jesus and the Restoration of Israel in Acts 1', *HThR* 79, 278–86

—, 1988: ' "Glory to Thy People Israel" ', in Tyson (ed.), 21–34

Trilling, W., 1959: *Die Täufertradition bei Matthäus*, BZ NF 3, 271–89

Tyson, J. (ed.), 1988: *Luke-Acts and the Jewish People. Eight Critical Perspectives*, Minneapolis

Ursinus, J.H., 1656: *Novus Prometheus. Prae-Adamitarum Plastes ad Caucasum relegatus & religatus*, Francofurti

van der Leeuw, G., 1986: *Religion in Essence and Manifestation*, Princeton

Volz, P., 1924: *Das Dämonische in Jahwe*, SGV 110, Tübingen

Vries, A. de, 1981 (1954): *Die Kinderbibel*, Constance

Wainwright, A.W., 1977–78: 'Luke and the Restoration of the Kingdom to Israel', *ExpT* 89, 76–9

Wansbrough, J., 1977: *Quranic Studies*, London

Warrior, R.A., 1991: 'A Native American Perspective: Canaanites, Cowboys, and Indians', in Sugirtharajah (ed.) 1991, 277–85

Watson, F., 1993: 'Liberating the Reader. A Theological-Exegetical Study of the Parable of the Sheep and Goats', in id. (ed.), *The Open Text*, London, 57–84

Watt, W.M., 1948: *Free Will and Predestination in Early Islam*, London

—, 1967: *Companion to the Qur'an*, London

—, 1970: *Bell's Introduction to the Qur'an, completely revised and enlarged*, Islamic Surveys 8, Edinburgh

Weinel, H., 1928: *Biblische Theologie des Neuen Testaments. Die Religion Jesu und des Urchristentums*, Tübingen (fourth edition)

Weiss, J., 1971 (1892): *Jesus' Proclamation of the Kingdom of God*, Lives of Jesus Series, Philadelphia and London

Werner, M., 1957: *The Formation of Christian Dogma: An Historical Study of Its Problem*, London

Wessels, A., 1991: *Images of Jesus. How Jesus is Perceived and Portrayed in Non-European Cultures*, Grand Rapids and London

Westerholm, S., 1988: *Israel's Law and the Church's Faith. Paul and His Recent Interpreters*, Grand Rapids

Wielandt, R., 1971: *Offenbarung und Geschichte im Denken moderner Muslime*, Wiesbaden

Wiles, M., 1967: *The Divine Apostle. The Interpretation of St. Paul's Epistles in the Early Church*, Cambridge

—, 1977: 'Myth in Theology', in J. Hick (ed.), *The Myth of God Incarnate*, London, 148–66

—, 1992: *Christian Theology and Inter-religious Dialogue*, London

Williams, M.A., 1996: *Rethinking "Gnosticism". An Argument for Dismantling a Dubious Category*, Princeton

Willis, W.L., 1985: *Idol Meat in Corinth. The Pauline Argument in 1 Corinthians 8 and 10*, SBL Diss. 68, Chico

Wilson, S.G., 1986: 'Marcion and the Jews', in S.G. Wilson (ed.), *Anti-Judaism in Early Christianity 2: Separation and Polemic*, Waterloo, 45–58

—, 1995: *Related Strangers. Jews and Christians 70–170 C.E.*, Minneapolis

Windisch, H., 1929: *Der Sinn der Bergpredigt*, Leipzig

Wink, W., 1968: *John the Baptist in the Gospel Tradition*, MSSNTS 7, Cambridge

—, 1988: 'Neither Passivity nor Violence: Jesus' Third Way', *SBL 1988 Seminar Papers*, Atlanta, 210–24

Wolff, O., 1955: *Mahatma und Christus. Eine Charakterstudie Mahatma Gandhis und des modernen Hinduismus*, Berlin
—, 1965: *Christus unter den Hindus*, Gütersloh
Wright, N.T., 1991: *The Climax of the Covenant. Christ and the Law in Pauline Theology*, Edinburgh

Zaehner, R.C., 1962: *The Comparison of Religions*, Boston
Zenger, E., 1993: *Am Fuss des Sinai. Gottesbilder des Ersten Testaments*, Düsseldorf
Zerbe, G.M., 1993: *Non-Retaliation in Early Jewish and New Testament Texts. Ethical Themes in Social Contexts*, Journal for the Study of the Pseudepigrapha, Suppl. Series 13, Sheffield
Ziesler, J., 1989: *Paul's Letter to the Romans*, TPI New Testament Commentaries, London and Philadelphia
Zmijewski, J., 1972: *Die Eschatologiereden des Lukas-Evangeliums: Eine traditions- und redaktionsgeschichtliche Untersuchung zu Lk 21,5–36 und Lk 17,20–37*, BBB 40, Bonn
Zöckler, O., 1878: 'Peyrere's (gest. 1676) Präadamiten-Hypothese nach ihren Beziehungen zu den anthropologischen Fragen der Gegenwart', *ZLThK* 39, 28–48
Zwemer, S.J., 1912: *The Moslem Christ*, Edinburgh

Notes

1. A Biblical Critic in the Global Village: Can Exegesis Serve Inter-Religious Harmony?

  1. Race 1983, 1f.; cf. Hick 1995, 12f.
  2. Ibid., 1.
  3. Ibid., xi.
  4. Küng 1987b, 441.
  5. Küng – Kuschel 1993.
  6. Ibid., 22.
  7. Race 1983, 72. It is questionable whether 'moral tolerance' alone will be enough in such a connection.
  8. Sugirtharajah 1995, 306–19 (= Sugirtharajah 1991, 352–63).
  9. The 'hermeneutical gap' between the biblical milieu and the present day is, he claims, a problem created by the historical-critical method (Sugirtharajah 1991, 436; id. 1993, 63f.), though in his campaign against 'objective scholarship' he actually agrees with many Western scholars who are criticized by him for individualizing the message, notably Bultmann.
  10. Borowsky 1995, 2.
  11. In itself, this is a controversial claim, but we can accept it here for the sake of argument.
  12. Likewise, Leonardo Boff writes that in Jesus' environment 'the real oppression did not consist in the presence of an alien, pagan power. The real oppression lay in a legalistic interpretation of religion and the will of God. In post-exilic Judaism careful cultivation of the law became the very essence of Jewish life . . . It degenerated into a terrible and impossible form of bondage proclaimed in God's name' (quoted by Riches 1993, 257.) Cf. also the negative attitude to Judaism displayed by J. Pathrapankal (as contrasted to his positive view of Hinduism): Fornberg 1995, 140.
  13. According to Sugirtharajah (1995, 312f.), the dialogical approach 'changes the understanding of what conversion is': it 'can

take place within a religious tradition itself' (but this is Stendahl's view too). 'One can be rooted in one's tradition and yet learn more and be open to its forgotten aspects.' Peter in the Cornelius episode is 'another case in point'. What we often overlook is that not just Cornelius was converted; 'Peter too was converted'. 'It was a rude shock to him, as it was to Jonah before him, that God's grace knows no bounds and extends to outsiders who are not normally recipients of such love.'

Yet it was precisely because of the impact of episodes like this that Christianity finally emerged as a new religion. 'Forgotten aspects' of the tradition actually made that tradition explode in the lives of certain people. Surely a multi-faith interpretation should not stop here, by admiring Peter's metamorphosis. It also has to look at the matters from the perspective of those who loved their traditional religion and scripture and were precisely therefore critical of Peter. How to assess new experiences in the framework of sacred tradition? For me, it is the task of historical exegesis to analyse and interpret such encounters as complicated, multidimensional processes.

14. Sugirtharajah's insight about the wisdom tradition (1995, 316f.) will concern us in the 'Conclusion'.

15. Cracknell 1986 also tries to show 'that the canonical scriptures taken as a whole are not exclusivist in their understanding of God's activity in this world' (5). 'The "Rainbow Sign" witnesses to the love and concern and graciousness of God the Creator towards the whole of his creation. The covenant with Noah is thus supremely important . . . this cosmic covenant was never forgotten . . . The Adamic and Noachic covenants make it impossible to picture the church as "the saved amid the damned"' (35). However, the Noachic covenant does condemn idolatry – and thereby most of humankind (see Ch. 3, p. 34).

16. Ariarajah's (1985, 11) criticism of the notion of election (which I deem justified) does not remove the notion from a central position in the Bible. It is another thing that the notion can be criticized: 'Such a self-understanding (election) is valid only insofar as it does not violate the doctrine of God as creator.'

17. Cf. Kraemer 1956, 242: 'Generally speaking, the Old Testament in its attitude towards surrounding religions is strongly condemnatory and hostile (cf. in very strong terms Deut. 7.2, 5).' 'In the New Testament one finds this same attitude of rejection towards paganism as a whole.' To be sure, Kraemer's position is equally

unbalanced, based as it is on the biblical misrepresentation of 'other' religions. Kraemer ignores in this evaluation e.g. the 'universalism' found in Deutero-Isaiah (but not the 'caustic scorn' with which idols are treated in Isa. 44!).

18. He admits to being selective, but thinks that the 'another side' he has focussed on is 'central to the spirit of the biblical message' (1985, 58). And surely '(t)here is *in* the Bible *a* more open, generous and inclusive understanding . . . than we seem aware of . . .' (71, my emphasis); or at least such an understanding can be deduced from central biblical tenets (God's unconditional love, creation). The point is precisely that one has to be rather selective to reach this overall understanding.

19. Race 1983, 10.

20. For an affirmation of the typology cf. e.g. Hick 1995, 18ff.

21. Hick 1995, 30 defines religious pluralism as the conviction that different religious traditions are seen as 'different valid human responses to the Real'. Unlike Hick (e.g. 1995, 103), I do *not* distinguish between a 'pluralistic religious' and a 'non-realist' understanding of religion. A pluralist is, for me, someone who gives up both exclusivist and inclusivist claims, and acknowledges the various traditions as different attempts to make sense of life, independently of whether he or she takes a realist or non-realist view of religion.

22. Race 1983, 10. For random confirmation cf. Levenson 1985a, 252: 'the Gospel of John takes a position of extreme exclusivism, which is the ancestor of the doctrine *extra ecclesiam nulla salus* . . . This exclusivism is closely related to the Johannine insistence that the Jews do not know God.'

23. Race 1983, 30f.

24. Ibid., 38.

25. Hick 1995, 20ff. finds religious inclusivism 'a vague conception which, when pressed to become clear, moves towards pluralism'.

26. Cf. also Acts 14.16f. and especially Acts 10.35: 'in every nation anyone who fears him (God) and does what is right is acceptable to him'; this verse is appealed to e.g. by Ariarajah 1985, 16f. But Cornelius is actually pictured in Acts 10.35 as a God-fearer in the Jewish sense, a Gentile sympathizer of the Jewish people (10.2). In order to get in into this group, one has to be a monotheist; an 'idolater' would not qualify.

27. Wessels 1991, 141.

28. Fornberg 1995, 135.

29. Race 1983, 39–41.

30. Ibid., 40. This would obviously correspond to Justin Martyr's view that 'those who live according to the Logos are Christians, notwithstanding they may pass with you for atheists; such among the Greeks were Socrates and Heracleitos . . .' (*Apol.* 1, 46).

31. Dibelius 1956, 76.

32. Kraemer 1956, 283f.

33. Dibelius 1956, 66 turns evasive: 'the perturbation may refer to the task and need not necessarily indicate anger'.

34. Kraemer 1956, 243.

35. Ibid., 283f.

36. Dibelius 1956, 56.

37. Ibid., 58.

38. Ibid., 55: not accusing, but enlightening the heathen.

39. Pregeant 1978, 151.

40. Cf. Lindemann 1995, 249f.

41. Dibelius 1956, 63: 'The speech is as alien to the New Testament (apart from Acts 14.15–17) as it is familiar to Hellenistic, particularly Stoic, philosophy . . . the main ideas of the speech . . . are Stoic rather than Christian.'

42. Race 1983, 40.

43. Seeley 1994, 83f. senses the problem in connection with the *Benedictus*: the rest of Zechariah's speech 'is oriented toward the sort of Messiah that Jesus definitely is not'; why Luke 'chose these verses for use here remains a mystery'.

44. McCurley-Reumann 1986, 287, 290.

45. Race 1983, 39.

46. For a fuller treatment see Chapter 2.

47. Cracknell 1986, 41.

48. Especially Gager 1983; Gaston 1987; cf. also Hall 1993.

49. Cf. the eschatological inclusivism in some of the later prophets: the nations will be peacefully won over, they will worship the God of Israel (and bring their treasures to Jerusalem!). The nations will find salvation – in and through Yahweh. They will become like us, they will be included among us. There will be no 'idolatry' – and no pluralism.

50. Race 1983, 38, quoted above.

51. Segal also mentions Stendahl, but this is a mistake (an error

which Segal shares with a number of writers).

52. Segal 1990, 281.

53. Baum 1979, 137f.

54. Ps.Clem. *Hom*. 8.6–7; cf. Ps.Clem. *Rec*. 4.5. Some of the
Christian interpolations into the (probably) Jewish Testaments of the
Twelve Patriarchs point to an astonishingly universalist vision,
especially Testament of Simeon 7.2: 'For the Lord will raise up
from Levi someone as a high priest and from Judah someone as a king,
God and man. He will save all the Gentiles (!, meaning Gentile
Christians?) and the tribe of Israel.' Yet it remains unclear whether
the basis for Israel's hope is, in the view of the interpolator, a conversion to Christ or God's original promise; perhaps he does not sharply
distinguish between the two. Cf. Wilson 1995, 107, 141.

55. Meeks 1993, 211.

56. Cf. Stendahl 1995, 21: 'A greedy hunger for relevance often
blinds the eyes of preachers and theologians.'

57. Cf. Race 1983, *x*: '. . . the encounter between Christianity and
other faiths is essential for Christian self-understanding.'

2. Saving God's Integrity: Paul's Struggle in Romans 9–11

1. See Introduction, p. 14.

2. For a comprehensive treatment see Räisänen 1987b, 1988,
1995a.

3. E.g. J. Piper (1983, 5) and Hübner (1984, 16) agree on this,
although their overall approaches differ greatly.

4. Bultmann 1951, 209 could still hold that Romans 'develops in
purely theoretical fashion the principle of Christian faith in antithesis
to the principle of the Jewish Torah-religion'.

5. Wright 1991, 231.

6. Cf. recently Fiedler 1990, 75–81; Segal 1990, 276ff.; Lüdemann
1996, 97–101; more cautiously Ziesler 1989, 237.

7. Largely in connection with Räisänen 1987a.

8. See esp. Wright 1991, 4ff., 143 etc. Cf. my review of Wright's
book in *SJT* 47, 1994, 117–19.

9. R.E. Brown 1983, 114 notes that 'it is curious that sometimes a
radical scholarship that has been insistent on the humanity of Jesus
balks at any real indication of the fallible humanity of Paul!'

10. Cf. e.g. the very different reconstructions by Gaston 1987 (see

my review in *TLZ* 114, 1989, 191f.) and Wright 1991. For some earlier attempts cf. Räisänen 1987a, 4 n.29.

11. Wright 1991, 251. Wright (250) wishes to take 'all Israel' in Rom. 11.26 'as a typically Pauline polemical redefinition' of Israel, overlooking, however, that 'all' in v.26 contrasts with *apo merous* in v.25.

12. In 9.3 Paul expresses the unreal wish that he could be 'accursed' and 'cut off from Christ' for the sake of his kinsmen; this implies that they must be 'in a plight as serious as the one he is willing to enter for their sake' (Piper 1983, 29). They are *anathema*. This can only be due to their unbelief when faced with the gospel.

13. Hübner 1984, 15.

14. Cf. ibid., 17: Paul 'juggles with the concept "Israel"'.

15. This is elaborated by Hübner 1984, 15–24; cf. Piper 1983, 54. By contrast, it is quite inadequate to summarize the point of Rom. 9.6ff. as Dunn 1991, 148 does: 'Those who are Israelites, but who fail to recognize the covenant character of their status as Israelites, have to that extent sold their own birthright . . .'; cf. Dunn 1988, 540: 'Paul's argument concerns the character and mode rather than the fact of election.' No, it concerns precisely the 'fact'! It is not a question of 'a schism within Israel' (*contra* Theobald 1987, 8). Hall 1993 portrays Paul as an 'inclusive' theologian on the basis of Romans 11, but he totally ignores the passage Romans 9.6–13 (and not just that).

16. It is hard to see why Gentile faith should be a problem for Paul (*contra* Johnson 1989, 143ff.). Israel's unbelief is the problem (9.3) which calls forth the statements concerning God's 'negative' acts in Romans 9.

17. This is not taken seriously enough by Johnson 1989, 148ff. (who focuses one-sidedly on 'God's creative mercy') or by Wright 1991, 238f.

18. Correctly Hübner 1984, 45.

19. Still, in vv.22–23 Paul's attention turns more to the 'vessels of mercy', predestined for glory. Paul dictates a sentence that implies double predestination. He is not quite at rest with the notion, however, and it is probably no coincidence that the sentence ends as an anacoluthon.

20. Such a view is indeed taken by some interpreters, e.g. Gaston 1987, 97.

21. Cf. Hübner 1984, 57; Lüdemann 1996, 98: 'The fact that we

know from ch. 11 that this is not Paul's last word on the problem of
Israel and salvation history must not be a reason for toning down the
sharpness of Paul's argumentation in an interpretation of 9.22f., or
doing away it in a dialectical fashion.'

22. It is unjustified simply to identify 'disobedient' with 'hardened
by God'; thus Johnson 1989, 140; Sänger 1994, 159, 162. Sänger
ignores v.20 altogether.

23. Verse 16, which forms a bridge to the allegory, is not very clear.
It seems to say that Israel as a whole is 'holy' because the 'first fruits'
and 'the root' are holy; most commentators think that this refers to
the patriarchs (cf. 11.28).

24. Gaston 1987 (originally 1979 and 1982); cf. now also Hall 1993.
For a more comprehensive critique cf. Räisänen 1988, 189ff.; Johnson
1989, 176ff.

25. This question is not even asked by Gager.

26. *sozesthai* vv.9, 13; *soteria* v.10.

27. Gager 1983, 251 defines *pistis* so that it includes both Jews and
Christians if they respond faithfully to God. The word *pistis* can
mean, for instance, that sonship lies in doing the Torah rather than
merely hearing it!

28. These include Rom. 3.21 (*choris nomou* is taken to mean alongside and in conformity with the law; Gager 1983, 251f.); Rom. 9.8
(250); Rom. 9.32 (250: Israel stumbled over the Gentiles, although the
stumbling stone is characterized as the object of 'believing' both in
9.32 and 10.11).

29. And if Paul was an apostate and he knew it, how could he still
put himself forward as an instance of those faithful Jews who constitute the remnant (Rom. 11.1–2)? Gager lays great stress on the fact
that Paul's treatment of the Torah and of justification is part of a
debate with fellow Christians, not with Jews (1983, 202 etc.). But this
is not very important, for precisely the Jewish identity of those
opposed to Paul was at stake. Gager (1983, 231) has adopted J.
Munck's implausible thesis that Paul's Judaizing opponents were
Gentiles.

30. The same applies to the older attempts to find Paul teaching a
doctrine of *apokatastasis panton* on the basis of Rom. 11.25ff.; thus e.g.
Weinel 1928, 315. In itself, the logic of 11.25ff. would undoubtedly
lead precisely to this conclusion.

31. Ziesler 1989, 285.

32. Mussner 1984, 33.; Beker 1980, 335.

33. Beker 1980, 334. Others, e.g. Mussner, refuse to speak of a 'conversion' of Israel at all. According to Mussner, God's sovereign initiative leads the Israelites to an act of faith (*emunah*). It is hard to see what the difference would be between this and a conversion.

34. Sanders 1983, 196; Becker 1989, 499ff.

35. Becker 1989, 500f.

36. Even according to Calvin, 'ministers and elders must proceed as if there were no predestination; must proceed indeed as if everyone had a free choice whether to accept or reject the offer of salvation in the Word', Höpfl 1985, 229.

37. Sänger 1994, 196 n.737 tries to harmonize I Thess. 2.14–16 with Romans 11 in a singularly unconvincing manner: Paul is aggressive in writing I Thess., as he knows that the Jews are sawing off their own branch, since the salvation of Gentiles is a necessary condition for the salvation of Israel. On this reading, the salvation of Israel is a special concern of Paul in I Thess. 2.14–16. No wonder Sänger omits to comment on the divine wrath *eis telos* of v. 16b. There is no getting round the fact that 'there is a direct contradiction between Rom. 11.25f. and I Thess. 2.14–16' (Lüdemann 1996, 101).

38. See Luz 1968, 279–286.

39. Ibid., 279. Hall 1993, 67ff., pleading for a totally different view, omits to discuss Gal. 3.19–25.

40. Cf. Luz 1968, 285.

41. Therefore it is hard to agree with those who find a theological development in Paul's thought from Galatians to Romans (notably Hübner). If there is development, that must have taken place, not between Galatians and Romans, but between Romans 9 and Romans 11 – if not between Romans 11.10 and 11.11!

42. See below, p. 70.

43. Cf. Räisänen 1992, 112ff., esp. 123ff.

44. Cf. Casey 1991, 121f.: Paul's 'dramatic redefinition' of the term 'Jew' (as in Rom. 2.28f.) 'shows how seriously assimilated St Paul himself was'. 'Observant Jews were bound to conclude that Paul had abandoned Judaism.' Casey rightly emphasizes that 'there are cases where the identity of individuals and of groups may be differently perceived' (12). The obvious fact that Paul himself perceived himself to be a Jew to the end of his life (to which e.g. Dunn 1991, 148f. refers) therefore does not at all solve the problem of the amount of his

continuity or discontinuity with average Judaism. Cf. already Riddle 1943, 244: 'Always regarding himself as a faithful and loyal Jew, his [Paul's] definitions of values were so different from those of his contemporaries that, notwithstanding his own position within Judaism, he was, from any point of view other than his own, at best a poor Jew and at worst a renegade.' See now the perceptive work of Segal 1990.

45. The claim that the Torah is 'paradoxically fulfilled whenever anyone confesses that Jesus is the Lord' or that 'when Christ is preached and believed, Torah is being paradoxically fulfilled' (Wright 1991, 244f., formulating Paul's point in Rom. 10.5–8) was (and is) bound to appear nonsense to most non-assimilated Jews.

46. Therefore I do not find it a fair description of my position to claim that I argue that 'Paul was totally alienated from his ancestral faith, from Judaism' (Dunn 1991, 140). It should be clear that I consider Paul's position to be more complex.

47. Ruether 1974, 105f. Sänger 1994 sets out to refute Ruether, but unintentionally ends up by confirming her point; see my forthcoming review in *JBL*.

48. Cf. Sanders 1977, 225ff.

49. Cf. 1 QpHab 8.8–13 (the wicked priest); CD 15.9f.

50. Sanders 1977, 247f.

51. Translation by G. Vermes. Less clear, but possible indications: 1 QH 6.7f.; 1 QpHab 5.3–6.

52. Casey 1991, 121.

53. Cf. Hübner 1984, 24f.

54. See above, n. 30.

55. On the issue of legitimation in general see Esler 1987. He notes that a particularly common characteristic of any symbolic universe erected to legitimate a new social order is 'the claim that it is not novel, but is actually old and traditional' (1987, 19).

56. Cf. P. Brown 1967, 403ff.

57. In 420, the Donatist bishop Gaudentius had retired to his basilica and had threatened to burn himself with his congregation. An imperial agent was worried. 'Augustine will now find it only too easy to answer this worried man; the fearful doctrine of predestination had armed him against feeling: "Seeing that God, by a hidden, though just disposition, has predestined some to the ultimate penalty (of Hellfire), it is doubtless better that [an overwhelming majority of the Donatists should have been collected and reabsorbed . . . while] a few perish in

their own flames: better, indeed, than that all Donatists should burn in the flames of Hell for their sacrilegious dissension,'' P. Brown 1967, 335f.

58. See Höpfl 1985, 231ff; McGrath 1990, 240ff.

59. McGrath 1990, 242.

60. It was because of his view of Scripture that Calvin was bound to teach double predestination. 'Scripture teaches nothing but what is necessary and beneficial for us to know. Scripture teaches predestination,' Höpfl 1985, 230, cf. 237. However, 'the entire edifice of scriptural demonstration of reprobation rests on Romans 9.18–23, and Jacob and Esau, as interpreted by St Paul in the same chapter', Höpfl 1985, 289 n. 34. Therefore, Calvin would not have taught *double* predestination (including reprobation), had it not been for Romans 9.

61. McGrath 1990, 241.

62. Ibid., 243.

63. Ibid., 259f.

64. Kötting 1968, 146.

65. For Duns Scotus it seemed enough that a handful were kept isolated on some island where they could observe their law; in them the prediction of Isaiah, quoted by Paul in Rom. 9.27, would be fulfilled: Eckert 1968, 220. Here the salvation of 'all Israel' is interpreted as the salvation of the *remnant* – an idea put forward by Paul a little earlier.

66. E.g. Bernard of Clairvaux and his pupils: Blumenkranz 1968, 122f., 131, 133. Bernard also quoted Rom. 9.4f. See further the idiosyncratic views of Isaac La Peyrère, presented in Chapter 9 below.

67. Cf. Friedrich 1988, 124ff., 138ff., 148.

68. J.M. Brown 1990, 394.

3. Co-existence and Conflict: Early Christian Attitudes to Adherents of Traditional Cults

1. Lane Fox 1986, 259ff. (quotation 261).

2. Ibid., 66f.

3. Ibid., 67f.

4. See e.g. I Enoch 99.7, 19.1; Jubilees 11.4; Or. Sib 5.80ff.; Epistle of Jeremiah 3ff.

5. *Spec.* 1.316; Sandelin 1991, 123.

6. Sandelin 1991, 125 n. 41 (quoting T. Seland).

7. *Spec.* 1.29; Sandelin 1991, 120.

8. W.C. Smith 1988, 55.

9. Barrett 1973, 37.

10. Dodd 1947, 25; cf. Lohse 1971, 61 on Rev. 9.20–21: 'Almost of necessity a vice-ridden way of life practised by godless people is associated with pagan superstition (cf. Rom. 1.23ff.).'

11. Kraemer 1956, 295, 298.

12. Ibid., 297.

13. Lane Fox 1986, 345f.

14. Sandelin 1995, 259.270.

15. Cf. I Cor. 5.9–13: 'Paul is concerned here with Christian discipline within the community; *synesthiein* with those outside, which would almost certainly involve eating *eidolothyta*, remains possible,' Barrett 1982, 47.

16. Cope 1990 has presented a suggestive case for regarding I Cor. 10.1–22 as a post-Pauline interpolation in the spirit of later Christianity which abhorred idol meat and developed a separatist attitude. This hypothesis, for which some arguments about vocabulary, style and coherence can be adduced, has the advantage that Paul emerges with a coherent stance on idol meat in I Cor. 8; 10.23–11.1; Rom. 14–15: 'meat and location are neutral so one may eat *unless* it offends a weaker brother's conscience'. Here, however, the question of how to pin-point Paul's view must be left open. In any case the thrust of his argument goes in the 'liberal' direction. If he wrote I Cor. 10.14–22, that passage signals a less than clear compromise.

17. Contra Willis 1985, 112ff. who denies that Paul basically agrees with the Corinthians' view as set forth in 8.1–6, 8. He even denies that Paul was on the side of the strong (119). But 9.22 shows that Paul had only become 'weak for the sake of the weak' for strategic reasons, just as he could be for the Jews 'as though he was a Jew'. Correctly Brunt 1985, 114f.: Paul 'is in basic agreement with the position of the strong', but 'this attitude does not govern Paul's treatment of the problem, for while he agrees with the position of the strong he never attempts to get anyone into their camp'.

18. Theissen 1979b, 275.

19. Ibid., 278f.

20. Ibid., 279f.

21. Ibid., 281.

22. Ibid., 241–5, 280.

23. Barrett 1982, 52.

24. Ibid., 50, 56. For the evidence see Ehrhardt 1964, 281ff.; Barrett 1982, 43.

25. Barrett 1982, 59 n. 53.

26. Meyer 1923, 194. Ehrhardt 1964, 280f. also notes that the Apostolic Decree 'caused the Christians to be separated from their neighbours'.

27. Fiorenza 1993, 122.

28. Ibid., 79f.

29. Ibid., 68.

30. Ibid., 119f.

31. Thus Bauckham 1993, 238ff.

32. See Räisänen 1995, 1602–44.

33. Collins 1989, 746; Thompson 1990; Klauck 1992, 153–6, 160–4. See, however, Lane Fox 1986, 433 for a somewhat different view.

34. Collins 1989, 741; Klauck 1992, 178f.

35. Ibid., 740f.

36. Collins 1986, 317.

37. Thompson 1990, 125.

38. It is becoming increasingly clear that 'Gnosticism' is a problematic category; in using the term I am actually speaking simply of groups that have conventionally been labeled 'Gnostic' (cf. Williams 1996, 5f. and passim).

39. See the evidence in Theissen 1979b, 282f.

40. Cf. Williams 1996, 103: 'In modern scholarship, it has become customary to cite these passages from Irenaeus about eating food offered to idols or attending pagan festivals as examples of rebellious "gnostic libertinism", the flagrant violation of traditional religious scruples. Yet the actions described are really socially deviant only if we think of Judaism and Christianity as the norm . . . Fewer dietary scruples and greater openness to the social interaction associated with community religious celebrations or public entertainment is behaviour that looks more like social conformity than like social deviance.'

41. Cf. Theissen 1979b, 285. Williams 1996, 96–115 convincingly refutes the thesis that 'Gnostics' were world-rejecting 'social dropouts' and argues on a broad basis that 'at least several of the important figures and groups among those usually classified as 'gnostics' . . . were moving precisely in the direction of *more* social

involvement and accommodation, and *less* tension with their social involvement' (97, his emphasis). To be sure, there were differences in the level of social tension between different 'Gnostic' groups, cf. ibid., 108ff.

42. Cf. Rudolph 1983, 251f. on festivals and circuses: 'Unfortunately we know nothing else about this aspect of the gnostic community life.'

43. Cf. Koschorke 1978, 137.

44. Rudolph 1983, 225f. with reference to NHC VI.6, 56, 10–14.

45. Cf. Williams 1996, 107f.

46. Perhaps one could go further and even speak of a kind of 'cultic universalism' (a phrase used with reference to the Naassenes by Frickel, cf. Williams 1996, 107).

47. Cf. Suetonius, *Nero* 16.2; *Claudius* 25.3; Pliny, *Ep.* 10.96; Tacitus, *Ann.* 15.4.

48. Cf. Fischer 1985, 172; Brox 1979, 29.

49. Cf. also I Peter 2.15f.; 4.4; 4.15–16 and Pliny, *Ep.* 10.96.7.

50. This should not be taken at face value as is done by Schutter 1989, 16f. and Thurén 1990, 122, 149.

51. Cf. Olsson 1982, 160.

52. See e.g. the following: Titus 3.3; 2.12; Eph. 4.17–19; 4.22; 2.1–3; II Thess. 3.2; I Peter 4.3–4; 1.14; 1.18; 2.1; 2.11; II Peter 1.4; 2.18; 2.20.

53. Luz-Lampe 1987, 201f., juxtaposing Titus 3.3 with Tacitus, *Ann.* 15.44.4.

54. Armstrong 1993, 109; cf. Fischer 1985, 163.

55. On this see Lane Fox 1986, 38, 98 etc.

56. Lane Fox 1986, 95.

57. Luz-Lampe 1987, 197; Lane Fox 1986, 432.

58. Thompson 1990, 131.

59. Klauck 1992, 181ff.

60. Ibid., 181. Even later, requirements such as that Christians should swear an oath by the Emperor's genius and the like 'are never cited as the cause of the Christians' arrest in the first place: provincials did not denounce them because of their refusal to pay cult to the Emperors. The issue is only aired in the courtroom by governors themselves, and at times they air it as an easier way out for people on trial', Lane Fox 1986, 426.

61. Thompson 1990, 163, with reference to S.R.F. Price

(Thompson's emphasis).

62. Lane Fox 1986, 40.

63. Thompson 1990, 131; cf. Lane Fox 1986, 425f.

64. Hanson 1985, 211.

65. Armstrong 1993, 61. On Israel cf. Levenson 1985, 65: 'Generally, the other cultures of the biblical world were, by comparison to Israel, remarkably tolerant.'

66. Lane Fox 1986, 335.

67. 'The Bible misrepresents idolatry by ascribing to worshippers the naive belief that the image is the deity . . . While the statue was the god in many respects, the god was not limited to its image. The idol's purpose was to allow the mortal a vision of the divine and to help god and worshipper focus their attention on each other,' Propp 1993, 261 (discussing Egypt, Canaan and Mesopotamia); cf. Levenson 1985b, 110; Armstrong 1993, 61.

68. Strong 1987, 97f.

69. '. . .that degree of idolatry is usually found only in the misguided pronouncements of monotheists or missionary ethnographers against "heathen" tribes who supposedly worship "sticks and stones",' Strong 1987, 97. On images see Strong 1987, 97f.; Ries 1987; Fredouille 1981; van der Leeuw 1986, 449–53; Heiler 1961, 106–18.

70. Levenson 1987, 109 n. 37. Cf. R.P. Carroll 1991, 113: 'What is going on in the Gospels . . . is an example of the standard demonization of the enemy so characteristic of political propaganda. Parallels can be seen in the Hebrew Bible . . . What the Jews did to the Canaanites in the Hebrew Bible, the Christians did to the Jews in the New Testament!'

71. 'The fifth-century BC citizens of Athens who banished their compatriot Stilpo for claiming that Phidias' statue of Athena was not the goddess herself must have been of this type', Strong 1987, 97.

72. Armstrong 1993, 64.

73. W.C. Smith 1988, 54–5.

74. Ibid., 57.

75. Ibid., 57f.

76. Ibid., 60.

77. Cf. Armstrong 1993, 64.

78. Smith 1988, 61.

79. Actually this is not so clear either. Cf. Knight 1993, 'The line between idol representations and permissible cultic objects may at

points seem unclear; the ark with its gold cherubim was not considered an idol but a manifestation of God's presence . . .; similarly ambiguous were the teraphim . . ., the ephod . . ., the bronze serpent . . . and the oxen supporting the molten sea in Solomon's Temple . . .'

80. Driver 1988, 214.

81. Ibid., 216.

82. Lang 1993, 115. See his whole chapter 'Religious Separation in the Hebrew Bible', 116–20. Recent study suggests that this exclusivist ideology was a late phenomenon in Israel's religious history. It was the catastrophe of the exile that necessitated attempts to find new ways to build up Israel's identity; in the end it turned out that exclusive intolerant monolatry functioned better in this regard than Deutero-Isaiah's universalist monotheism. Here I am indebted to a Finnish article by Dr Risto Lauha.

83. Cf. Jewett 1984, 150.

84. Hill 1994, 257; see his whole chapter on 'The Decalogue and Idolatry' (253–63).

85. Ibid., 258.

86. Ibid., 257, with reference to Richard Sibbes.

87. Ibid., 256.

88. Lane Fox 1986, 23.

4. The Redemption of Israel: A Salvation-Historical Problem in Luke-Acts

1. See Chapter 1 above.

2. Jervell 1972, 64. For a similar view see George 1968, 521; Conzelmann 1960, 163; Eltester 1972, 129. These scholars differ among themselves on Luke's view of the law and on whether the church has separated itself from the Jewish people or whether Israel is restored in the shape of the church. But they share the view that all unrepentant Jews have forfeited their membership of the people of God.

3. Leaney 1966, 69–72 attributes a coherent eschatological scheme to Luke: the Parousia will be preceded by the restoration of Israel, which is the establishing of God's kingdom on earth and is 'but one step towards the final consummation' (263). Wainwright 1977–78 has the restoration of Israel following the Parousia rather than preceding it.

4. Mussner 1984, 38. Tiede (1986, 1988) argues for a rather similar

view on the basis of Lukan texts.

5. Tannehill 1985, 72. Tiede 1988, 25f. concurs.

6. Thus Moessner 1988, 38–46. Correctly J.T. Carroll 1988, 42.

7. In the *Magnificat*, the aorists in Luke 1.51–53 refer to salvation through the death and resurrection of Jesus (R.E. Brown 1977, 363). These verses show that political language was already being applied to the non-political salvation accomplished by Jesus in the group from which the psalm stems. Luke is probably responsible for applying the *Magnificat* (and *Benedictus*) to Jesus' conception and birth (Brown 1977, 346–55).

8. Cf. J.T. Carroll 1988, 46: 'The Jewish hope will not be disappointed! At the same time, . . . a process of redefinition of that hope is already under way. For the salvation that the Davidic King will bring seems to focus on release from sins and freedom for service as much as on rescue from enemies.' The point is, for me, that this 'process of redefinition' remains hidden; it is not made explicit by Luke.

9. The emphasis rests on the 'fall' of many, as the mention of a 'sign that is spoken against' (v. 34) shows. Cf. Lohfink 1975, 30. Tiede 1988, 28 puts great weight on a dubious interpretation of 2.34: the falling has taken place, but the rising lies ahead, waiting to be fulfilled.

10. Cf. J.T. Carroll 1988, 51: Israel's hope, which is about to be fulfilled, 'appears to embrace national (an unending kingdom of David's son) and religious (forgiveness of sins) concerns in tension (or unreflective ambiguity)'. My assessment is that the ambiguity is all-important.

11. J.T. Sanders 1987, 61: 'the well-merited destruction of the Jews at the Second Coming'. Tannehill 1985, 84 n. 29 has problems with Luke 19.27: 'In the light of the call to repentance and offer of forgiveness in Acts, this judgment must be understood as an indication of what will happen if those who reject their king do not finally repent.' But 19.27 agrees with the end of Acts which suggests that the mission to the Jews has come to an end. Cf. Sanders 1987, 81f. Luke 19.27 can*not* refer to the destruction of Jerusalem by the Romans, for the punishment is to take place in connection with the Parousia. Sanders 1987, 61f.

12. Leaney 1966, 70–2; Wainwright 1977–78, 76f.

13. This is a necessary inference from the contents of 21.12–19, which outweigh the fact that the circle of listeners is not defined in

21.5, 7.

14. In 21.31, the 'kingdom of God' seems to be identified with this 'redemption' of the faithful; cf. Zmijewski 1972, 260. Verse 28 refers to Christians: Zmijewski 1972, 254, 257.

15. Cf. J.T. Carroll 1988, 124: in Acts 1.8, 'Jesus redefines the content of "restoration of the kingdom to Israel"'.

16. Several interpreters point out that Jesus does not correct the question about Israel: Conzelmann 1960, 163; Wainwright 1977–78, 76; Mussner 1984, 38; Tiede 1986, 278: '. . .Jesus' final words respond positively to the question of restoration by revealing the deployment of theocratic dominion . . .' Differently Maddox 1982, 106: 'Jesus' answer includes an indirect denial that it is Israel to whom the Kingdom will be given.' But it is artificial to apply v.7 to Israel ('God has determined "times and seasons" for dealing with Israel') rather than to the final consummation; in this verse, standard Parousia language is used.

17. Tannehill 1985, 77 takes Luke's repeated 'to you' statements at face value, as demonstrating that especially to the people Israel the promise has meaning, 'for it is the fulfilment of their hope and history'.

18. Tannehill 1985, 84 presupposes it without further ado 'as the similarities in wording between Acts 3.20–21 and 1.6–7 make clear'; likewise Mussner 1984, 38.

19. Cf. Jervell 1972, 58; Haenchen 1974, 209: 'the Jew who does not turn to Christ is no longer a member of God's people!' The Christians are the true Israel. See also 211. Mussner 1984, 259f. n. 49 claims that neither here nor anywhere else in Acts is there a single syllable (!) about God excluding his people Israel from eschatological salvation, even though it rejected Jesus as Messiah; in the Old Testament such juridical threats as this also belong simply to the prophetic style of teaching!

20. Mussner 1984, 38 thinks that an actual kingdom for Israel is in view 'on the basis of the entire context which refers to the salvific fate of Israel (prediction of this "establishing" by the prophets of Israel!)'. The parenthetical clause – and not least the exclamation mark – shows how efficiently Luke did his work. He misled Mussner to think of the actual contents of the prophetic predictions in the Old Testament, whereas Luke is thinking of the prophets as reinterpreted through his Christian lenses. The same applies to Tannehill 1988, 87f.: 3.2–26

shows 'that the narrator still understands the scriptural promises quite concretely as promises to the Jewish people'.

21. This is an implication of *proton* in v. 26.

22. Luke is drawing on Isa. 55.3, where *ta hosia David ta pista* stands in parallel to 'an eternal covenant' (an expression omitted by Luke). Haenchen 1974, 412 n. 1 notes that it would not fit here.

23. Tannehill is led astray in his interpretation because he clings to the Old Testament content of the promises which are twisted by Luke to serve his new creed. He finds (1988, 86f.) that 'the emphasis in 13.34 fits well with the Messiah in the angel's announcement to Mary' (he will reign over the house of Jacob for ever, Luke 1.33) and that Paul 'affirms the promise of the messianic kingdom for the Jewish people'.

24. Correctly Jervell 1972, 52f.; Lohfink 1975, 59. The view of Haenchen (1974, 448) that the rebuilding means 'the story of Jesus, culminating in the resurrection' fits other Lukan statements (Acts 2.30ff.; 13.32ff.) but does not do full justice to this particular context.

25. Tannehill 1985, 78 notes that 'this is peculiar': 'Paul is insisting that the issue of the trial is something quite different from what everyone else thinks it is.'

26. J.T. Sanders 1988, 57 rightly speaks of 'fairly unconvincing apologetic'.

27. Tannehill (1989, 12f.) interprets Acts 26 in the light of Luke 1.33! 'If we assume that resurrection of the dead simply means life after death for individuals we will miss the point.' Paul speaks of 'a hope for the Messiah's rule with all its benefits for the Jewish people', 'established through resurrection and characterized by resurrection life corporately shared. That is why it is so important to Israel.'

28. Cf. Fredriksen 1988, 194 (on Luke 4): 'This abrupt and inexplicable reaction of murderous rage scarcely suits the immediate context of the pericope (cf. 4.14, 22), much less the generally irenic tone of this gospel. But it establishes the paradigm repeated continuously in Acts, once the church's mission goes to the Diaspora: initial openness, despite Christological ignorance; mild contention; Gentile response; jealousy, wrath, attempted murder; moving on to the next town.' Fredriksen notes that the Jews of the Diaspora, acting 'from malice and jealousy' against the church, are 'the true villains of Luke's piece' (1988, 194, 193).

29. See Cook 1988, 104–9.

30. Tannehill 1988, 98. He states that the remark in v.30 that Paul welcomed 'all' those coming to him 'should not be dismissed as an idle remark': v.24 stated that some Jews were persuaded, and v.30 indicates that they were welcome to talk to Paul later. However, the converse point can be made: although the response to Paul's message is, according to v.24, divided (not just negative), Luke has Paul subsequently focus only on the negative part of the response. Even Tannehill (1988, 98f.) must admit that the emphatic place of 28.28 at the end of the narrative 'grants the final situation a certain permanence'; at the very least the narrator is aware that 'the possibility of Christians preaching to a Jewish assembly . . . has become very remote'.

31. He thinks that the same idea may be found in the reference to the 'times of the Gentiles' in Luke 21.24: Tannehill 1985, 84f.; 1986, 155f. Cf. also Mussner 1984, 263 n. 116. But the reference to Gentiles need mean no more than that the Parousia will put an end to the Roman rule in Jerusalem. Alternatively, it may indicate that the present time is a period of mission to Gentiles. Nothing suggests that it would be followed by a time of salvation for Israel *qua* Israel. See Zmijewski 1972, 216–20.

32. Evans 1990, 565; J.T. Carroll 1988, 162: 'The close verbal correspondence between Luke 13.35c and 19.38 indicates that the former prophecy is, after all, fulfilled in Jesus' entry into Jerusalem . . .'

33. Alternatively, one could interpret Luke 13.34–35, in the light of 19.41–44, as follows: 'The time will come when you will be ready to call me "Blessed", but then it will be too late', Manson 1949, 128; cf. Fitzmyer 1985, 1035f.

34. Cf. Luke 1.77; 4.16ff.; 19.38, 24.21, 44ff.; Acts 1.6ff.; 2.39; 3.24ff.; 13.32ff.; 15.14ff.; Acts 26.

35. Luke 2.10f.; 2.34.

36. Luke 2.30ff.; 4.16ff.; Acts 2.39; 15.14ff.

37. Luke 19.27; 21.22ff.; Acts 3.23; 13.41; 28.28.

38. Some interpreters think that such a confrontation does take place at this point. 'The temptations . . . are unequivocal (!) in *rejecting* a way for the anointed Son as outlined in Mary's and Zechariah's expectations and hopes', Moessner 1988, 43. That may once have been the point of the story when it circulated in the tradition, but Luke does nothing to make that point clear.

39. J.T. Carroll's conclusion (1988, 163) is correct as far as it goes: all 'emblems of the fulfilment of Israel's hope' (the covenant-promise to Abraham, etc.) 'find their place in relation to Jesus Messiah, and the early church's proclamation of him. This *is* the definitive process of Israel's restoration!' Only, Carroll does not seem to find any problem in this redefinition of Israel's hope which is not spelt out in so many words.

40. Syreeni 1987, 219; cf. 119 on the relationship between Matt. 1.23 and 28.20: 'In the former context, the name "Immanuel" or "God with us" is clearly taken for "God with *Israel*". At the close of the Gospel, Jesus promises to be "with" his disciples, i.e. *the Church*. A purposeful relatedness probably exists between these "with" statements. Hereby Israel and the Church are tacitly assimilated: in one way or another, the Church *is* Israel . . . the evangelist sincerely connotated [sic] "Immanuel" as "God with Israel"; and equally sincerely recorded that the exalted Jesus will be "with" the Christian community; and believed that the latter pronouncement is the adequate realization of the promise of God's presence among Israel.' All this, I think, applies *mutatis mutandis* to Luke's handling of 'salvation' for Israel and for the Christian community. A related assimilation is his use of *laos* both for Israel and for the church.

41. Bovon 1983, 408.

42. Hecht 1987, 149, listing the following texts: *Conf. Ling.* 62–63; *Virt.* 75; *Vita Mos.* 2.44; 2.288; *Op. Mundi* 79–81.

43. On the passage see Hecht 1987, 149f. Unlike Luke, here at least Philo clearly differentiates between a 'corporeal' and a 'spiritual' interpretation, letting the reader know why he chooses the latter.

44. Cf. Hecht 1987, 161, quoting Gershom Scholem.

45. Gaston 1986, 152 notes that the consequences of Luke's solution for the relationship between Christians and Jews are 'deplorable'. Cf. Cook 1988, 123.

46. Gaston 1986, 152.

47. 'Quite different from his presentation of the past, Luke's present is characterized by an implacable enmity between the church and "the Jews" . . . Luke is unable to defend the legitimacy of the (Gentile) Christian movement without declaring the Jews as such to be enemies of the church of God', Gaston 1986, 140.

48. Cook 1988, 122.

49. Gaston 1986, 153; cf. Cook 1988, 116.

50. Jervell 1972, 58, on Acts 3.12–26.

51. This 'profound dilemma of the development of christology' is finely analysed by Ruether 1979: the standard Christian view of redemption is 'a non-messianic soteriology that insists on calling itself a "christology", thereby laying claim to fulfil the Jewish messianic tradition' (243). 'The spiritualizing of the messianic is basically the denial of the messianic, while claiming to fulfil it' (245f.). That this critique hits not only Christians but also Philo or modern Hasidism is another matter. Mussner's answer (1984, 231) to Ruether's claim that the world remains unredeemed is naive: '. . .two things now exist which were not there previously: The gospel and the Church. Their effective history in the world was much, much greater than one commonly assumes. Without the gospel would one have known, for example, that history really should be the history of freedom?'

5. Attacking the Book, Not the People: Marcion and the Jewish Roots of Christianity

1. Chadwick 1967, 40. Gager regards Marcion's point of view as 'an extreme form of Christian anti-Judaism'; his is 'the most thoroughgoing and systematic repudiation of Judaism in early Christianity' (Gager 1983, 162, 175). Bright 1967, 69 claims that 'Marcionism and anti-Semitism undoubtedly have affinities' (though he perceives that 'Marcion's answer to the problem of the Old Testament is not necessarily motivated by anti-Semitism'). Zenger 1993, 7 intentionally evokes sinister associations in speaking of Marcion's 'judenfrei' Christian Bible. As for older assessments, Conybeare (1958, 329) called Marcion 'the greatest anti-Semite of antiquity'! Cf. Holmquist 1907, 66: 'Paul's anti-Judaism became in Marcion a glowing hatred of Jews'. Lietzmann 1949 put forward a remarkably positive assessment of Marcion, but thought it possible that 'he was affected by anti-Semitic influences' (251).

2. Harnack 1985, 198 and passim; cf. also Lietzmann 1949, 249–63; Lüdemann 1996, 159–69.

3. Barr 1971, 34, voicing a general view (which he himself does not share). Barr shows that the comparison of modern doubters of the validity of the Old Testament with Marcion is not valid; such people are not 'modern Marcionites'; their position may even 'come closer to being the reverse of the Marcionite position' which was world-

denying, ascetic and gnostic (32–6). So he frees modern people from the accusation of being 'Marcionites', but does nothing to vindicate Marcion himself.

4. Bright 1967, 73f.

5. Mussner 1995, 241.

6. Zenger 1993, 7 misleadingly suggests that Marcion 'even staked large sums of money in order to persuade the Roman church to dispose of the Old Testament and the "Jewish" passages of the New Testament'. Actually Marcion made his donation before getting engaged in his reform project (besides, a New Testament was not yet in existence).

7. See Lampe 1989.

8. Hoffmann's (1984) attempt to date Marcion's activity earlier has been rightly rejected (see e.g. May 1987–88, 131; Aland 1992, 90), and so has his concomitant thesis that Ephesians and perhaps Colossians 'represent orthodox versions of letters originating in the Marcionite community of Laodicea' (Hoffmann 1984, 274).

9. Cf. Justin, *Apology* 20.5–6; Tertullian, *Adv. Marc.* 5.19. Celsus only knew two branches of Christianity, one of which was Marcionism: Origen, *Contra Celsum* 2.6; 5.54; 6.57; 7.25–6. Still in the fifth century a Syrian bishop reports, not without pride, his success in uprooting survivals of Marcionite belief in several villages (Wilson 1995, 208). It was only the persecutions of heretics, conducted by the brethren of the faith with the support of state authorities, that put an end to this remarkable denomination.

10. Harnack 1985, 143.

11. Harnack still reconstructs Marcion's New Testament. E.g. Hoffmann 1984 now longer attempts this, nor is it possible; see May 1987–88, 132ff. It is unfortunate that Tertullian, who has the *Antitheses* before him (this is denied by Hoffmann 1984, 192), does not cite the work directly, but comments on it, criticizes and edits it. Harnack 1985, 83f. points out that it is difficult to know whether Tertullian is criticizing Marcion himself or later Marcionites in a given passage.

12. Harnack 1985, 93; cf. Aland 1992, 93.

13. He is neither Ahriman nor Satan: Harnack 1985, 97.

14. Aland 1992, 96.

15. See *Adv. Marc.* 4.16.6: 'if such forbearance . . . is imposed upon me by one who is not going to be my defender, in vain does he enjoin

forbearance: for he sets before me no reward . . .'; cf. Aland 1992, 96.

16. Had they belonged to him, he would not have needed to buy them!

17. Irenaeus: May 1978–88, 139. Harnack 1985, 131 comments: 'What an exaggerated Paulinism, but at the same time – what a conviction . . . of the omnipotence of merciful love and the inferiority of morality which, wherever it rules alone, becomes the deadly enemy of the good.' Contrast Blackman 1948, 110: 'This was Paulinism run mad!'

18. Hoffmann 1984, 304.

19. Paul had already stated that total sexual asceticism is better than marriage (I Cor. 7.1), though marriage is preferable to unchastity or 'burning'. Marcion radicalized and generalized this side of Pauline ethics (Lüdemann 1996, 163).

20. Tertullian had to be content with the assertion that Marcion was illogical: since your God who does not punish wrongdoers is not to be feared, why don't you sin?! Marcion's answer to such a *reductio ad absurdum* echoed Paul's *me genoito*: *absit, absit.* Harnack 1985, 135 n.4 is correct in noting that Tertullian's criticism is awkward here. For Marcion, the imperative flowed from the indicative.

21. See Williams 1996 in particular.

22. Therefore Harnack denied Gnostic (and almost any other contemporary) influences altogether, regarding Marcion merely as a representative of exaggerated Paulinism. Marcion's negative view of the world may in fact be a feature that singles him out as being more 'world-rejecting' than 'typical' Gnostics; cf. Williams 1996, 108ff.

23. Hoffmann 1984, 177f.

24. Ibid., 170.

25. Wilson 1995, 214. He continues: 'His sessions with Cerdo in Rome presumably exposed him to ideas that were both congenial and suggestive and that could, with some adaptation, be used to articulate and extend the views he had already formed.' Cf. Lüdemann 1996, 165f. Actually Marcion's separation of redemption and creation may be to some degree paralleled by the unresolved tension between apocalyptic evaluation of the present aeon and the sapiental praise of creation within the New Testament itself. Cf. Harnack 1985, 6.

26. May 1987–88, 148.

27. Contrast Origen, *Contra Celsum* IV.2.1–2. For him, reading the scriptures in their spiritual sense is the solution both to the problem

of the 'hard-hearted and ignorant members of the circumcision' who 'refused to believe in our Saviour' because they could not get beyond the literal sense and to the problems of Marcion, who also read things 'according to the bare letter': Efroymson 1979, 107. Origen's point of view is largely shared by Blackman, who blames Marcion for 'literal-mindedness', a 'literalist and prosaic' bent of mind and blindness 'to any figurative meaning' (Blackman 1948, 113, 115). Marcion's 'lack of imagination', which 'was bound to misinterpret much of the prophetic literature', is seen, according to Blackman (115), e.g. in the fact that Marcion refused to understand Ps 72.10, 15 ('the kings of Arabia and Saba shall offer him gifts . . .') as referring to the Wise Men honouring Jesus at his birth. For a sensible account of the Christian use of the Old Testament ('philological games without precedent', as Nietzsche had put it) down to the time of Marcion see Lüdemann 1996, 148–59.

28. Blackman 1948, 116 (who is both appreciative and critical of this faculty).

29. Apelles developed Marcion's view in a more radical direction: what Moses wrote about God is not right but wrong; Hoffmann 1984, 164.

30. Origen, *Hom.* XII, 1ff.: Harnack 1985, 272*–3*. Cf. *Nihil humanitatis habuit Jesus filius Nave* (Josh. 9; Origen, *Hom.* X, 2).

31. Megethius in Adamantius, *Dial.* I, 13; Harnack 1985, 281*.

32. Adamantius, *Dial.* I, 11; Harnack 1985, 281*. For Tertullian, the Amalek passage conveys a type of the cross.

33. Epiphanius, *Ancorat.* 111: Harnack 1985, 281*.

34. Tertullian replies that the Hebrews had to get recompensation for wages not paid for their labour (*Adv. Marc.* 2.21). In *Adv. Marc.* 4.24 he adds a practical point: the Hebrews were being moved out into the wilderness, but the disciples were being sent into cities!

35. Megethius, *Dial.* I,16: Harnack 1985, 282*; Tertullian, *Adv. Marc.* 4.23.4–5.

36. Even Tertullian, *Adv. Marc.* 4.23.8, admits the difference between the creator's sternness – Elijah brings fire upon the false prophet – and Christ's gentleness in Luke 9.56ff. He notes that 'this gentleness of Christ is promised by the same stern Judge' (Isa. 42.2).

37. Tertullian, *Adv. Marc.* 2.21, replies: divine labours are not forbidden on the Sabbath, only human ones.

38. Tertullian explains, weakly, that creating evil things refers to

punishments (*Adv. Marc.* 2.14).

39. Tertullian, *Adv. Marc.* 2.25.2, explains this away, suggesting that one has to read 'Adam, where art thou!', as meaning 'Thou art in perdition . . .' He stands in an exegetical tradition, cf. R.Braun 1991, 230ff.

40. Cf. Harnack 1985, 92.

41. Eaton 1989. Cf. the not unjustified eulogy of the 'continuing appeal' of the Old Testament for 'anyone who becomes really familiar with its contents' by Rogerson 1995, 82.

42. Lüdemann 1996, 164.

43. Hill 1994, 76.

44. Marcion subjected Galatians, too, to editorial criticism, but 'his editing of Romans was the most drastic of all, which is what we might expect from someone brought up on Galatians'. And indeed, 'if the view of Paul that Marcion got from Galatians is exaggerated, distorted, or truncated, then so is any view of Paul that knows him only through this epistle – as is shown by the difficulty some of us have in bringing the views expressed in Galatians into line, for example, with those expressed in Romans', Wilson 1995, 214.

45. Simon 1986, 74. Cf. Drane 1975, 112f.: '. . . taken in isolation from his other epistles, Paul's statements on the Law in Galatians can with a great deal of justification be called blatantly Gnostic . . . The natural and logically necessary outcome' of Gal. 3.19, 'whatever may have been its original justification . . ., was the belief that the Law was the product not of the supreme God . . . it was but a short step from Paul's statements to the assumption that the Law was the work of some evil angelic Demiurge.'

46. See Origen, *Comm. in Rom.* IV, 4 on 4.14f.; *Comm. in Rom.* V, 6 on 5.20f.: Harnack 1985, 277*. Tertullian (*Adv. Marc.* 5.13.14) emphasizes against Marcion that 'it was not the law that led astray, but sin'. It can perhaps be inferred that Marcion had claimed that the law led astray (a 'dangerous perversion' of Rom. 7.11 according to Aland 1992, 94). Yet the law did contribute to the increase of sin according to Rom. 5.20 and 7.7, and this was its intention; if this was the case, what else can such statements of the Old Testament which connect the law with life and speak of the eternal character of its commandments be but misleading claims which lead people astray?

47. Harnack 1985, 202f.

48. He goes on: 'From here, it is a stone's throw to the Johannine

demonization of the servants of that diabolical deity and to the notion that they worship the devil' (cf. Rev. 2.9; 3.9). Levenson 1985a, 247.

49. Martyn 1991, 173.

50. Luz 1967, 322. Cf. Martyn 1991, 174: 'the singularity of the seed (sc. in Gal. 3.16) spells, in fact, the end of *Heilsgeschichte* as a view that encompasses a linear history of a people of God prior to Christ'. This paragraph is indebted to the doctoral thesis of Kari Kuula (in preparation in Helsinki).

51. Cf. Räisänen 1992, 273ff.

52. Gager 1983, 183.

53. Cf. Harnack 1985, 204–6; Kotila 1988, 209f.

54. In Origen, *Contra Celsum* VII.18.

55. See Ariarajah 1985, 9, quoted Ch. 1, p. 5.

56. Cf. Wiles 1967, 49: Marcion's 'attack upon the law . . . struck at the roots of the fundamental Christian conviction that the revelation of Christ was in direct continuity with the revelation of the same God in the era of the Old Testament . . .'

57. Tertullian emphasizes (*Adv. Marc.* 2.1.6) against Marcion that a novelty must needs be a heresy, 'precisely because that has to be considered truth which was delivered of old and from the beginning'. In view of what actually happened to the Old Testament in Christian interpretation, this comes close to self-condemnation.

58. Wiles 1967, 50: 'Where Marcion's emphasis had fallen with extreme one-sidedness on Paul's criticisms of the law, the emphasis of the orthodox commentators falls almost equally heavily on the other side . . .'

59. Thus Origen. Wiles 1967, 52: 'No other writer shows the same degree of reluctance as Origen in this matter; but . . . all are careful to defend the law itself from ultimate blame.'

60. Cf. *Adv. Marc.* 4.33.8: the New Testament statement that 'the law and the prophets were until John' (Matt. 11.12 par.) means that the Baptist 'has been set as a sort of dividing-line between old things and new, a line at which Judaism should cease (!) and Christianity should begin . . .'

61. Cf. 'Christ has always (!) acted in God the Father's name, has himself ever since the beginning associated with, and conversed with, patriarchs and prophets' (*Adv. Marc.* II.27.3). On this common doctrine see R. Braun 1991, 162 n. 1.

62. The figurative nature of the law is derived from Romans 7,

where Paul affirms that the law is 'spiritual'!

63. Efroymson 1979, 108. 'What Marcion did was to draw conclusions from premises that had been built into the "mainstream" gentile Christianity he knew . . . a God whose change of mind (replacement of Jews with gentiles; abandonment of much of his ritual law) seemed insufficiently accounted for . . .; a Bible supposedly sacred to Christians, but whose ritual law they did not keep; an emphasis on newness which seemed inconsistent with a claim to continuity or antiquity. Something was wrong . . . Justin, Irenaeus, Tertullian, and Origen succeeded in getting Marcion's case ruled out of court, but their case was hardly a solution to the original problem.'

64. The Pastorals and Hebrews are missing from Marcion's Pauline corpus.

65. E.g. *Adv. Marc.* 4.7, 4.9 and passim.

66. Campenhausen 1984, 161.

67. Harnack 1985, 71: 'an honest moralism will find it more difficult to excuse the Fourth Evangelist than Marcion, especially as Marcion does not conceal his cards, which can hardly be said of the Fourth Evangelist. But in neither case is the moral criterion appropriate.' Cf. Campenhausen 1984, 160f., who adds the example of Tatian, who did not shrink from making major excisions (e.g. Matt. 1–2, Luke 1–2).

68. See Campenhausen 1984.

69. Cf. Hoffmann 1984, 226–34; Wilson 1995, 207–21.

70. Hoffmann 1984, 228.

71. Blackman 1948, ix–x totally misses the mark in speculating that what he calls 'Marcion's anti-Judaism' might have been 'a merit in Tertullian's eyes' (though it was not), as Tertullian was no friend of the Jews either.

72. But note Marcion's irony: 'Such a very good God, if when calmed down he gives back what he took away when angry . . .' (ibid.)

73. Efroymson 1979, 101.

74. Gager 1983, 172.

75. Efroymson 1979, 102. We found a similar emphasis already in Luke (above, Chapter 4).

76. Efroymson 1979, 104.

77. Hoffmann 1984, 233, my emphasis. In this sense one could perhaps even speak, if only *cum grano salis*, of 'the pro-Jewish orientation' of Marcion's theology (Hoffmann 1984, 227).

78. Gager 1983, 172. For a discussion of the attitudes to Jews and Judaism in the Nag Hammadi texts, concerned to refine Gager's claim, see Wilson 1995, 199–207.

79. Wilson 1986, 58. However, this very sentence is omitted from the updated version of Wilson's study (1995, 221).

80. von Reventlow 1995, 145–6.

81. Ibid., 146.

82. Harnack 1985, 217: transl. Barr 1971, 33f.

83. Blackman 1948, 122 is typical. Even Wilson 1995, 209 scarcely does justice to Harnack here: 'a judgment that was doubtless, in its turn, influenced by the inadequate view of Judaism and its law that prevailed in the scholarship of Harnack's day'.

84. Harnack 1985, 220. Cf. Prickett 1995, 153: 'To Oliver Cromwell, fighting against Catholics in Ireland, it seemed . . . appropriate to justify the brutal obliteration of Catholic society and, if necessary, the massacre of his opponents, by supporting the Protestant Plantation in Ulster with images of the Israelites occupying Canaan appropriated from the book of Joshua.'

85. Harnack 1985, 222.

86. Ibid., 223: 'but the question today is not one of "rejection"; rather the character and significance (the Prophets) of the book is only valued and prized everywhere when the *canonical* authority which is not its due is withdrawn from it'. Blackman's question 'is there nothing in the Old Testament which should be conserved?' (1948, 122) misses the mark. Aland (1973, 447) even writes: 'Harnack's call to the twentieth century to follow Marcion's example in rejecting (*sic*!) the Old Testament needs no refutation, nor even a commentary'.

87. Hill 1994 is full of examples; see especially his chapter on political sermons (79–108).

88. Bernard Mandeville, quoted in Hill 1994, 76.

89. Niditch 1995, 3f.

90. Niditch shows in her superb work that the 'crusading idea' is 'not unique to Israelite culture' and that 'within the Hebrew Bible the sort of war of extirpation waged against the Canaanites in Joshua is one among many war ideas . . ., a war ideology with which the authors of Chronicles and Jonah, some Deuteronomic threads, and post-biblical authors such as Josephus are uncomfortable' (1995, 5 and *passim*). '. . . the history of attitudes to war in ancient Israel is a

complex one involving multiplicity, overlap, and self-contradiction' (154).

91. '. . . ancient Israelite authors do worry about the ethics of killing in war and make peace with themselves in various ways,' Niditch 1995, 21. 'We have sought to understand the banning and other ideologies of war . . . as expressions of varying cultural threads in ancient Israel and in terms of human responses toward manifestations of the "Other", asking how people react to and employ violence, power, and oppression' (127).

92. Warrior 1991, 289.

93. Ateek 1991, 281.

94. Ruether – Ruether 1989, 179.

95. Mayes 1990, 369.

96. Ateek 1991, 283.

97. Cf. Luz 1994, 32–4, 82, 92, asking critical questions e.g. about Matt. 27.25; 12.31–32 and I Cor. 14.34–35.

98. Parkes 1979, x–xi.

99. Levenson 1985a, 245.

100. Beck 1985, 285; he gives as an example John 8.13, where 'the Pharisees' 'can be rendered as "some of the people there", since obviously not all of the Pharisees alive at that time would have addressed Jesus simultaneously in one unified chorus' (261). To change consistently all passages where something 'obviously' could not have happened that way would mean to rewrite the whole Bible drastically.

101. Beck's other suggestion (1985, 285) that 'we will be more selective in our choice of lectionary texts, providing readings that are less blatantly anti-Jewish' is acceptable. However, the alternative that one keeps anti-Jewish texts, but preaches against them in the sermon might be worth considering.

102. It is hardly in doubt that Marcion 'greatly excelled' his adversary Tertullian 'in profundity and originality': Meijering 1977, ix, 168. 'That the battle (in Tertullian's work) goes Tertullian's way is simply due to the fact that Marcion . . . is given no chance to fight back' (1977, ix).

6. Jesus between Christianity and Islam: Muhammad's Portrait of the Jewish Prophet

1. Maqsood 1991, ix, xi.

2. Ibid., 176, cf. 4. Despite this impressive testimony, it is not quite clear to me why she became specifically a Muslim and not a Quaker or a Jew. Maqsood also reveals that she has already run into trouble with authoritarian representatives of her new religion. She has feminist leanings and a passion to question any Islamic tradition which she finds not to be based on the Qur'an itself. See her comments on some Muslims' 'obsession with literal obedience to minutiae' which can create 'blind guides' (57); cf. 53, 131, etc.

3. Küng 1987b, 123.

4. For a full treatment see Räisänen 1971; cf. also Michaud 1960; Parrinder 1965; Schedl 1978; Robinson 1991. The Qur'an is cited according to the official Egyptian counting of the verses, which differs slightly from the edition of G. Flügel, whose numbering was earlier common in the West. Watt 1970, 202f. gives a convenient table for converting verse-numbers.

5. It is found in the Nag Hammadi Library in the 'Second Treatise of the great Seth': 'I did not die in reality but in appearance . . . they nailed their man unto their death' (NHC 55,18–19, 55,34–35).

6. See Räisänen 1971, 7f.

7. Zwemer 1912, 8 (typical of many others).

8. Henninger 1945, 135. Yet the cry has been inevitable: 'How sadly attenuated is this Christian prophet as Islam knows Him!', Cragg 1956, 261.

9. Rafiq 1980, 106.

10. *Review of Religions (Rabura)* 1978, 204.

11. Cf. the references in Räisänen 1971, 11. On the portrait of Jesus in particular see now the treatment of its Monophysite roots by Risse 1989.

12. Masson 1958, 7.

13. Al-Husayni 1960, 299, 302; cf. Ayoub 1980, 117.

14. E.g. Zaehner 1962, 209, 216.

15. Cf. Chapter 1, p. 15.

16. The angel says to Mary: 'Even so thy Lord has said: Easy is that for Me; and that We may appoint him a sign unto men and a mercy from us' (19.21).

17. E.g. Abraham, Moses or certain Arab figures.

18. Muhammad seems to have taken over this designation from Christians who had applied it to Jesus (it is found in Tertullian's *Adversus Iudaeos* 8.12); see Colpe 1987.

19. Lüling has set forth the speculative thesis of a 'primitive Qur'an' which consisted of Christian hymns. Despite a basic sympathy (see below, n. 29) with his critical approach to doctrine (which is indebted to his mentor, Martin Werner), I cannot but regard his ideas concerning a primitive 'angel christology', supposedly preserved in the Qur'an, as highly idiosyncratic. Cf. Rudolph's balanced judgment in his review (1980, 3): 'That Muhammad was initially strongly dependent on Christian notions . . . has been recognized. We must also reckon with a "revision" of earlier surahs of the Qur'an . . . However, none of this justifies the reconstruction of a Christian Ur-Qur'an with a method which subjects the Arabic text to very arbitrary and violent exegesis.'

20. Räisänen 1971; cf. 1980. My exposition has been taken up by others, notably by Rudolph 1975 and Küng 1987b.

21. We recall that Ariarajah in his effort to outline a pluralistic theology of the New Testament turns from John's exclusivism ('I am the Way and the Truth . . .' [John 14.6]; 'there is no other name by which we can be saved' [Acts 4.12], 1985, 19f.) to the portrait of Jesus in the Synoptic Gospels. Jesus lived a 'God-centred life', making 'no claim to divinity or to oneness with God'. 'In the Synoptic environment it would be strange if Jesus were to say "I and the Father are one", or "I am the way . . ."' (21). Unlike Paul, Jesus 'claims that he has come not to abolish the Law' (21f.). This witness to Jesus 'in some ways stands in contradiction' to that of the exclusive sayings (22).

22. On the non-soteriological interpretation of the death of Jesus see e.g. Dunn 1990, 17f., 218f., 284f., and the summarizing statement (224): 'As regards the death of Jesus: Jesus himself probably regarded it as the beginning of the messianic woes which would bring in . . . the final rule of God; the earliest churches and/or Luke apparently made little of it as a soteriological factor; whereas Paul in particular developed a theology of the suffering and death of Christ . . .'

23. Casey 1991.

24. Wilson 1995, 79.

25. Even if the spearhead of Muhammad's criticism is directed against *Monophysite* views, as is shown by Risse (216 and *passim*), mainstream christology is no less hit by it.

26. See Küng's summary of scholarship on the Jewish background of Muhammad's 'christology' (1987b, 122–6).

27. Dunn argues powerfully that 'the heretical Jewish Christianity of the later centuries could quite properly claim to be more truly the heir of earliest Christianity than any other expression of Christianity. It was rejected (in Dunn's view, justly!) because in a developing situation where Christianity had to develop and change, it did not', Dunn 1990, 244.

28. For a recent discussion of Jewish Christianity see Wilson 1995, 143–59.

29. On this general level my view is not very far from Lüling's contention that 'the Prophet Muhammad is the last theological defender of early Christian theology against its Hellenistic-Western deformation' (1981, 21). If the lack of a confrontation with 'early Christian angel christology' exhibits the 'reactionary spirit' of German evangelical-theological faculties (thus Lüling 1981, 347 n.1 on my 1971 book), then so be it. Lüling accepts Werner's thesis of an angel christology as normative. However, other scholars had their good reasons for rejecting Werner's view (cf. Hurtado 1988, 72f.). For an attempt to examine, from another angle, 'whether Jewish angelology may have assisted early Jewish Christians in coming to terms theologically with the exalted Christ' cf. Hurtado 1988, 75ff. For a critical discussion of the radical reconstruction of the origins of Islam by Crone and Cook ('Hagarism') see Robinson 1996, 47ff.

30. The 'adoptionism' of the Ebionites is well attested, the clearest expression being found in Epiphanius, *Panarion* 30.18.5–6; cf. Dunn 1990, 242.

31. It is possible, however, that Eusebius' account is 'muddled' (Wilson 1995, 358 n. 60). Origen (*Contra Celsum* 61) also knows of two types of Ebionites, but only ascribes a low christology to one of them; the other is said to be fairly orthodox. Cf. Wilson 1995, 156. If Eusebius is inaccurate, the adoptionist 'low' christology of a group of Jewish Christians remains the best traditio-historical parallel to the Qur'anic view of Jesus.

32. Küng 1987b, 124.

33. Ibid., 93. Cf. 95: 'I wonder: if a Muslim or a Jew should be expected to recognize the Hellenist councils from Nicaea to Chalcedon, what would Jesus of Nazareth, the Jew, have done?'

34. Muslim-Christian Research Group 1989, 80. Rahman 1980,

170 even states: 'The Qur'an would most probably have no objections to the Logos having come in the flesh if the Logos were not simply identified with God and the identification were understood less literally.' However, 'the Muslim faith categorically rejects the idea that Jesus could really be the son of God, eternally begotten of the Father in the bosom of the Trinity. The God of Muslim faith is not a God to be born and to die like the Christian deity' (Muslim-Christian Research Group 1989, 80f.). By contrast, the Christians in the Muslim-Christian discussion group still affirm that 'for the Christian faith . . . the Creator has taken the initiative of becoming a creature (!) in Jesus Christ' (ibid., 74).

35. Lindars 1972, 54.

36. Käsemann 1964, 32.

37. Fitzmyer 1985, 1558. For modern Old Testament scholars there is not a single saying in the Old Testament that could be taken as a reference to Jesus when read in its original context.

38. Muslim-Christian Research Group 1989, 100 n. 38.

39. Cf. especially von Rad 1962–65.

40. Von Rad 1962, 350.

41. Wink 1968, 105.

42. Becker 1972, 13.

43. Trilling 1959, 286.

44. Translation according to Arberry 1986.

45. Ayoub 1980, 116f.

46. Glassé 1989, 208f. Note also the claim of Balic (1987, 544) that the Qur'anic stories about Jesus belong to 'Prophet Stories' which are 'often regarded as legends' and have a 'pedagogical-literary auxiliary role'.

47. In both cases it should be realized that originally the statements were hardly meant to be symbolic. They were regarded as 'factual' by their originators.

48. See the account in Wessels 1991, 43–56.

49. Ibid., 55f.

50. 'Do not even think of fighting. One who tries to bring people happiness cannot lightly think of shedding their blood' (in Wessels 1991, 53). Mahfuz views Jesus' work as spiritual, not political. 'He was known as the man who delivered people from evil spirits and gave them happiness and health, all for the sake of God alone', Wessels 1991, 51. If Mahfuz's picture of Jesus is a challenge to Muslims, it is

likewise 'a genuine challenge for a Christian to see here how a Muslim pictures Jesus' way of non-violence, his non-attachment to power and possessions, and his utterly 'spiritual' type of ministry . . ., action experienced by those in power as a threat', Wessels 1991, 159.

7. Arbitrary Allah? Predestination in the Qur'an

1. For a comprehensive treatment of the issue see Räisänen 1976. I follow Arberry's translation of the Qur'an (1986), with occasional adaptations.

2. See e.g. Watt 1948; Stieglecker 1962, 100–20.

3. See e.g. Nygren 1956; McSorley 1967; McGrath 1990, 240ff.

4. Migne, *Patrologia Graeca* 94, 1585ff.

5. E.g. Schlunk 1953, 113.

6. Kraemer 1938, 221.

7. Cf. Volz 1924.

8. Dodd 1947, 158f.

9. Cf. Kiddle 1941, 250f. on Rev. 13.8: 'It is hardly possible not to feel distaste' at the deliberate predestinarianism of the book which 'leaves little to commend' in the seer's conception of God.

10. I follow the classical chronological analysis of Theodor Nöldeke (and Friedrich Schwally). For a fresh discussion of its merits and possible faults see Robinson 1996, 76–96. The broad distinction between Meccan and Medinan surahs is not in doubt (and there is little difference on this between Nöldeke and the classical Muslim view). What may be more questionable is Nöldeke's assignment of the Meccan surahs to three distinct periods, though this still seems a viable working hypothesis.

11. Cf. Ringgren 1955, 115f.

12. The translation here follows that of Bell 1960. Arberry 1986 translates 'the Word has been realised *against* most of them, *yet* they do not believe'. On this reading any predestinarian shade would disappear from the passage.

13. Paret 1966 thinks of the predestining word; Watt 1967, 201 also offers the alternative 'the sentence of damnation'.

14. Cf. the occurrence of *haqqa* during the second Meccan period in the following cases. What has been fulfilled is in 38.14 the 'vengeance', 50.14 the 'menace', 37.31 God's 'sentence'; in 36.70 the word has been fulfilled 'concerning the unbelievers'. See Räisänen 1976, 19 with n. 5.

15. Cf. Wansbrough 1977, 72f. The thought is repeated in 17.45–46. In the third Meccan period, biblical influence is apparent in the account of the exodus in Surah 10. There Moses prays to God to make Pharaoh and his Council 'go astray'; he asks God to 'harden their hearts so that they do not believe' (10.88). The idea of the hardening of Pharaoh's heart must ultimately go back to the biblical story. In 41.4–5 (third Meccan period) the notion of veiled hearts is rather ingeniously put into the mouth of Muhammad's hearers who say: 'Our hearts are veiled from what thou callest us to, and in our ears is a heaviness, and between us and thee there is a veil . . .'

16. A version of the Christian legend of the 'seven sleepers'.

17. Watt 1948, 14.

18. Here the verb *qaddara* occurs which was to become an important technical 'fatalistic' term in Islamic theology. In the Qur'an, however, the word does not yet carry a firmly established theological meaning; it simply denotes 'deciding' in a quite general sense. See Ringgren 1955, 97–103; Rahbar 1960, 108–15.

19. Regarded as predestinarian by Brandon 1962, 244.

20. Arberry 1986 translates 'against'; likewise Bell 1960. I follow the translation of Paret 1966 and others.

21. Thus Margoliouth 1939, 35.

22. Cf. Ringgren 1955, 94f.

23. Brandon 1962, 244–5.

24. Paret 1980, 109f.

25. Cf. Rahbar 1960, 80f.

26. So also 38.84 from the second Meccan period.

27. Grimme (1895, 109) thought that this verse represented the final stage in Muhammad's development from a preacher of free will to a teacher of absolute, eternal predestination. The results of the Islamic expositors Rahbar 1960 and Rauf 1970 suffer from the fact that they curiously neglect this verse altogether. (Rauf 1970, 215 does cite the latter part of the verse, but omits the first part which speaks of creation for Gehenna!)

28. Cf. Rahbar 1960, 84.

29. Arberry 1986 translates 'hypocrites', which is an often used alternative rendering.

30. For Seale 1964, 22 even this verse is 'purely predestinarian'.

31. The classical presentation is Grimme 1895, 105–9.

32. This is the correct conclusion by Rahbar 1960.

33. Thus, the interpretation of Otto (1959), shared e.g. by Heiler 1961, 153f., which traces the predestinarian language directly back to Muhammad's numinous experience of God (cf. also Bouman 1980, 262f.), is *not* supported by our analysis. A further argument against this interpretation is the fact that it is not only God who leads men astray according to the Qur'an; in more rationalistic terms Satan also figures in this role, if only by God's permission.

8. Word of God, Word of Muhammad: Could Historical Criticism of the Qur'an be Pursued by Muslims?

1. Antes 1981, 181 calls attention to the great similarity between Islamic exegesis and traditional Jewish exegesis of the Hebrew Bible.

2. Cf. Goldziher 1952; Baljon 1968; Jansen 1980; Gätje 1976.

3. Rippin 1987, 242, cf. 237.

4. Küng here refers to the view of Fazlur Rahman, to be discussed further below.

5. Küng 1987a, 86f.

6. On the Muslim side, e.g. S.H. Nasr is of the opinion that in Christianity biblical criticism has become 'a diabolic enterprise' (quoted in Antes 1981, 179).

7. Hick 1995, 121.

8. E.g. Adams 1987, 173f. A minority (the 'Mu'tazilites') have held that the Qur'an was created by God (cf. Watt 1970, 170f.).

9. Rahbar 1958a, 47.

10. Wielandt 1971, 42.

11. Rahbar 1958b, 279.

12. Cf. Wielandt 1971, 43: 'The metaphysical problem, how abrogations, i.e. changes, are possible in a pre-existent text which is as eternal as God himself, has never been clearly perceived, let alone solved, by the theologians . . .'

13. Especially Sayyid Ahmad Khan in India, Muhammad Abduh in Egypt. Cf. Baljon 1968, 21–32, 88–98.

14. Jansen 1980.

15. This was Muhammad Abduh's view; it is not, however, typical of Abduh's approach as a whole, cf. Jansen 1980, 33f., 39, 43. There are other expositors who are much more extreme in their 'scientific' exegesis. The positive drive behind scientific exegesis is the wish to maintain that 'Islam is tolerant of all scientific investigation' (Jansen

1980, 34). The approach 'antedates the impact of the Western technology . . . on the Islamic world' (37).

16. Jansen 1980, 50. The references are, respectively, 17.1; 41.53; 55.33 and 74.33–35.

17. The same point had been made before, e.g. by G.Parwez, see Baljon 1968, 85.

18. Jansen 1980, 43.

19. Cf. Prot.Jac 8; Ps.-Matt 6.

20. Baljon 1968, 22.

21. See ibid., 69f.

22. Ibid., 27f.

23. Differently, however, al-Mashriqi for whom 'the speaking ant is accounted representative of insects charged to spread bacteria into Solomon's camp . . . for the protection of his soldiers from these insects Solomon prepared all the scientific means which modern nations nowadays prepare'. Baljon 1968, 73.

24. Baljon 1968, 23. Bucaille, who denies the occurrence of any scientific error in the Qur'an, does not even mention any of these cases.

25. Barr 1977, 40–55, qualified in Boone 1990, 44f. (Barr is correct insofar as he restricts his analysis to 'relatively scholarly evangelicals').

26. Cf. Barr 1977, 40f.

27. Jansen 1980, 7 (cf. 53) notes that 'scientific' exegesis 'not only has zealous adherents, but also ardent opponents, who argue passionately that it is a "stupid heresy" . . .'

28. Jansen 1980, 33. On al-Khuli's method see Jansen 65–9. His work was carried out by his widow Bint as-Shati; cf. Jansen 1980, 69–76. For her 'the purpose of the narrative element of the Qur'an is to provide moral and spiritual guidance, not to provide history or "facts"': Rippin 1987, 243.

29. Jansen 1980, 65f.

30. Stendahl 1984, 11–44.

31. He was able to find support in individual statements in the writings of some older modernists (Baljon 1968, 38ff.). On Khalafallah see Jomier 1954; Baljon 1968, 38–42; Wielandt 1971, 134–52.

32. Jansen 1980, 68. Jansen, 15f. n.54, points out Khalafallah's use of a 'typological' method, when he writes e.g.: 'The picture the Koran gives of the Prophets Hud and Shu'ayb and of how they debated with their fellow-tribesmen, is a general picture which applies to every

Prophet. It applies to the Arab Prophet Mohammed.' 'If we try to understand the spiritual excitement of Abraham and Moses [when they destroyed the idols of their fellow-tribesmen] we inevitably understand the circumstances under which Mohammed preached.'

33. In fact, Khalafallah's aims were apologetic: he wished to do away with historical difficulties seized on by 'atheists, orientalists and missionaries': Jomier 1954, 66.

34. Jomier 1954, 65; Wielandt 1971, 151. However, there is no reason to doubt Khalafallah's subjective sincerity in this regard.

35. In his later production Khalafallah reverted to conventional apologetics, Wielandt 1971, 152.

36. Rahbar's book was concerned to show by way of contextual analysis that the doctrine of predestination is *not* found in the Qur'an. See the previous chapter.

37. Rahbar 1958b, 281. A Western reader might wish to know whether this entails the admission that some of the passages about Jesus go back to apocryphal Christian material, but such outspoken questions are not taken up by Rahbar.

38. Al-Ashmawy 1989, 39f., goes in the same direction.

39. Cf. Boullata 1990.

40. Al-Ashmawy 1989, 39f. Cf. the work of Muhammad al-Nuwayhi (Boullata 1990, 22, 63f., 66ff.).

41. See An-Na'im 1990, xi–xii. An-Na'im is carrying on the work and developing the thoughts of the famous Sufi thinker and civil rights fighter M.M. Taha, executed in old age in the last days of the Numeiri regime.

42. Those Qur'anic passages which explicitly put women into a position different from that of men, indeed come from the Medinan period, e.g. 4.34. On the other hand, An-Na'im does not appeal to a single Meccan verse with a positively egalitarian content. An argument from silence can hardly be convincing here. Cf. Jansen, 94 on similar devices in connection with attempts to remove the death penalty for apostasy or to abolish the seclusion of women: 'It is difficult to see how the Koran by being silent could influence people to adopt a set of new opinions.'

43. E.g. 16.125: 'Call thou to the way of thy Lord with wisdom and good admonition and dispute with them in the better way'; |29.46: 'Dispute not with the People of the Book save in the fairer manner, except for those of them that do wrong; and say, "We believe

in what has been sent down to us, and what has been sent down to you . . .'"

44. E.g. 2.190–193: 'Fight in the way of God with those who fight with you . . . And slay them wherever you come upon them . . . Fight them, till there is no persecution and the religion is God's . . .'; 9.29: 'Fight those who believe not in God and the Last Day . . . being of those who have been given the Book – until they pay the tribute out of hand and have been humbled.'

45. While the theory is at least as old as Origen, J.S. Semler can be singled out for his use of it in the eighteenth century. Cf. Baird 1992, 123f.; ibid., 186 on Gabler; 188, 192 on G.L. Bauer; 346 on Thomas Arnold.

46. On Rahman's contribution cf. Denny 1989; Sonn 1991.

47. Morgan 1990, 585.

48. Ibid., 27.

49. Ibid., 25, 28–29.

50. Ibid., 35–37. See on the subject of wine Powers 1988, 128f. 'After first praising wine as one of the signs of His grace to mankind (Q. 16/67), God refers to this substance as a mixed blessing in Q 2/219; in Q. 4/43, He orders believers not to come to prayer "when you are drunken until you know what you are saying"; finally, God prohibited wine entirely in Q. 5/90 . . .' (129). Cf. also Robinson 1996, 64–9.

51. Rahman 1968, 37.

52. Baird 1992, 188 (discussing the New Testament theology of G.L. Bauer).

53. Rahman 1970, 330.

54. In a similar vein, Al-Ashmawy 1989, 31 underlines that the main interest of the Qur'an is to 'form the conscience of the believer' (rather than legislate).

55. Al-Ashmawy 1989, 42f. develops the case of the punishment for theft in an interesting direction: the practice of amputation of a hand is pre-Islamic, already found in the code of Hammurabi, and practised in Mecca before Islam. If the Qur'an did not abstain from borrowing from 'pagan' law, why should it be an act of infidelity to borrow today details from the law of a Christian country?

56. Rahman 1970, 330f.

57. In an inter-religious dialogue, S.H.Nasr called Rahman 'an anomaly'; to refer to such an 'isolated case' in the course of a dialogue is to destroy 'the possibility of understanding and creating peace' and

to 'overlook the beliefs of a billion Muslims'. Nasr 1987, 98f. However, the billion Muslims are not a homogeneous block. Eickelman 1993 reports that 'a publishing event is sweeping the Middle East; a modernist interpretation of the Qur'an by a Syrian civil engineer has become a bestseller' (163). The broad appeal of the book 'suggests that Islamic liberalism is alive and well, and perhaps even on the verge of effectively asserting its voice' (165). The author, Muhammad Shahrur, seems to share Rahman's approach.

58. Cf. e.g. Arkoun 1982, 50. See on Arkoun, Boullata 1990, 79ff.

59. Boullata 1990, 84.

60. Cf. Arkoun 1982, xxviii: his programme entails 'a freedom to think, describe and publish which contemporary Muslim societies do not yet guarantee'. Ibid., xxxii: 'The most difficult obstacle seems to me to be a conservative attitude in Arabic and Isalmic studies . . . my objective is above all to open up ways and involve young researches in them.' Cf. ibid., 35.

61. Arkoun endorses the work of Khalafallah (1982, 2 n.1).

62. Cf. Arkoun 1982, 3, 41. In a similar vein Ayoub 1989, 44: 'We know now that no religion can claim an exclusive monopoly on salvation and truth. We must accept the fact that our forebears knew far less about world religions than we know. Hence we must see our faith in global perspective as one among many, each having its own spiritual heritage and civilization. In light of this, no religious community or religio-ethnic group can claim a special and exclusive mission to humankind.'

63. Boullata 1990, 85.

64. He was Professor of Law and Vice-Chancellor of the University of Jammu and Kashmir as well as former visiting professor at Cambridge University and UCLA.

65. Cf. Fyzee 1963, 101: 'For instance, great emphasis need not be laid on the virgin birth of Jesus, or the descriptions of Heaven and Hell in the Koran. Their *literal* truth need not be emphasized, their *poetic* truth is cardinal and supreme.' Ibid., 102: 'The Koran . . . may (at times) speak in the language of poetry, metaphor, myth or legend.'

66. Quotation in Baljon 1968, 68 n. 2. Here Fyzee is following up Daud Rahbar's opinion.

67. Their works are to be studied with care 'so that we may not be misled by the mistakes and guesses of the medieval Arab lexicographers', Fyzee 1963, 98. 'The true interpretation of Koranic verses,

studied in the chronological order, with all the *apparatus criticus* of Semitic scholarship, will have to be determined afresh . . .' (103).

68. Fyzee 1963, 113 footnote.

69. Cf. Halide Edib Adivaz's conclusion from Fyzee's view (quoted in Baljon 1968, 43): because some parts of the Qur'an were meant for ancient people and others for all humans and for all time, one ought to seek some of the latter values from the Qur'an.

70. Boullata 1990, 139.

71. Wielandt 1971, 168. Cf An-Na'im's view (1990, 61) of the *ulama* as the gravest obstacle for a renewal of the *shariah*.

72. Rahbar has pointed out that 'it is the historical study of the Qur'an, and a scientific review of the classical discussions of *Asbab al-Nuzul* . . . which will reorientate the Muslim mind and enable him to share scientific attitudes with the Westerner', Rahbar 1958a, 47.

73. Cf. Ch. 9 on La Peyrère.

74. He expressed the wish (in 1958): 'A modern and satisfying exegesis of the Qur'an, with a scientific insight into revelation like that of the rich modern exegesis of the Bible, has yet to appear', Rahbar 1958a, 44.

75. Fyzee 1963, 107. Fyzee calls the new kind of Islam he is longing for not just 'liberal' but also 'protestant' (104). The religious pluralism of the Indian scene has deeply affected his thought (95). Of course, his picture of Luther may be somewhat exaggerated.

76. Arkoun 1982, 2; cf. ibid. 38.

77. Cf. Räisänen 1990, 122–36.

78. Cf. Räisänen 1992, 271f., for a brief statement of the issue.

79. An-Na'im 1990 (e.g. 157, 187).

80. But cf. Khalafallah's procedure in comparing two different versions of the Lot legend in the Qur'an, with the result that 'the disparity of both records' can be reduced to 'a difference in function and aim'; see Baljon 1968, 38f.

81. A Christian reader of the Bible might be in a comparable situation, if the old church had not accepted the Jewish Bible as canonical or had not accepted the whole collection of what is now the New Testament. We may speculate what would have happened if only one writing, say the Gospel of John (or Marcion's purified New Testament for that matter), had been canonized. Then the chances for critical questions on a text-immanent basis would be small.

82. Cf. its role in the conceptions of Rahbar, Al-Ashwamy and An-

Na'im. Antes 1981, 181 notes that here (and, almost only here) 'there are at least the beginnings of a possibility of understanding along the lines of historical-critical exegesis which should be taken up carefully and developed further in the dialogue with Muslims.'

83. See the lists of abrogated verses according to the standard work of Ibn Salama in Powers 1988, 137f.

84. Powers 1988, 130: 'In many cases, the exceptive, abrogating clause occurs in the same verse as the abrogated verse.'

85. Cf. Powers 1988, 119: 'it becomes essential to determine the relative chronology' of the discrepant verses 'because, if one mistakes the abrogating verse for the abrogated, Muslims would be adhering to a legal ruling that has been suppressed and, at the same time, they would be neglecting a ruling that has been commanded'. In Muslim tradition, 'there was considerable disagreement over the scope and parameters of abrogation' (125) and even 'considerable disagreement over the scope of abrogation within the Qur'an itself' (126). The 'sword verse' (9.5), which abrogated no fewer than 124 other verses, 'is itself considered to have been abrogated by the conditional clause with which it concludes' (131)!

86. See Watt 1970, 42–4.

87. Antes 1981, 182f.: theologically the redaction history of the Qur'an is a problem to which hardly anyone has so far called attention.

88. 'Uthman's commission decided what was to be included and what excluded'; even if it 'must be adjudged to have achieved a wonderful piece of work' (Watt 1970, 44), this is a far cry from the inerrancy of an uncreated heavenly book.

89. Antes 1981, 183: every educated Muslim knows the fact, but no one seems to be aware of the implications.

90. Even An-Na'im (1990, 19) can state that 'the text of the Qur'an is accepted as accurate and beyond dispute by all Muslims' and add: 'This is my belief as a Muslim. Some Western scholars (he refers to John Burton) have disputed this . . .'

91. They were collected and published by Jeffery (1937).

92. Watt 1970, 44f.; Adams 1987, 164. Even if the variant readings 'chiefly affect the vowels and punctuation', cases of a different consonantal text do occur as well: Watt 1970, 45. It may be true that a text-critical edition which would satisfy a Western scholar 'familiar with the way in which textual studies have elucidated the stages in the development of early European literary texts' cannot be achieved

(Watt, ibid., 46). But 'the available information is insufficient' (ibid. 47) because of the intentional destruction of early material by Uthman, and not because of any conspicuous unity in the textual tradition. In the light of his own account, Watt's conclusion (ibid., 46) that 'there was no great variation in the actual contents of the Qur'an in the period immediately after the Prophet's death' seems overly optimistic. But even if it is accepted, the existing variation is great enough to cause problems for the orthodox Muslim view of the Qur'an.

93. That of of Ibn-Mas'ud (d. 653).

94. On the other hand, the other respected early collection (that of Ubayy) includes these three surahs, but it also seems to have contained 'two other suras which are not in the standard text of the Qur'an': Watt 1970, 46. Even apart from that, 'we cannot be certain that no part of the Qur'an delivered by Muhammad has been lost' (ibid., 54). The issue is further complicated through peculiarities in the script in which the Qur'an was originally written (a *scriptio defectiva* which, besides omitting vowels, also left many of the consonants open to different interpretations). The process of improving the script was completed more than two centuries after the Prophet's death. As a consequence, different reading traditions had developed. Of these, seven came to be officially accepted in the tenth century. The new standard Egyptian edition of the Qur'an (of 1924) reproduces one of these seven versions 'and thus gives it a certain canonical supremacy', Watt 1970, 47–50: 49.

95. Exception: Wansbrough 1977.

96. Watt (1970, 51) concludes that this revision 'was honestly carried out, and reproduced, *as closely as was possible to the men in charge of it*, what Muhammad had delivered'.

97. Smith 1957, 25f. n.13; Jansen 1980, 2.

98. Cf. Smith, ibid.; historical scholarship of these traditions is being conducted within Islam.

99. Cf. Hill 1994.

100. Boone 1990, 31 rightly notes a parallel 'between the fundamentalist doctrine of the Bible and the Islamic doctrine of the Koran, despite explicit denials of any parallel'.

101. Of course, the nature of the sources may not predict great success regarding the former.

102. 'One of the most important reasons for an expected flowering

of North American Muslim religious thought . . . is the freedom of expression found in the West. Although there are many in the traditional Muslim countries and societies who have long acknowledged the necessity for updating and independent intellectual searching in matters religious, the penalties for going public with such have sometimes been severe.. It is not reckless to anticipate that the new élan of Muslim discourse . . . will be generated in North America, even more than in Europe', Denny 1994, 1082.

103. Denny 1994, 1080 (with reference to Salman Rushdie as only the 'most dramatic' recent example). Indeed, the 'cultural Muslims' might be in a key position; they might voice a critical position from within.

9. The Bible and the Traditions of the Nations: Isaac La Peyrère as a Precursor of Biblical Criticism

1. For the modest beginnings of the pre-Adamite theory before La Peyrère see Popkin 1987, 26–41.

2. Allen 1963, 133 regards La Peyrère as the father of the modern study of prehistory.

3. La Peyrère is 'one of the most peculiar figures of the seventeenth century', as well as one of its 'most interesting phenomena in terms of the history of ideas', Schoeps 1952, 3, 17.

4. Bowden 1988, 23.

5. Ibid., 27.

6. Ibid., 25.

7. Popkin 1987, 42.

8. Popkin 1987, 42 refers to Richard Simon's view of La Peyrère's lack of linguistic knowledge. In several places of his work, however, La Peyrère does appeal to the Greek text (*Exerc.*, chs. 5, 10, 13, 20, 25; *Syst.* I, ch. 6 etc.); once he even puts forward a Greek conjecture to 'correct' the original (*Exerc.*, ch. 10). (For the reference system used see p. 139.)

9. See especially Popkin 1987, 5–25.

10. This year is more likely than 1594; see Popkin 1987, 5.

11. Strauss 1930, 60; Schoeps 1952, 14–16; cautiously Popkin 1987, 22f.

12. La Peyrère cites him in *Syst.* IV, ch. 14.

13. See Popkin 1987, 54–8.

14. On the relations of Christina and La Peyrère see also Åkerman 1988, 147–50.

15. *Praeadamitae* appeared in 1655 in four editions and the *Systema* in three; in addition one edition appeared which combined both.

16. See McKee 1944, 457.

17. See on these Frank 1865, 72–4; Allen 1963, 136 n. 103. The refutation published by Samuel Maresius (Desmarets) in 1656 became a classic; it was 'the only one that was usually cited' (Popkin 1987, 81).

18. Popkin 1987, 14–16.

19. Summaries are given by Strauss 1930, 32–61; McKee 1944, 460–8; Klempt 1960, 90–6; Scholder 1990, 82–7; Popkin 1987, 42–59, 69–79.

20. Death is no longer a simple and natural matter. Even a pre-Adamite had to die, but not 'surely die' (*Exerc.*, ch. 18). Before Adam there was a *mors naturalis*; from Adam on there was *mors legalis*. Adam died a 'legal and spiritual death' the day he transgressed God's law; his natural death followed much later (*Syst.* I, ch. 3).

21. *Exerc.*, ch. 8. Genesis is now consonant both with Chaldean and Chinese sources and with the traditions of the Mexicans discovered by Columbus.

22. Popkin 1987, 47.

23. Klempt 1960, 95.

24. That is, the Jews and those Gentiles who had mixed with them. La Peyrère takes 'the sons of God' in Gen. 6.2 to mean Jews and 'the daughters of men' Gentiles! Those Gentiles who had mixed with Jews were destroyed in the same flood.

25. He devotes special attention to Grotius, who is criticized in *Syst.* IV, ch. 14. La Peyrère is embittered about Grotius' polemic against the manuscript La Peyrère had confidentially sent to him. Grotius regarded the Indians as descendants of the Norwegians; the Vikings for their part, as Europeans, naturally descended from the sons of Noah. La Peyrère shows that this theory founders on the Eskimos whom the Vikings encountered in Greenland and who could not possibly descend from Vikings.

26. *Syst.*, V. Adam's sin was necessary for all humans to become beneficiaries of the work of Christ; all had first to die in Adam. Christ's work, then, was not the consequence of Adam's transgression, but its presupposition.(This is an interesting, if coincidental,

parallel to the idea put forward by E.P.Sanders 1977 that Paul thought 'backwards', from solution to plight.)

27. Maresius 1656, LXXXXIV–LXXXXV, noted that La Peyrère was looking for contradictions 'with the method of the impious Socinians'. Cf. Strauss 1930, 34ff.; Scholder 1990, 84f.

28. Maresius 1656, 189ff.

29. *Quaest. in Gen.* I. 1: Zöckler 1878, 35 n. 1.

30. Maresius 1656, 195.

31. Similarly Ursinus 1656, 121–6.

32. Occasionally La Peyrère can postulate a copyist's error in Romans as well (*Exerc.*, ch. 10); he even proposes a theory of the origin of the false reading (*ellogeito* instead of *ellogeitai*). However, this conjecture is not of great significance for his interpretation of the verse.

33. This is apparently seen by Ursinus 1656, 49 who asks: 'Do you call as your witness Moses whose knees you have smashed and whose neck you have broken . . .?'

34. The starting point for the apograph theory is the view of some that everything that has happened must be mentioned in the books of Moses; if pre-Adamites are not mentioned there, then they have not existed. Yet this claim could have been refuted simply by showing that it is not the aim of Genesis to tell everything. As we saw (above, p. 144), even the critics of La Peyrère accepted this assumption (it was assumed that Adam and Eve had a great number of descendants not mentioned in the Bible).

35. Klempt 1960, 96.

36. Strauss 1930, 46f., 54f. He has got the impression that La Peyrère does not really want to combine his 'naturalism' with salvation history, but only tries to cover up his unbelief with ecclesiastical terminology (54); it is questionable whether his 'theological system' was meant to be taken seriously (55). Popkin, too, claimed in 1979 (218) that La Peyrère 'obviously did not want a way of harmonizing Scripture with his data. Rather he wanted to raise a basic kind of religious scepticism about Scripture in order to justify his own religious views.' In his 1987 book Popkin has, however, justly given up this interpretation.

37. Popkin 1987, 21. He refers in addition to the fact that La Peyrère 'chose to live in a very pious monastery', and to the Pope's benevolent attitude towards him.

38. Maresius 1656, LXXXIV.

39. See ibid., XXVIII–XXIX.

40. Popkin 1987, 72. Scholder 1990, 164 n. 85 wrongly belittles the significance of the critical thoughts of La Peyrère. Better justice is done to him by Kraus 1982, 60f.

41. Schoeps 1952, 5f. claims that La Peyrère is looking for rational explanations for miracles. The rationality is, however, limited to the fact that La Peyrère is content with miracles of a 'reasonable' size; they are still miracles. Correctly Popkin 1987, 51: 'La Peyrère's way of making religion more reasonable is to interpret miracles as *local* events rather than *natural* events' (my emphasis).

42. Contra Strauss 1930, 46, who thinks that La Peyrère explains the miracle away rationalistically (sic) and disguises only slightly the fact that he actually denies it; cf. also McKee 1944, 466.

43. Maresius 1656, 630ff. notes that La Peyrère was not the first to deny that the sun moved back or stood still in the sky. He himself sticks to literal miracles: how could the shadow have moved back if the sun did not (631f.)?

44. Barr 1977, 243–5, with reference to H.J. Blair and B. Ramm; the citation comes from Ramm, *The Christian View of Science and Scripture*.

45. B. Ramm, in Barr 1977, 244.

46. K.A. Kitchen, quoted by Barr 1977, 358 n. 9.

47. Harrison 1970, 558.

48. Scholder 1990, 84.

49. Zöckler 1878, 31. Zöckler is mistaken, however, in claiming that La Peyrère ignores Acts 17.26, which tells against his theory. La Peyrère (*Exerc.*, ch. 25) takes that verse to mean that God created all men out of the same matter (rather than that he made all mankind out of one person).

50. Schoeps 1952, 4 justly speaks of an 'acute and consistent argument'.

51. Schelkle 1959, 184. Similarly now Cranfield 1975, 282.

52. Such problems made some people, among others Gregory of Nyssa, long before La Peyrère, think that Rom. 5.13 speaks of a commandment given to Adam (Schelkle 1959, 184).

53. On the discussion on the 'imputation' in Rom. 5.12–14 see Räisänen 1987, 145–7.

54. Westerholm 1988, 183f.

272 Notes to pages 149 to 152

55. Ibid., 184.

56. Bultmann 1951, 252. One could add that the understanding of sin implied in Rom. 5.13 runs counter to the argument of Rom. 1–2, where Paul is anxious to show that Gentiles who live outside the Mosaic law are nevertheless not without a law, being actually a 'law' to themselves. Again, in Rom. 5.20 Paul attributes a considerably more negative role to the coming of the law: it actually increases sin.

57. Strecker 1979, 249 shows that Paul has artificially inserted the question of the law (which intrigues him) into an Adam–Christ-typology to which it is in itself alien.

58. Popkin 1987, 58.

59. For a summary of the contents of this work see ibid., 54–8.

60. *Exercitatio* contains 'a map of Terra Sancta which would please the most expansionist Israelis, and would horrify even the most pacific Arabs. It even has the Holy Land, Eretz Israel, including much of what is now Saudi Arabia and Yemen', Popkin 1987, 46.

61. Stendahl 1984, 213.

62. Cf. above, Ch. 5.

63. For the 'French nationalist messianism up to La Peyrère' see Popkin 1987, 60–8.

64. Cf. above, Ch. 2.

65. Thus still Zöckler 1878, 40.

66. Allen 1963, 136. Cf. also Kraus 1982, 59.

67. Schoeps 1952, 4, even speaks of 'a whole system of positions critical of the Bible'.

68. Popkin 1987, 73.

69. Kasher and Biderman (1988, 138–41), in a thorough study of the excommunication of Spinoza, reach the conclusion that an essential reason may have been the adoption of La Peyrère's theory of pre-Adamites by Spinoza. On La Peyrère's influence on Simon see Popkin 1987, 87f. Simon rejected the pre-Adamite theory, but availed himself of La Peyrère's individual observations. Jean Astruc (1753), who is considered the father of the modern study of the Pentateuch, criticized La Peyrère, but based himself on Simon, and thus indirectly on La Peyrère's work; see Popkin 1987, 88f.

70. Kraus 1982, 59–61; Hayes-Prussner 1985, 25–7: 'The most radical reinterpretations of the Bible during the seventeenth century were produced by La Peyrère and Spinoza, whose works . . . opened the door to new theological approaches to the Bible' (25).

71. See McKee 1944, 468–85; Popkin 1987, 114–45.
72. Scholder 1990, 87; cf. also Klempt 1960, 95.

10. A Bible-Believer Improves the Bible: Joseph Smith's Contribution to Exegesis

1. Barlow 1991, 26.
2. Ibid., 45.
3. Ibid., 8; cf. 3–10.
4. 'Substantially before the organization of Mormonism into a church, Smith had begun to see events in his own life as a continuation of the Bible narrative', Barlow 1991, 21. (One thinks here of the analogous role-taking in John Wesley's life, cf. Källstad 1974.) It is easy to understand his experience as Ström 1994, 313 interprets it: Smith had heard countless Christian sermons and adopted the material in his memory; in his auditions he reproduced, more or less unconsciously, parts of it. Ström has also identified Red Indian elements in early Mormonism (summary, 313f.).
5. Barlow 1991, 11f.
6. Ibid., 68.
7. Ibid., 69, 75ff.
8. Ibid., 221.
9. Mormonism is mentioned neither in Richardson's *Dictionary of Christian Theology* nor in Blackwell's new *Encyclopedia of Modern Christian Thought*. Stendahl 1984, 99 regrets 'how cavalier we biblical scholars have been in our attitude toward the biblical "after-history". Every scrap of evidence for elucidating the origins of Christianity and its formative periods receives minute attention and is treated with great seriousness, however marginal. But . . . the laws of creative interpretation by which we analyse material from the first and second Christian centuries operate and are significantly elucidated by works like the Book of Mormon or by other writings of revelatory character: Swedenborgian, Christian Science, Jehovah's Witnesses, or the Divine Principles of the Unification Church.'
10. The (conservative) *Dictionary of Christianity in America* (1990) recognizes Mormonism as 'a vigorous all-American religion' which may have 'the potential to become the first world religion to emerge since the birth of Islam' (I. Hexham, 777 on 'Mormonism'). Smart 1989, 360 observes: 'Some of the doctrines – that God is material, that

there are many Gods, and that human beings may become Gods – have been modified, and in many ways Mormonism is now a conforming evangelical kind of Protestantism, with the colorful additions of the Book of Mormon and the charismatic memory of the genial and masterful Joseph Smith.'

11. Davies 1978, 91.

12. 'In any case, the Mormon believes his position is . . . a repossession of a New Testament understanding that reconciles Paul and James', Dillenberger 1978, 175.

13. Benz 1978, 216.

14. Stendahl 1978, 139–54.

15. Actually the first Beatitude demands the hearers to pay heed to the words of the Twelve: the apostolic authority is stressed.

16. Stendahl 1978, 142 notes that this is 'one of the most striking differences perhaps between the Sermon on the Mount and its equivalent in Nephi'.

17. Ibid., 152.

18. Cf. ibid., 150.

19. Ibid., 151.

20. Ibid., 145.

21. See Koch 1986, 186–98 and passim. Koch shows that Paul goes far beyond his contemporaries in his freedom in handling the texts.

22. Stendahl 1978, 154.

23. 'Genuine biblical words have been changed according to the ideals which the falsifier had in his mind', Meinhold 1962, 577; cf. 575.

24. Stendahl 1978, 154.

25. O'Dea 1958, 55.

26. Hullinger 1980.

27. See Barr 1977, 280–4.

28. See on the IV Barlow 1991, 46–61. Barlow, a Mormon scholar, interprets the IV in 'redaction-critical' terms as a product of Smith's creative interpretation, finding a close analogy to Smith's 'prophetic licence' in the work of biblical writers, especially Paul. Barlow's study is strikingly free from the apologetics displayed by Matthews 1980, who still tried to describe, through complicated hermeneutics, how and why the 'inspired translation' really is a 'translation'. It remains to be seen whether the new liberal trend can assert itself within Mormonism.

29. Cf. O'Dea 1958, 27: the Book of Mormon is 'an almost completely neglected primary source for the intellectual history of the common man'.

30. Yet compare annotated Bibles such as the Geneva Bible and the Scofield Reference Bible – or the recent translation of the New Testament, published by the Oxford University Press, in which – to give just one instance – Matt 11.25 is rendered 'No one knows the Child except the Father-Mother . . .'

31. Cf. Hendriksen 1982, 949f.: 'If he hanged himself from a tree located on a high cliff, above a valley, and if then the rope broke and the traitor fell on rocky ground, the result could very well have been as pictured in the book of Acts'; Maier 1980, 422.

32. Cf. Maier 1979, 281 on the demoniacs; Hendriksen 1983, 1053 on the angels at the tomb.

33. In the case of Mark this happens indirectly: 'they that were crucified with him reviled him' (KJV) is altered to 'one of them . . .' (IV).

34. See Merkel 1971.

35. Matthews 1980, 347. For points of comparison in evangelical literature see Guthrie 1981, 794–8.

36. Matthews 1980, 328. In the Book of Mormon, too, prophets and preachers repeatedly proclaim the future coming of Jesus Christ which is described in detail in advance. 'It is as if the author could not imagine Hebrew messianic hopes in any other terms than Christian', O'Dea 1958, 39.

37. Matthews 1980, 328.

38. Cullmann 1967, 253f., 310f.

39. Bultmann 1955, 201.

40. Hullinger 1980, 122; cf. ibid., 148 n. 19.

41. Cf. ibid., 135 n. 4.

42. Another reading: God.

43. Adduced as a parallel by Charlesworth 1978, 120f.

44. De Vries 1981, 14 (translated from the German version available to me).

45. Ibid., 21, cf. 25. Jacob too thought of Lord Jesus when he died; this is made clear in a long interpolation (ibid. 56).

46. The Book of Mormon too makes it clear that the law of Moses is a type of Christ (Alma 26.15–16). Its commandments are to be observed until Christ comes, but not after that (3 Nephi 9.19–20).

After the appearance of Christ, his commandments alone are valid (3 Nephi 15.10; 4 Nephi 12). Although Smith's view is not clear in all its details, the constancy of the divine plan is unmistakeable.

47. On Christ as the giver of the Old Testament law in patristic writings see Werner 1957, 88f. E.g. the 'mediator' in Gal. 3.19 is identified with the pre-existent Christ.

48. Cf. Wiles 1967, 57; Werner 1957, 91f.

49. No wonder Joseph Smith could not imagine that Paul had ever lived 'without the law'.

50. By contrast, it is not clear why Paul had to be 'under sin' while being 'under the law': on this point, Rom. 7.14 has gone unchanged in the Inspired Version (see below); or why the law was 'to the administration of death' (thus an addition in a Pauline vein to John 1.17 IV). But the tension between negative and positive statements on the law is, of course, a Pauline legacy for which his interpreters are not to be blamed.

51. Wiles 1967, 57, with reference to Chrysostom, *Hom. in Rom.* 12.5.

52. Cf. Meyer 1912.

53. Ibid., 39.

54. Ibid., 137.

55. Hutten 1953, 447.

56. This is so despite the fact that the Book of Mormon itself has been transferred to a subsidiary position, its role being mostly of a legitimating nature.

57. Quoted in Tanner – Tanner 1980, 92.

58. In 1985 a curious event shattered the Mormon church. An early letter of 1830 was found in the archives of the church in which Martin Harris, one of the classic 'witnesses' to Smith's gold plates, described Smith as utterly superstitious; when he found the plates he had been led by a spirit in the form of a white salamander. As a consequence, a number of members left the church, pointing out that since Smith had eight years later changed the salamander into an angel (in his autobiography of 1838), the Book of Mormon had turned out to be unreliable. The crisis was overcome, as World President Joseph Fielding Smith declared that Harris's letter, though authentic, could have no effect on the faith of the church: Ström 1994, 312f.

59. Barlow 1991, 143–7.

60. Ibid., 132–4.
61. Ibid., 141 n. 91.
62. Ibid., 146f.
63. Ibid., 223.

11. **Ideas and Problems of Universal Wisdom: Mahatma Gandhi and the Sermon on the Mount**

1. Aula 1967, 129–31.
2. Likewise, W. Mühlmann thought that it was the Sermon on the Mount that gave Gandhi (1893 in South Africa) the idea of passive resistance and 'the immediate impulse for the political conclusion' (1950, 33f.). Gandhi actually 'seems to be a Christian' (4).
3. Heiler 1926, 41.
4. Ibid., 37, 50.
5. Hick 1977, 183; Gnilka 1986, 285 with n. 1.
6. I have used the Penguin edition of 1982.
7. See e.g. Borman 1986, 237f.
8. Historians point out that India would have gained independence even without him. J.M. Brown 1990, 385. She notes that '. . . non-violent forms of opposition to the British raj rarely achieved major or immediate political concessions' (386). The same point is made polemically by Edwardes 1986. Gandhi's celebrated work in South Africa did not bring lasting results either; cf. J.M. Brown 1990, 46.
9. This tendency is visible in Hick's Foreword in Chatterjee 1983, ix–xii, but Chatterjee's fine book itself, concerned with 'identifying essential structures' of Gandhi's thought, also lacks any criticisms whatsoever.
10. Wolff 1955; Edwardes 1986, esp. 258–60: Gandhi, a maimed personality, lacked ordinarily human love and caused incalculable damage to the cause of the poor.
11. Borman's book serves to emphasize both the relevance of Gandhi and the necessity of correcting his ideology on certain points.
12. See e.g. Tähtinen 1964; Bondurant 1965; Borman 1986; Richards 1991, 31–63.
13. Cf. Borman 1986, 8f., 20f.
14. He is alarmed by the exploitation of Gandhi by Hindus, especially by Radhakrishnan, in a fight against Christianity's claim to absoluteness. In a later book (Wolff 1965), polemics has yielded to a

more positive attitude.

15. He even found himself temporarily in a state of inner turmoil, with both Muslim and Christian friends endeavouring to convert him. He turned for help to a Jain sage who convinced him that 'no other religion has the subtle and profound thought of Hinduism' (*Autobiography*, Part 2, Ch. 15).

16. Cf. Tähtinen 1964, 115; Richards 1991, 34.

17. Of course, Gandhi was perfectly capable of interpreting what he read in his own way. But if he interpreted Matt. 5.38 (ff.) in terms of resistance, then that idea must already have been in his mind, and it must have been so powerful that it was able to suppress the literal meaning of the text as it stands.

18. '. . . when Indians in South Africa resorted to passive (*sic*) resistance they did so as the natural reaction to their situation of a weak group without other forms of leverage, rather than as the direct result of any of the ideas Gandhi had been studying or of his personal contacts with contemporary exponents of passive resistance. Gandhi's correspondence with Tolstoy, for example, only started after passive resistance had begun, and he only read Thoreau's essay on civil disobedience when he was in prison for that very offence', J.M. Brown 1972, 6f.

19. Tolstoy's books especially helped him articulate his preexistent vision of nonviolent action (*Autobiography*, Part 2, Chs. 15, 22): '*ahimsa* and "universal love" fell into place' in his thought, J.M. Brown 1990, 84.

20. Cf. *Autobiography*, Introduction: 'What I want to achieve – what I have been striving and pining to achieve these thirty years – is self–realization, to see God face to face, to attain *moksha*. I live and move and have my being in pursuit of this goal.' Edwardes 1986, 258 comments that 'Gandhi's life was a Hindu life, and his message was Hindu also. Hindu morality is centred upon the self and self-realization'. Perhaps one could speak of an inherent tension between the ideal of self–realization and the communal vision (the latter is stressed by Chatterjee 1983, 56). On self-realization as Gandhi's goal see also J.M. Brown 1977, 15.

21. Wolff 1955, 128.

22. Chatterjee 1983, 69. For critical comments on the political use of vows see Wolff 1955, 73f.

23. See Chatterjee 1983, 71–3; Borman 1986, 217–20; for

criticisms of the method see Juergensmeyer 1989, 39–43.

24. Gandhi once commented that Matt. 5.22, where Jesus threatens with hell, is 'inconsistent with the *ahimsa* of Jesus': Chatterjee 1983, 51f.

25. Devaraja 1969, 83 comments on the temple scene: 'This too, one feels, was not altogether an exemplary piece of behaviour.' Also, Luke 12.8f. is a statement 'unworthy of Christ and inconsistent with the ethics of love for enemies'; so is the cursing of the fig tree (ibid., 82).

26. Quoted in Chatterjee 1983, 47.

27. In ibid., 51.

28. Cf. Wolff 1955, 135 (with some polemical distortion); id. 1965, 147f. In speaking to Ceylonese Christians, Gandhi did not omit to appeal to Buddha: *MPW* 1, 500. In Burma (1929) he talked on Buddha and *ahimsa*, asking why light and peace are not seen 'in a land that professes the law of *ahimsa*', the answer being that 'the message of Buddha . . . has only touched but the surface of the heart of Burma' (*MPW* 1, 508). And at a meeting commemorating Muhammad's death (1934) he appealed to the Prophet who 'had renounced everything' (*sic*), *MPW* 2, 513.

29. Thus, addressing an economical society in Allahabad in 1916 he quoted Matt. 6.34, and read the whole passage Mark 10.17–31 on Jesus and the rich man. But he went on: 'I will not insult you by quoting in support of the law stated by Jesus passages from the writings and sayings of our own sages, passages even stronger if possible than the Biblical extracts I have drawn your attention to. Perhaps the strongest of all the testimonies . . . are the lives of the greatest teachers of the world' (*MPW* 1, 359).

30. He concedes that Jesus said 'I am the way', but claims that 'any teacher who has dedicated his life to the service of God and humanity and attained to complete purity can say that' (*MPW* 1, 509f.).

31. Windisch 1929, VI.

32. See below, n.52.

33. In Q, Jesus' death is seen as the typical fate of a prophet (Matt. 23.29f., 34f./Luke 11.47f.; Matt. 23.37/Luke 13.34) which also awaits his followers (Matt. 5.12/Luke 6.23).

34. Cf. Wolff, esp. his more balanced presentation in 1965, 149–54. Chatterjee 1983 recognizes inconsistencies, but passes over them rather easily (see 3f., 9, 29f.). She never mentions e.g. Gandhi's actual

attitude to wars.

35. Wolff 1965, 149.

36. This assertion is taken at face value by Hick 1983, xi, who sees part of Gandhi's challenge to the liberation movements to lie in his 'absolute commitment to non–violence'.

37. 'It must be noted that Gandhi's final value is *not* non-violence. Whatever his disclaimer and arguments, he in fact always preferred violence to cowardice – without exception', Borman 1986, 252.

38. Cf. Wolff 1965, 150f. Borman 1986, 217 concludes: '*Satya-graha*, contrary to both Gandhi's analysis and the canons of strict non–violence, is an essentially coercive force.' Albert Schweitzer, of all people, commented that 'there is the risk that this concealed use of violence produces more bitterness than an open use of it' (quoted in Wolff 1955, 265). Many critics hold indeed that non-violent resistance is impossible. All resistance implies at least spiritual violence and may well, if it continues long enough, also destroy life. The point was made in 1932 by R. Niebuhr (Niebuhr 1963, 240ff.). Niebuhr, a former near-pacifist, argued that there is no intrinsic difference between violent and non-violent resistance. Later he commented that Gandhi did not teach us anything new on the 'perplexing problem' of love and justice. 'He made the pretension of sainthood into an instrument of political power. That may have seemed plausible in the environment of India, but it must be ultimately intolerable anywhere', Niebuhr 1984, 526.

39. Edwardes 1986, 258. On the strange sides of Gandhi's *brahmacharya* (the exercise of 'total self-control'), which required him to prove his purity of heart by taking naked girls to bed, see e.g. Mehta 1977, 179–213.

40. Wolff 1955, 210f.

41. Ibid., 66ff., 210–13.

42. Ibid., 211. The consequences were interesting: villagers refused to co-operate with Gandhi in his recruiting efforts, exercising a kind of non-violent resistance to Gandhi himself!

43. Niebuhr 1963, 247. Cf. Borman's analysis of Gandhi's views on war (1986, 161ff.).

44. Wolff is right on this: we might understand Gandhi, if he frankly appealed to *realpolitisch* points of view; but then he logically ought to reject his doctrine of *satyagraha* altogether! Wolff (84) has analogous criticisms of Gandhi's strike weapon. See also the criticisms

of Gandhi's inconsistencies by Mühlmann 1950, 199–211.

45. Wolff 1965, 154.

46. On the reception history see Kissinger 1975; Berner 1985; Kantzenbach 1982, 21–81; Luz 1989, esp. 218–23, 318–22, 331–37, 347–51; G. Barth 1980, 611–15.

47. 'Do you want to know what your duty is as a prince or a judge or a lord or a lady . . .? You do not have to ask Christ . . .' Quoted in Luz 1989, 334.

48. We are reminded of the phenomenon that conservative exegesis is often far from 'literal'; cf. Barr 1977.

49. I omit here the exegetically best-founded history-of-religion interpretation, as it has hardly influenced the larger audience. This limits the options so far to three.

50. On Tolstoy's interpretation see Laurila 1946; for dogmatic reasons the author takes a polemical attitude to Tolstoy.

51. Cf. e.g. Justin, *Apol.* 16. But see on the other hand Did. 6.2 (keep what you can!).

52. The picture of a non–violent, apolitical Jesus has been challenged by Horsley 1987. He paints a social revolutionary rather reminiscent of Gandhi's Jesus. Jesus 'consistently criticized and *resisted* the oppressive established political–economic–religious order of his own society' (319). Like Gandhi's, Horsley's Jesus implies that taxes should not be paid to Caesar (313); in the temple he goes further than Gandhi's in performing 'a minimally violent prophetic demonstration' (299). However, Horsley rejects the pacifist picture of Jesus altogether. Jesus had nothing to say on non–violence. The original context of the sayings in Matt. 5.38–48 par is 'that of social–economic relations in a village or town' (270). If this were true, the theme of 'universal love', so dear to Tolstoy and Gandhi, would totally disappear from the message of Jesus. Subsequent research has challenged Horsley's reading of the socio–political situation in Galilee, but the thesis that local relations are in view in the passage on non–violence has stimulated further thought. The focal interest, though, has moved from Jesus to the 'Q' group, the ethos of which is more clearly visible in the Lukan parallel to Matt. 5.38ff.; Luke 6.27–36. Such passages are taken to reflect 'a profound lack of confidence among the Q people regarding the social and judicial institutions active in their sphere' (R. Piper 1995, 60). These people are located 'among the lower administrative sector of the cities and

villages in Galilee', former minor officials with 'scribal' abilities (ibid., 62; Kloppenborg 1991) who have opted out from the system (R. Piper 1995, 65f.). The implication (which is so far seldom spelt out) would seem to be that the roots of the crucial passage in the Sermon on the Mount (Matt. 5.38–48) may be found in the situation of the later 'Jesus movement' rather than with Jesus himself, a view strengthened by tradition-historical considerations (cf. below, n. 70). Cf. Douglas 1995, 120 (criticizing Horsley's tacit assumption that sayings such as Luke 6.27–36 originated with Jesus): 'The various sayings may be "authentic", but this should not be merely assumed and cannot be easily determined.'

53. The difference is overlooked by Pelikan 1985, 213. Nor does Chatterjee (1983, 50f.) sense a problem in Gandhi's relation to Tolstoy.

54. Wink 1988, 210 n.1 praises Gandhi for refusing to submit to an unjust law, but eventually lumps Gandhi and Tolstoy together among 'those who have lived by Jesus' words' (224).

55. Borman 1986, 122, 125 correctly points out the difference between Gandhi's *satyagraha* and the 'passivity of the Christian peace witness' of the 'peace churches'.

56. Wink's (1988, 221) suggestion that *antistenai* refers to armed resistance does not carry conviction.

57. Cf. Windisch 1929, 14.

58. Windisch 1929, 87, 133, rightly defends them against Christian dogmaticians.

59. He could obstinately cling to his quiet little 'voice'. Juergensmeyer 1989, 43, speaks of the 'stubbornness and coerciveness' of Gandhi's *satyagraha*.

60. Cf. Bauer 1967, 246.

61. For the different possibilities of interpretation see e.g. Zerbe 1993, 185f.

62. Evans 1990, 867. Even if the prayer stemmed from Luke's pen, its historical authenticity would be anything but credible, just like the Lukan incident of the 'penitent thief'.

63. Harvey 1990, 101.

64. Ibid., 101. Harvey concludes, somewhat weakly, that 'if we wish to say that he did personally "love his enemies", we shall have to take it on trust that he maintained a deep interior love for them despite his apparently adversarial or merely submissive demeanour'.

65. The sharpness of these sayings goes back to Matthew; the Lukan parallel (Luke 11.39) is somewhat milder. Nevertheless it is difficult to distinguish sharply between Matthew and Jesus. Even Tertullian noted the tension: Christ 'forbids the return of cursing for cursing, not to mention taking the initiative in it, yet hurls his Woe against the pharisees and doctors of the law' (*Adv. Marc.* 4.27.1), but uses this as an argument in favour of the Creator: this text proves that even Marcion's Christ (Marcion did not delete this text) is 'changeable, variable, capricious, teaching one thing, doing another . . .'

66. Luke 23.34.

67. Montefiore 1909, 521.

68. Some of these people were, for various reasons, despised by the community, so that mixing with them makes Jesus look like a philanthropist.

68. Luz 1993, 326f.

70. Even the authenticity of the command, though generally counted to the 'bedrock' tradition, is far from certain (cf. Sauer 1985). The oldest New Testament statements on non–retaliation are directly connected to biblical or Jewish tradition (I Thess. 5.15; Rom. 12.17–21). In Romans 12 Paul does not cite Jesus, but Proverbs (Prov. 25.21–22), probably following a tradition of parenesis which in turn draws on Jewish (and Greek) moral lore. Paul never mentions a command to love enemies (cf. Sauer 1985, 26)! Likewise, the oldest New Testament statements about blessing one's persecutors are found in Paul (I Cor. 4.12–13; Rom. 12.14). Paul does not refer to Jesus. This raises the question, Were Christians in the fifties not yet exhorted to pray for their persecutors because Jesus had said so? Was the motivation suggested simply that this was what love demanded? Why should Jesus have taken up the subject of persecution, which is more understandable in Paul's situation?

71. Zerbe 1993, 294. See also Klassen 1984, 43–71. The best-known instances include Joseph and Asenath 23.9–10; 28.3–4; Test. Benj. 4.2–3; 5.1–5; Test. Gad 6.3; 6.7; Josephus, *BJ* 2.351; 2.169–74.

72. For the Greek tradition see Klassen 1984, 12–26.

73. Cf. Schottroff 1975, 209.

74. Cf. ibid., 212f.

75. Broer 1992, 28 with n.31.

76. Klassen 1984, 5.

77. J. Piper 1979, 27.

78. Sauer 1985, 16.

79. Thus the demand to love enemies serves, for its part, to strengthen the identity of the group – and, paradoxically, to establish a wall between the subject and the objects of this love. As a motive for love for enemies and non–retaliation even the expectation of a reward is mentioned in the Sermon on the Mount (Matt. 5.46; Luke 6.35). Thus, love is not necessarily purely unmotivated (as 'Christian love' is often thought to be). In the middle of the second century Christian apologists speak much of the love shown by Christians towards their enemies. Yet the old martyr stories display mostly a neutral or even hostile attitude to the persecutors (Bauer 1967, 243). Pious Polycarp says concerning the people: 'Those there I do not regard worth defending myself before them' (Mart. Pol. 10.2), thus sharing the attitude of philosophers. Polycarp does not pray for the persecutors either.

80. The recommendation of non–retaliation is common moral wisdom; love for enemies and prayer for persecutors goes beyond it (cf. Bauer 1967, 249f.), but then the situation of persecution for one's religious conviction is exceptional as well.

81. See Ch. 1, p. 1.

82. Sugirtharajah 1995, 316f.

83. For a succinct account see J.M. Brown 1990, 389f. A vivid description is found in Mehta 1977, 214–51.

84. Gould 1989, 8.

85. See Smith-Zepp 1975.

86. Ibid., 57.

87. Pelikan 1985, 218.

88. Niebuhr, who in spite of much appreciation took a critical stance on Gandhi's thought and action (see above, n.38), responded enthusiastically to King's non-violent practice; see Smith-Zepp 1975, 97.

89. Borman concludes his evaluation (1986, 228): 'While Gandhi's practical claim fails and he does not close the debate over the justifiability of violence, his work may be a key factor in averting large scale violence and even nuclear conflict', if it is adapted in certain ways. Cf. also Juergensmeyer 1989.

12. Conclusion: The Pluralist Imperative

1. Knitter 1985, 173, cf. 171: traditional Christian claims (exclusive and inclusive claims alike) 'are insufficiently sensitive to the way they contradict contemporary awareness of historical relativity'.

2. Wiles 1992, 13.

3. Ibid., 14f.

4. Recall the self-critical question of Wesley Ariarayah, a Christian participant in the dialogue (above, Ch. 1, p. 5).

5. Cf. Räisänen 1987, 154–6.

6. See above, Ch. 6, n.22.

7. Käsemann 1964, 103.

8. Dunn 1990, 376.

9. Cf. Räisänen 1990, 82f.

10. Dunn 1990, 244f.

11. Race 1983, 97.

12. Theissen 1979a, 3.

13. See above, Ch. 8, 133f.

14. Stendahl 1984, 241.

15. Hick 1988, 18.

16. Cf. Räisänen 1990, 122–36.

17. Knitter 1985, 18f.

18. Gilkey thinks that this happened largely 'with the help of the Enlightenment', Gilkey 1988, 38.

19. Cf. Räisänen 1990, 137–41.

20. Watson 1993, 63f.

21. Ibid., 65.

22. This is noted by Watson himself (ibid., 81 n. 10).

23. Ibid., 66.

24. Ibid., 65.

25. Ibid. 79.

26. Ibid. 70.

27. Cf. ibid. 80.

28. Ibid. 67.

29. Seeley 1994, 85–97.

30. Ibid., 86.

31. Ibid., 87.

32. Ibid.

33. Ibid., 88f.

34. Ibid.

35. Cf. Cracknell 1986, 40.
36. Eaton 1989, 131.
37. Ibid., 131.
38. Ibid., 134.
39. Weiss 1971, 57–60, 131–6.
40. Wiles 1977, 164.
41. Ariarayah 1985, 23.

42. Stendahl 1984, 239f. Among others, Knitter 1985, 184f. follows him.

43. See above, Ch. 6, p. 91.

44. Hick 1989, 209. Hick's christology is adopted by Race 1983 (cf. 106ff. on incarnation, 127 on pre-existence); the net result (135f.) is that the traditional view of incarnation is mythological, but Jesus is still 'decisive' – 'for the vision he has brought in one cultural setting'.

Index